STAGNATION AND DRIFT IN THE WESTERN BALKANS

INTERDISCIPLINARY STUDIES
ON CENTRAL AND EASTERN EUROPE

Vol. 10

Edited by
Christian Giordano, Nicolas Hayoz & Jens Herlth

PETER LANG
Bern • Berlin • Bruxelles • Frankfurt am Main • New York • Oxford • Wien

CLAIRE GORDON
MARKO KMEZIC
JASMINA OPARDIJA (EDS)

STAGNATION AND DRIFT IN THE WESTERN BALKANS

The Challenges of Political, Economic and Social Change

PETER LANG
Bern · Berlin · Bruxelles · Frankfurt am Main · New York · Oxford · Wien

Bibliographic information published by die Deutsche Nationalbibliothek
Die Deutsche Nationalbibliothek lists this publication in the Deutsche Nationalbibliografie; detailed bibliographic data is available on the Internet at ‹http://dnb.d-nb.de›.

British Library Cataloguing-in-Publication Data: A catalogue record for this book is available from The British Library, Great Britain

Library of Congress Cataloging-in-Publication Data

Stagnation and drift in the Western Balkans : the challenges of political, economic and social change / Claire Gordon, Marko Kmezic, Jasmina Opardija (eds).
pages cm. – (Interdisciplinary studies on central and eastern Europe ; v. 10)
ISBN 978-3-0343-1152-6
1. Balkan Peninsula–Politics and government–1989- 2. Balkan Peninsula–Economic conditions. 3. Social change–Balkan Peninsula. 4. Democratization–Balkan Peninsula.
I. Gordon, Claire E.
DR48.6.S695 2013
949.605–dc23

2013009858

Cover illustration: "Swing of Change" by Amer Kapetanović.

ISSN 1661-1349 pb. ISSN 2235-7025 eBook
ISBN 978-3-0343-1152-6 pb. ISBN 978-3-0351-0581-0 eBook

Hochfeldstrasse 32, CH-3012 Bern, Switzerland
info@peterlang.com, www.peterlang.com

Printed in Hungary

Table of Contents

Claire Gordon, Marko Kmezic and Jasmina Opardija

Introduction: The Challenges of Political, Social and Economic Change in the Western Balkans

This edited volume on *Stagnation and Drift in the Western Balkans: The Challenges of Political, Social and Economic Change* is the product of the Regional Research Promotion Programme (RRPP)[1] in the Western Balkans. It offers insights into the contemporary work of mostly younger social scientists from the Western Balkan region and beyond who are researching political, social and economic changes in the region. The chapters in this volume were initially presented and discussed at the third annual RRPP scientific conference in Budva, Montenegro, in May 2011. They were selected from among some 45 contributions in cooperation with the discussants from the eight thematic workshops that were held at the 2011 conference.

Annual conferences and the publication and dissemination of research are only two aspects of the work of the RRPP. The programme also supports a cooperation platform for social scientists working on the region with three interrelated pillars:

- support and financing of regional research projects conducted by researchers from Albania, Bosnia-Herzegovina, Kosovo, Macedonia, Montenegro and Serbia;
- provision of methods training to scholars in the region by well-established international scholars;
- the facilitation of regional and international cooperation and networking, in particular through the organization of international conferences.

1 This programme is run by the University of Fribourg and is fully supported by the Swiss Agency for Development and Cooperation (SDC), Federal Department of Foreign Affairs.

The RRPP for the Western Balkans was initiated in 2008 by the Swiss Agency for Development and Cooperation, motivated by the idea that social science research can contribute to higher quality evidence-based policy making and thus influence much-needed reforms in the political, social and economic domains in the region. Considering the difficult post-conflict context in the countries of the former Yugoslavia, and the EU-driven transitional processes that are still taking place throughout south-eastern Europe, the RRPP has emerged as one of the key actors enabling research that has direct relevance for these ongoing transformation processes in the region. For this reason the RRPP is particularly committed to supporting research in the following areas:

- the rule of law and democracy;
- economic development;
- social and economic change and the challenge of (new) social disparities;
- managing diversity (national, ethnic and religious identities, gender, youth, and minorities, including Roma);
- states, networks and informality.

It is hoped that the current volume will not only contribute to raising awareness of the particular political, social and economic challenges that the countries of the Western Balkans continue to face in the wake of the conflicts that ravaged the region in the 1990s and early 2000s and the resulting stalled postcommunist transition but that it will also highlight the range and diversity of the burgeoning researchers in the region and beyond. These researchers are working creatively in this area to expand knowledge and scholarship, to build academic communities and to develop departments and faculties in the social sciences in higher education institutions.

This introduction provides a brief overview of the current challenges that the region has been grappling with as a means of contextualizing the work of the young generation of scholars who have contributed to this volume. It briefly discusses the process of European integration as well as the problematic of external leveraging on the part of the EU, which has been beset by a combination of enlargement fatigue and internal preoccupations with the future of the Eurozone in the midst of the current global economic crisis. We then turn to consider the constraints on democratic consolidation and state building before touching on the impact of the global economic crisis on the countries of the Western Balkans, underlining in particular the toll this has taken on youth across the region. The introduction concludes with an overview of the chapters that make up this edited volume.

The processes of democratic and socio-economic consolidation and the accession to the EU in south-eastern Europe have been fraught with difficulties. Romania and Bulgaria joined the EU in 2007 as laggards of the 2004 enlargement round to Central and Eastern Europe and Croatia will follow in 2013 but the rest of the region remains a long way behind with no prospect of accession for the foreseeable future. In addition to the dual political and economic transformations from authoritarian communist rule to pluralistic democracy and from a planned economy to market liberalism, Albania, Bosnia-Herzegovina, Kosovo, Macedonia, Montenegro and Serbia remain weak states with dysfunctional institutions, notwithstanding the considerable diversity among these countries. Transformation in the former Yugoslavia was marked by state dissolution and violent conflict, necessitating reconstruction and reconciliation. The legacies of this period of violent conflict continue to shape political, social and economic conditions across the region.

Without disregarding continuing enlargement fatigue in EU institutions, which are currently preoccupied with the economic and financial crises and the very survivability of the Eurozone, it is exactly these multiple challenges that explain the current delay in the processes of transformation and EU integration in the Western Balkan countries (WBCs) and that have resulted in the replacement of the phase of accelerated transformation immediately after 2000 with a period of stagnation and drift. Although functionally separate, transition processes are intimately interwoven with the famous Copenhagen conditions, which were originally issued at the 1993 European Council for the countries of Central and Eastern Europe that were to form the 2004/2007 enlargement round. The year 2000, the so-called *annus mirabilis* for the WBCs, marked by the collapse of Slobodan Milošević's regime in Serbia and Montenegro, and the 'second' democratic revolution following general elections in Croatia, provided new preconditions for the start of democratic consolidation and economic reform in the region. The same year, the EU launched its new policy initiative for the Western Balkans in the form of the Stabilization and Association Process (SAP). Although shaped in part by the Central and Eastern European enlargement model, in its design the SAP sought to take into account the peculiarities of post-conflict stabilization as well as the particular transformation and integration challenges facing the countries of the region. While offering an upfront 'perspective' of EU membership to the WBCs, at the same time the structuring of the SAP enabled the EU to introduce additional stages of conditionality into the process in view of the complex post-conflict conditions in the countries of the region while at the same time building on the perceived success of the instrument of conditionality in delivering transformative change in the countries of Central and Eastern Europe (Phinnemore, 2003; Gordon, 2009).

Despite the fact that the SAP was launched in 2000, the WBCs continue to be characterized as weak states with societies severely divided along ethnic lines. (Kostovicova and Bojicic-Dželilović, 2008; Ramet and Wagner, 2010). The momentum generated following the democratic changes in the region in 2000 has stalled and the current situation can at best be described as the consolidation of unconsolidated democracies (Bieber, 2012a). The latest edition of the *Nations in Transit* report presents a record of stagnation and backsliding in all key governance indicators across the countries of the region (Walker and Habdank-Kołaczkowska, 2012). Liberal democratic governments seemingly identify themselves with the EU but a large number of formal and informal economic and political elites persist that continue to manipulate ethno-nationalist mobilization for their own private economic interests in the preservation of political power. Despite the initial steps that have been made, reconciliation after the violent conflicts from the 1990s is far from complete and conversely elite-level political decision making in some cases is still driven along the old ethno-national lines and these fault-lines are also reflected in widespread public attitudes. Thus in pre-election campaigns politicians are wont to resort to ethno-nationalist rhetoric abandoning trust-building and reconciliation discourses for ethno-nationalist discourses (Volcic and Dzihana, 2012; Bieber, 2012b).

Bilateral relationships, particularly that between Serbia and Kosovo, often remain overburdened by historical legacies, negatively influencing the advance of processes of regional cooperation, a new dimension of conditionality under the SAP. While the dynamics of the EU integration offered the prospect of a new phase in political relations across the region, with incentives for enhanced regional cooperation and an end to the post-conflict phase, a relapse into the doctrine of the ethnically pure state and ethnic extremism cannot be totally ruled out. Moreover, Bosnia-Herzegovina and Kosovo – notwithstanding the latter's declaration of independence in 2008 – remain at least partially internationally administered territories with high levels of inter-ethnic contestation (Weller, 2009; Bieber, 2010; Oisin, 2010). Macedonia managed to avoid a full-scale war at the turn of the century and to reduce inter-ethnic tensions with the mostly successful implementation of the Ohrid Framework Agreement of 2001, but the political system is far from fully consolidated (Ilievski and Taleski, 2009; Irwin, 2010). Although an EU candidate since 2005, the country's Euro-Atlantic integration has been stalled by Greece's veto as a result of the ongoing dispute over the country's name – a dispute that remains deadlocked despite efforts at international mediation. The lack of progress in the country's EU integration has contributed to the rise of a destabilizing strand of populist politics in the domestic arena.

Serbia, after the dissolution of the common state with Montenegro in 2006 and Kosovo's declaration of independence in February 2008, faces the prospect of the return of Milošević's 'reformed' political allies. Meanwhile its political elites have failed to solve the contradictions over state and nationhood issues and, in particular, to move beyond the unworkable 'Kosovo and the EU' strategy (Becker, 2008). Having gained independence in 2006, Montenegro has nearly completed its state-building processes. However, the country's newly achieved independence has not resulted in the swift resolution of the key challenges that Montenegro faces today, in particular weak governance and the widely perceived corruption in the polity (Trivunović, Devine and Mathisen, 2007). Albania did not have to cope with violent state dissolution as was the case with the countries of the former Socialist Federal Republic of Yugoslavia (SFRY) and, consequently, did not have to undergo a phase of reconstruction and reconciliation. Consequently, Albanian society has faced fewer challenges to democratic consolidation but it has, nonetheless, experienced very slow democratic and economic transition and it is still hampered by internal political polarization of the ruling elites, the dominant influence of informal centres of power and high levels of corruption throughout all branches of government (Fischer, 2010).

Effective economic transformation has yet to be implemented in the countries of the region so that the economies of the WB could be considered capable of withstanding the competitive pressures of the EU market. Throughout much of the region economies remain undeveloped, dependent on aid and prone to high levels of state intervention coupled with low levels of institutional complementarity with other EU markets. For years, in the WBCs, consumption has been higher than production and has been financed primarily by foreign investments. Unemployment runs at very high levels, especially among the youth, and has further increased in the wake of the global and European economic crisis. The private sector remains underdeveloped while the majority of the working population continues to be employed in state-owned enterprises. The structural changes that have taken place have primarily favoured the expansion of services rather than production (Uvalic, 2010). The 2008 global financial and economic crisis has only deepened existing economic problems in the region by adding two further external shocks: reduced capital inflow from abroad and the collapse of export demand. Bartlett and Prica (2012) suggest that variability in 'demands for export … access to credit, and in inflows of foreign investment and remittances' were the main cause of the negative impact of the crisis in the region. The entire WB experienced rather modest overall decline in GDP during the crisis and in most countries industrial production and exports fell more steeply, while the unemployment rate increased, particularly in Bosnia-Herzegovina (27.2%) and Serbia (19.2%) (Statistical Bulletin No. 3, 2011). Consequently, the crisis has had wider social consequences, resulting in increased poverty and lower living standards for the citizens of the Western Balkans. Finally, in the absence of a sustainable solution to the ongoing debt crisis in the Eurozone periphery, it can be assumed that negative effects will continue to spill over to the WB region, thus importing new factors spurring economic instability.

The current generation of youth in the region is facing all of the challenges mentioned above at a highly precarious moment in their development. The youth population peaked in the WB before 1990. Now, with the exception of Kosovo and Albania, the share of young people is falling at a rate of 2% annually (*Young People and their Transition to Decent Work in the Western Balkans*, 2008). The violent conflicts which raged during the 1990s throughout the WB are now finished but they have left many scars and traumas behind them, maybe even more so on the generations whose first memories are based on television and real-time images of atrocities committed in the former Yugoslavia. While their aspirations – to participate in society in decent and well-paid jobs – remain the same as those of their parents' generation, the setting is rather different as the youth of today seek employment in labour markets structured on the basis of a free market of supply and demand as compared to the planned economic system of the socialist period, which guaranteed universal full-time employment to their parents.

Another complicating factor lies in the fact that, whereas globalization, technological change and intensified competition have changed the world economy, education and training systems in the WB have not followed the same dynamics (Marko, 2010). While the literacy rate and primary education surveys both show satisfying results, the picture changes significantly when examining the secondary and tertiary enrolment rates of young Roma and children from refugee and internally displaced families (*Young People and their Transition to Decent Work in the Western Balkans,* 2008). Due to the unusually high tuition fees for universities and scholarships that do not correspond to average regional salaries, youth stemming from socially vulnerable families often remain excluded from receiving higher education. Finally, at the end of the educational cycle, the economy is not able to create enough jobs in the formal market, so large numbers of young people are forced to seek informal employment where they do not enjoy basic rights at work such as health insurance coverage or pension contributions.

After an apparent halt to the widespread immigration that occurred during the 1990s, high levels of international migration of young and often highly educated people are once again causing a brain-drain problem throughout the region. On a more positive note, it is worth mentioning the positive effects of the EU visa liberalization which all WB states except for Kosovo now enjoy. Visa liberalization is of crucial importance for young people anywhere to be able to move freely and be able to communicate with their peers from different cultures and social contexts. However, this more positive development is rather eclipsed by the difficult socio-economic situation that young people in the region too often find themselves trapped in today. The difficulties they face in breaking out of conditions of socio-economic deprivation have arguably also been one of the factors that have contributed to an entrenchment of ethnically based stereotypes and nationalist attitudes, which remain one of the legacies of the decade-plus of conflict in the WB region. Of course, political elites have had a hand in this too.

It is these particular challenges of transition and change that the diverse contributions to this book seek to address from various national, regional and disciplinary perspectives. The book is organized in four parts. Part I attempts to deconstruct perspectives on the state of democracy in the countries of the Western Balkans. Part II addresses the challenges of state-building processes in the region bearing in mind the continued difficult legacies of the violent conflicts of the 1990s and early 2000s. Part III takes as its special focus the problems that political, economic and social change have posed for young people in the Western Balkans which have been thrown into stark relief by the effects of the global economic and financial crisis. Part IV, which only contains one chapter, opens the lid on the problematic of social reform and the challenge of balancing equity, efficacy and economic viability in the context of pressure of fiscal constraint and economic hardship. Due to the interrelatedness and complexity of transitional processes, the contributions to this volume include perspectives from different disciplines: politics, law, anthropology, history, cultural studies, sociology and economics. Some of the chapters stem from research projects funded within the framework of the Regional Research Promotion Programme in the Western Balkans, whereas others are from scholars who are dealing with the region and who are a part of the growing RRPP network of social scientists working on the Western Balkans, which together add to the richness, diversity and value of the volume.

Part I of this book explores the state of democracy in the Western Balkans from a range of different perspectives. This is timely given the apparent stalling of the democratic transition in the region and the emergence of a state of unconsolidated democratic consolidation in a number of countries in the Western Balkans (Bieber, 2012a). This phenomenon appears to have some similarities with Carothers' earlier conceptualization of the so-called 'grey zone', which designated countries undergoing democratic transition that fell somewhere between liberal democracy and authoritarianism (Carothers, 2002). The notion of unconsolidated democratic consolidation suggests a set of countries (in this case in the Western Balkans) that have moved closer along the continuum towards full-fledged democracy but have stalled. At present, as a concept, it remains understudied and undertheorized. The rich and diverse insights in Part I may in due course contribute to a new understanding and conceptualization of this phenomenon in the Western Balkan region.

Ana Stojanova's study on 'Defective Democracies: Challenges to Democracy Consolidation in the Western Balkans' fills a gap in the diverse transitions literature in its attempt to quantify empirically various explanatory factors that account for the successful outcome of democratic transition in Central and Eastern Europe compared with the more problematic record in the Western Balkans. Deriving hypotheses from the key approaches in the academic literature on transitions including modernization theory, social structural approaches and the seminal 1996 work of Linz and Stepan on the role of 'stateness', Stojanova's analysis leads her to the conclusion that, rather than the degree of ethnic and religious diversity, the key factors impeding the process of democratic consolidation in the Western Balkans are economic backwardness and political instability as a result of unresolved 'stateness' issues. Taken together, these drivers may pose potential dangers to future stability and consolidation given the continuing resort by political elites to populist politics that threaten to fan the ethno-nationalist sentiments that ravaged the region in the 1990s and early 2000s.

Snjezana Milivojevic's chapter explores how the media have fared in the process of political and economic transition and in the face of the current challenges posed by the global economic crisis as well as by the ongoing rapid technological changes in the media industry. The development of free, open, transparent media is a critical aspect of the democratization process and thus an important topic for assessing the state of democracy in the Western Balkans. Taking as its specific focus journalism in Serbia, the study explores the quality of journalism and its capacity to respond to a changing media environment. The study highlights the considerable levels of political and economic pressure that journalists in Serbia find themselves working under. The author concludes with a note of concern that Serbian journalists do not perceive these pressures or the spread of information-communication technologies as a major challenge to their profession, which leads her to suggest that journalists are caught in a state of limbo between the delayed transition processes in Serbia and the rapidly evolving information society.

The third chapter in Part I, by Mina Petrovic and Jelisaveta Vukelic, shifts its focus to another dimension of democratization, that of civil society whose role at different stages of democratic transition has been widely debated in the academic literature. The study, which investigates the participation of civil society in environmental decision making in Serbia, not only provides a means of analysing and assessing the place of civil society in Serbia's democratic transition – it also, as the authors highlight, considers the nature of the evolving partnership between civil society and the public sector, an important factor in the development of new environmental governance regimes, which is an integral aspect of the country's path to EU accession. The authors conclude that the combination of low trust in institutions and low levels of social capital with the difficult socio-economic conditions limits the levels of participation of the public and other civil-society actors in environmental decision-making and, as a consequence, impedes a shift away from centralized executive patterns of governance towards more decentralized forms of governance regimes. Thus it constitutes another critical case study whose findings potentially extend far beyond the question of civil society's role in environmental decision-making and also beyond the borders of Serbia.

The final chapter in Part I, 'Social Space in Serbia' by Predrag Cveticanin, Jasmina Nedeljkovic and Nemanja Krstic, comes from a rather different point of departure. It is informed by the work of Pierre Bourdieu although its exploration of social, economic and cultural capital and patterns of social differentiation dovetails well with the preceding chapter. It sheds interesting light on the resources (or 'capitals') that different occupational groups in Serbian society draw on in shaping their life strategies and how far these are likely to be individualist or collective, reactive or proactive. In particular the chapter explores the strategies of farmers, qualified workers and representatives of the upper classes and identifies key fault lines in terms of the availability of global or local cultural capital, levels of economic capital and different types of social capital (so-called political social capital and social capital of solidarity). It raises interesting questions about the role of informal networks and limited possibilities for social mobility even in times of transition such as Serbia is continuing to experience.

Part Two of the volume focuses on the challenges of state building in the Western Balkans. These processes follow the dynamics of the post-communist and post-conflict transformations of the region. Challenges on the path of state-building are perhaps best understood in the context of the fact that, at the time of the cessation of hostilities, none of the states under scrutiny could claim the ability to exercise legitimate monopoly over basic physical security within its borders. In an effort to overcome the problems of weak states and divided societies the countries of the Western Balkans have been seeking to address the so-called 'fours Rs': rehabilitation, restitution, reconstruction and reconciliation. The ultimate goal of the interplay of the 'four Rs' is to tackle the root and proximate causes of the previous conflicts in order to prevent a return to violence. It is also crucial to create a stable political and constitutional framework for sustainable economic growth and management of cultural diversity, and effective representation and participation at the various municipal, regional, state and supranational levels. Kostovicova and Bojicic-Dzelilovic (2010) have suggested that the main challenges of the state-building processes in the Western Balkans lie beyond the observable practices of formal politics or the workings of the formal economy. Therefore any assessment of the establishment of the functional triangle of stability, efficiency and democracy in the region must take into account the informal actors who manifest themselves in the form of nationalistic 'predatory' elites, interested in the preservation of political power for their private economic interests. The main debate addressed in the second part of the volume is the extent to which the state-building process has evolved in the WB. This is explored through the diverse contexts of weak states, municipal decentralization and protection of minorities.

Marius Calu's contribution considers the question of Kosovo's state weakness through the perspective of liberal interventionism and the role of the international community in the postconflict state-building process on one hand, and the difficult legacy of the past on the other. Taking the contested domestic sovereignty of Kosovo's state institutions as its point of departure, Calu, in his analysis, comprehensively debates the EU's efforts at democratization and institutional capacity building. He claims that state weakness in Kosovo comes from the perpetual state–society rift, which is further cultivated by both the external influence of international administration (supra-state authority) and the political authority of informal social networks (sub-state authority).

Aisling Lyon's chapter explores municipal decentralization in the Republic of Macedonia and its capacity to manage ethnic difference. While the decentralization process in Macedonia has been widely regarded as a success story, Lyon looks beyond the legislative framework and introduces us to the poor and inconsistent implementation of consociational power-sharing arrangements at the local level. In so doing she raises the critical question of whether the perceived dichotomy between integrationist and accommodationist ideas for the constitutional design of divided societies need necessarily be mutually exclusive. Finally, Simonida Kacarska explores minority policies in the EU accession process to the WB and focuses particularly on the role of the Framework Convention for Protection of National Minorities (FCNM) in the Republic of Macedonia. Bearing in mind the vagueness of the EU minority rights conditionality, using a process-tracing method Kacarska examines how far the FCNM serves as a benchmarking tool during the EU integrations in the case of Macedonia.

Part III of this book has a special focus on youth. The consequences of years of transition and stalled transition, conflict and the aftermath of conflict, and most recently the effects of the global financial and economic crisis have all taken their toll on young people in the Western Balkans. As noted earlier in this introduction, unemployment rates among young people are disturbingly high, socio-economic prospects are limited and there is clear, though not entirely surprising, evidence to suggest that political and social identities and the resulting attitudes of young people have been shaped by their experience of growing up in conflict and the aftermath of conflict. The contributions to this part of the volume shed interesting light on these issues. The chapter by Turjačanin and Majstorović examines the identities of youth in Bosnia-Herzegovina (BiH) today with a particular focus on attitudes to ethnicity and the state. In postwar BiH, which remains politically and constitutionally fragmented along ethnic lines, ethnicity remains a key point of reference and a dividing line for young people irrespective of their background. This is also underscored by the rejection of a national state Bosnian identity by most Croats and Serbs. In the case of Bosniaks, the authors found a marked tendency for Bosniaks to equate state (i.e. Bosnian) identity with Bosniak identity. The one area where these different groups appear to find common ground is in regarding Europe as an acceptable overarching identity. This would suggest that, despite the continuing constitutional quagmire in the country and repeated delays in the accession process, future reconciliation and state consolidation in Bosnia-Herzegovina will only be found on the road to Europe.

The other two chapters in Part III concentrate on the socio-economic status of young people in the region. In Chapter 11, Stanojević and Tomanović present the fascinating findings of their longitudinal study on the financial and housing situation of young people in Serbia between 2003 and 2011, highlighting degrees of dependence of young people from their parents and investigating the place of education and employment in this mix. The authors conclude that eight years on there continue to be high levels of financial and economic independence among young people in Serbia on their families, which underlines the slow pace of socio-economic progress in the country during this period. Nonetheless there has been a process of diversification in line with differing levels of personal income, suggesting there have been selected improvements in the financial position of some young people but no significant changes in their housing status. In terms of economic independence, the authors identify a clear though not entirely surprising correlation here with levels of education. It remains to be seen whether the effects of the financial and economic crisis will once again stall the modest developments identified in this research.

Chapter 12 by Korunovska, Korunovska and Maleska investigates the characteristics of unemployed youth in Macedonia, the so-called 'getting nowhere' generation with a view to identifying the individual predictors in terms of demographics of youth unemployment in this country. As the authors note rather eloquently, the failure to integrate young people into the labour market has broader consequences for the future prosperity and development of the country. Potentially the most positive finding highlighted in this chapter in the Macedonian context is that there were no telling differences between the different ethnic groups in the country, between male and female respondents or between respondents from urban or rural communities when it comes to predicting youth unemployment. On the other hand this might simply be a reflection of the parlously high level of unemployment in the country, with some 57% of Macedonian youth currently without jobs. Moreover evidence abounds in the broader literature of the damaging social and individual effects of (particularly long-term) unemployment on young people. The other interesting and worrying result of this research is that the educational level of the survey's respondents has no significant influence on their employment status. Given the potential implications of this finding for investment in higher education in Macedonia, it would seem imperative that the research of Korunovska, Korunovska and Maleska is replicated and the relationship between the quality of higher education (where 80% of youth were enrolled in 2009–10 – of course this may in part be due to the absence of available jobs) and the structure of the labour market in Macedonia be further scrutinized as this has may have very real policy implications for the government in Macedonia and other countries, the economies of which share similar structural features.

Last but not least we turn to Part IV. Though somewhat of an outlier with regard to the rest of the volume Milevska-Kostova's work on equity in health in Macedonia is a welcome contribution to this book, which would have been incomplete without a consideration of the question of social policy reform in the Western Balkans. Since the collapse of the communist system and the previous system of universal and level social provision, governments across the Western Balkan region have all been faced with the ongoing challenge of reforming their welfare systems under the combined and conflicting pressures of fiscal constraint, limited administrative capacity, transitional pressures to claw back the state and significant levels of economic and social hardship. In the process they have sought, to differing degrees, to navigate a path between efficacy, equity and economic viability. This case study of reform of primary health care and access to prescription medicines and other services in Macedonia sheds a timely spotlight on these issues. Although the improvement in the quality, efficiency and effectiveness of health services were among the key priorities identified in the agenda for reforming the healthcare system in Macedonia, Milevska-Kostova's study shows that there have been no significant improvements either in the quality of service delivery or in terms of savings at the very least within the primary health care sector though further research would need to be carried out to explore the impacts and linkages to secondary and tertiary health care levels.

In conclusion we would like to thank all those who have supported the development of this edited volume from inception to completion. Starting with the Swiss Development Agency for Development and Cooperation whose generous funding of the RRPP programme enabled the organization of the conference in Budva, Montenegro on the shores of the Mediterranean in the late spring of 2011 and the commencement of this book project, progressing to the constant support, thoughtful questioning and gentle diplomatic nudging of the RRPP Programme Director Professor Nicholas Hayoz who has helped us to keep this book project on track and finishing with the highly professional and committed shepherding of the editing process by Jan Kreuels, which meant that this book has seen the light of day. We would also like to offer our special thanks to the following experts on the Western Balkans who participated in discussions on the panels at the Budva conference and played a critical role in the paper selection process: Denise Efionayi-Maeder, Didier Rudan, Bashkim Iseni, Lea Sgier, Lejla Turcilo, Kolb Steffen, Jasna Capo Zmegac, Nadege Ragaru, Arben Hajrullahu, Nicolas Hayoz, Simone Baglioni, Maria Theiss, Eric Gordy and Vjeran Pavlakovic. We hope that readers who are new to the Western Balkans will find that the richness and variety contained in this book provide broad insights into the current challenges that the countries of the region are grappling with today, and that those who have long followed developments in this part of the world will also find something new in the presentation of the latest research findings contained in this volume. All that remains to be done is to thank our contributors for their hard work, patience and active engagement in the book project. We wish them future success in their own individual careers as well as in their endeavours to build research and educational capacity in the Western Balkans region.

References

Bartlett, W. and Prica, I. (2012) *The Variable Impact of the Global Economic Crisis in South East Europe*, LSEE - Research on South East Europe, London, p. 2.

Becker, J. and Engelberg, A. (eds) (2008) *Serbien nach den Kriegen*, Suhrkamp, Frankfurt am Main.

Bieber, F. (2010) Bosnia and Herzegovina since 1990. In *Central and Southeast European Politics Since 1989* (ed. S.P. Ramet), Cambridge University Press, Cambridge, pp. 311–28.

Bieber, F. (2012a) EU and the Western Balkans - current status and research perspectives. Keynote address to RRPP Conference in Sarajevo.

Bieber, F. (2012b) The Western Balkans are Dead – Long Live the Balkans! Democratization and the Limits of the EU. In *Unfinished Business: The Western Balkans and the International Community* (eds V. Dzihic and D. Hamilton), Brookings Institution Press, Washington D.C.

Carothers, T. (2002) The end of the transition paradigm. *Journal of Democracy* 13 (1), pp. 5–21.

Dzihana, A. and Volicic, Z. (n.d.) *Media and National Ideologies, Analysis of Reporting on War Crime Trials in the Former Yugoslavia*, Mediacentar, Sarajevo, available at www.rrpp-westernbalkans.net/en/library/Research-Results.html (accessed 4 October 2012).

Fischer, J. (2010) Albania since 1989: the Hoxhaist legacy. In *Central and Southeast European Politics since 1989* (ed. S. Ramet), Cambridge University Press, Cambridge, pp. 421–45.

Gordon, C. (2009) The stabilization and association process in the Western Balkans: an effective instrument of post-conflict management. *Ethnopolitics* 8 (3), pp 325–340.

Ilievski, Z. and Taleski, D. (2009) Was the EU's Role in Conflict Management a Success? *Ethnopolitics* 8 (3), pp. 355–67.

Irwin, Z. (2010) Macedonia since 1989. In *Central and Southeast European Politics since 1989* (ed. S. Ramet), Cambridge University Press, Cambridge, pp. 328–58.

Kostovicova, D. and Bojicic- Dželilović, V. (2010) Human security in a weak state in the Balkans: globalization and transnational networks. In *Transnational Terrorism, Organized Crime and Peace-building: Human Security in the Western Balkans* (eds W. Benedek, C. Daase, V. Dimitrijević and P. van Duyne), Palgrave Macmillan, Basingstoke.

Kostovicova, D. and Bojicic-Dželilović, V. (eds) (2008) *Transnationalism in the Balkans*, Routledge, New York, NY.

Marko, J. (2010) Human Rights and Ethnopolitics', in Cordell, K. and Wolff, S. (eds.) *Handbook of Ethnic Conflict*, Routledge, London, pp. 236–48.

Oisin, T. (2010) *Regime-Building: Democratization and International Administration*, Oxford University Press, New York, NY.

Phinnemore, D. (2003) Stabilisation and association agreements: Europe agreements for the Western Balkans? *European Foreign Affairs Review* 8 (1), pp. 77–103.

Ramet, Sabrina P. and Wagner, F. Peter 'Post-socialist models of rule in Central and Southeastern Europe' in Ramet, Sabrina P. (ed.), *Central and Southeast European Politics since 1989*, Cambridge University Press, Cambridge (2010).

Statistical Bulletin No 3, Centre for Public Employment Services of South East European Countries, Zagreb (2011).

Trivunović, M., Devine, V. and Mathisen, H. (2007) *Corruption in Montenegro 2007: Overview over Main Problems and Status of Reforms*, Chr. Michelsen Institute, Bergen.

Uvalić, M. (2010) *Serbia's Transition: Towards a Better Future*, Palgrave Macmillan, New York, NY.

Walker, C. and Habdank-Kołaczkowska, S. (eds) (2012) *Nations in Transit Report 2012: Fragile Frontier- Democracy's Growing Vulnerability in Central and Southeastern Europe*, Freedom House, Washington DC, http://www.freedomhouse.org/report/nations-transit/nations-transit-2012.

Weller, M. (2009) *Contested Statehood: Kosovo's Struggle for Independence*, Oxford University Press, Oxford.

Young People and their Transition to Decent Work in the Western Balkans (2008) International Labour Organization, Geneva.

Jasmina Opardija

Building Social Science Research Capacities in the Western Balkans: RRPP Experiences and Perspectives in the Light of EU Integration

Introduction

This chapter explores the current status of social science research in the Western Balkans. It looks at major issues and possible steps forward while taking into account the impact of European Union (EU) accession processes that are relevant for all the countries in the region.[1] The EU accession process is of particular significance considering that the EU and its member states are deeply involved in adjusting their higher education and research systems, striving to become a knowledge-based society fit for ever-growing global competition.[2]

The chapter will put into perspective the major obstacles currently undermining the speed of modernization, the development of institutions and human capital and the much-needed internationalization of social science research in the Western Balkans. It contends that increases in focused investments, political ambition to transform systems, combined with more transparency and cooperation across party or entity lines, are urgently needed. Considering that the countries in question are in one or another way involved in EU accession processes, timely and serious reforms would enable the region to catch up more easily with the EU and its members states,

1 Albania, Bosnia-Herzegovina, Macedonia, Montenegro, Kosovo, Serbia.

2 With the EU's 2020 strategy, it aims to better position itself in relation to the rest of the world, especially in contrast with the USA and Japan. The most important project aiming at unifying standards across the EU in terms of teaching and researching is the Bologna Process.

which are themselves undergoing transformations in their research and education systems.

Such efforts would significantly accelerate progress within the Bologna Process, an initiative that was undertaken in order to unify higher education standards across Europe, improve student mobility and create a European Higher Education Area (EHEA). Furthermore, such efforts would improve the region's position in co-creating and strengthening the European Research Area (ERA), which aims to be 'an internal market for research making Europe the world´s most competitive knowledge-based economy' (Marko and Unger, 2010: 5).

I will present some issues found in the field of social sciences in the Western Balkans and a set of priorities, which have been elaborated through a number of consultations with researchers and decision makers within the framework of the Regional Research Promotion Programme in the Western Balkans (RRPP).[3] The RRPP strives to help bring forward the necessary changes and thus promotes and funds not only regional cooperation, regional and national research teams and their projects, but also reform initiatives targeting higher education research systems in each of the countries in question. The programme endeavours to do this by building up regional networks consisting of social science research institutions and researchers, paying special attention to the inclusion of younger generations (PhD students) and women. Over a period of five years, the programme has managed to develop a large network of social scientists from the region and beyond, offering them opportunities to conduct empirical research and improve their research skills through a number of regional methods colloquia and regional/international networks. By doing so, the programme has contributed to the emergence and strengthening of a new generation of researchers in the region that utilizes necessary state-of-the-art research methods while conducting regional research projects. Hence, the RRPP is enabling cooperation across ethnic and national lines and contributes to better

3 See http://www.rrpp-westernbalkans.net. The programme is fully funded by the Swiss Agency for Development and Cooperation, Department of Foreign Affairs, and implemented by the University of Fribourg. It focuses on Albania, Bosnia-Herzegovina, Kosovo, Macedonia, Montenegro and Serbia. The programme is implemented in cooperation with participating partner institutions.

understanding of shared problems in a divided region. This is significant considering that many researchers supported through the RRPP either already serve or will serve as experts in their countries and therefore have the possibility to influence policy making and public opinion. A number of chapters in this volume stem from researcher supported by the RRPP.

Based on the experience of the RRPP, this chapter proposes several steps towards improving the status of social sciences in the Western Balkans. These include the establishment of high-quality PhD programmes; the introduction of research methods trainings; intensified regional and international mobility; enhanced research structures and programmes at universities; the removal of bureaucratic hurdles at public institutions; and making state-of-the-art social science research results available to the wider public, including policy makers, media and nongovernmental organizations (NGOs).

The chapter consists of four closely interweaved parts.

The first part, 'Investing in Knowledge-Based Societies: the EU versus the Western Balkans', presents today's major investments in social science research while looking into expenditures (percentage of GDP) on research and development in selected countries, hence providing an assessment of where the region stands today in its level of science and research promotion when compared with the EU and some of its individual member states. Taking this comparison as a starting point is of central importance considering the chronic underinvestment in research in the Western Balkans. The comparison is also provided in order to emphasize the need for countries to change their policies in order to enable them to catch up more quickly with other countries of the EU. This is a necessary stage as the Western Balkans countries are all seeking accession to the EU.

The second part, 'Social Sciences in the Western Balkans: Between Hurdles from the Past and Insufficient Capacity for the Future', is an assessment of social science research capacities. It looks into 'why' research capacities have been so weak and which challenges need to be addressed in order to move forward. This part explores the difficult process of 'change' in a postconflict context. It is introduced in order to explore the causes of the core problems that must be urgently addressed by all relevant actors, including policy makers on different levels, researchers and donors.

The third part, 'Research, Teaching and Policy Making – the Missing Links', addresses urgent current issues (and their consequences), especially those that relate to the impact of old-fashioned and inadequate bureaucracies and procedures in higher education institutions combined with the lack of connectedness between research and teaching. This constitutes the core of the chapter providing justifications as to why social science research and teaching need to be improved and substantially supported.

Finally, the fourth concluding part represents a summary of 'Challenges and Priorities', defining areas wherein investment and initiatives are urgently needed, including PhD programmes, regional and international mobilization, improvements in scientific productivity, institutional reforms, removal of administrative hurdles and improvement in management policies, especially at public institutions.

Investing in Knowledge-Based Societies: The EU versus the Western Balkans

Western Balkan countries – Albania, Bosnia-Herzegovina, Kosovo, Macedonia, Montenegro and Serbia – are still marked by difficult transition trajectories that are the consequences of ethnic conflicts (violent) and unfinished nation-state building processes (except Albania). Recent economic crises and political dynamics in the EU have significantly affected the region, contributing to a further deterioration in the socio-economic situation and the fragile trust in a postconflict context. As a consequence, recent research shows that previously shared hope for a better life envisaged with eventual EU membership has faded: 'the people in the Balkans feel disillusioned with the Union, their own societies and the two-decade long transition' (Kacarska, 2012: 2).

Despite the crisis and EU 'enlargement fatigue', the international community continues to play a crucial role in reform processes in the Western Balkans; it remains a particularly important player.

Daskalovski (2011: 51) notes that the EU conditionality approach[4] in the Balkans, through the Stabilization and Association Process (SAP) and subsequent accession processes, contains two dimensions: 'a) the EU as *an active player* in the mediation and conflict resolution and b) the EU as *a framework* providing a possibility of participation in decision making and equipping (…) with models of governance and policy-options.' Hence, higher education and research are fields wherein countries from the region can benefit widely in terms of 'models of governance and policy-options' (Daskalovski, 2011: 51) especially considering EU strategies and initiatives, such as Europe 2020, the Bologna Process or the FP7 programme. Marko and Unger (2010: 53), citing Horvat and Bonas, note that 'In the past, research and technological development have played a pioneering role in European integration.'

Considering this 'pioneering role' of research in development and the fact that many innovative and well-educated people from the region remain or wish to stay connected to the sector, more investment into this field should be among the top priorities. This is especially true if we consider the brain-drain process and its devastating consequences on bringing forward the necessary political and socio-economic changes. As Horvat (2004: 90) puts it '… if a large number of elites emigrate, there will be severe hardships in implementing transitional reforms.' At present, despite the urgent need to accelerate development and to benefit from the brightest people in the region, current levels of investment in higher education and research are poor or even non-existent and the brain drain continues to be among the region's major problems.

At the EU level, constant investment is made to boost research and development capacity, setting 'research and innovation at the top of its agenda for growth and jobs.'[5] With the EU's Europe 2020 strategy, the union is attempting to increase competitiveness and better position itself in relation to the rest of the world, especially

4 The EU conditionality approach is in essence an EU-designed system for eastward expansion, guiding the accession process of aspiring countries and rewarding them for complying with EU conditions and standards with EU membership status.

5 See *European Union, Research and Development,* http://europa.eu/pol/rd/ (accessed 1 March 2012).

the US and Japan. To this end, the EU's goal is to raise investment to '3% of its GDP (public and private combined) in R&D/innovation',[6] which has yet to be achieved (European Commission, 2012). There are significant disparities in the investments of individual countries within the EU's 2012 average of 1.9%.[7] In order to achieve the 3% target, the union has developed several specific instruments, including the Socio-Economic Sciences and Humanities (SSH) Programme[8] that is most relevant for social sciences. It is an integral part of the FP7,[9] 'EU's main instrument for funding research (...) designed to respond to Europe's employment needs, competitiveness and quality of life in Europe' (European Commission, 2012).[10] Finally it should also help in unifying the European Research Area (ERA) (Marko and Unger, 2010: 37).[11]

All countries from the Western Balkans, except for Kosovo, have started integrating into the ERA with the signing of the EU Stabilization and Association Agreements that specifically require meaningful regional cooperation in different fields. Today, all countries from the region, except for Kosovo, are eligible to participate in FP7 and have already established National Contact Points (NCP), providing information and guidance in local languages to enhance cooperation (European Commission, 2012).[12]

6 *The Seventh Framework Programme for Research, Technological Development and Demonstration, 2007–2013,* http://ec.europa.eu/europe2020/reaching-the-goals/targets/index_en.htm (accessed 5 October 2012).
7 See WEB INCO NET, http://wbc-inco.net/object/news/2855 (accessed 4 April, 2012).
8 See http://ec.europa.eu/research/social-sciences/index_en.html (accessed 1 March 2012).
9 See *Seventh Framework Programme for Research and Development,* http://ec.europa.eu/research/fp7/ (accessed 1 March 2012).
10 See *Understanding Seventh Framework Programme,* http://ec.europa.eu/research/fp7/index_en.cfm?pg=understanding (accessed 1 March 2012).
11 'An open space of knowledge composed of all research and development activities, programmes and policies in Europe which involve a transnational perspective. Together, they enable researchers, research institutions and businesses to increasingly circulate, compete and co-operate across borders.' See What is ERA? http://ec.europa.eu/research/era/understanding/what/what_is_era_en.htm (accessed 3 April 2012)
12 See CORDIS, http://cordis.europa.eu/fp7/get-support_en.html (accessed 03 April 2012)

Looking at the situation at the national level, it is apparent that the best performing countries in Europe are the Scandinavian states, considering their individual investments or share of GDP in research and development (R&D): Finland (3.87%), Sweden (3.42%) and Denmark (3.06%).[13] As shown above, these countries already exceed the EU's general target of 3% (Eurostat, 2012). However, disparities within the EU are significant and members from south-east Europe seem to be particularly poor in this respect, 'with Romania having the lowest R&D investment of 0.5% of its GDP' (Eurostat, 2012). Looking at the Western Balkans, the situation looks even less promising, with no state even reaching the level of the investment of Romania. According to the data provided by WEB INCO NET,[14] Bosnia-Herzegovina, after suffering huge destruction of research infrastructure and loss of human capital during and after the war, only invests some 0.07% of its GDP into R&D. As for Albania, which was not directly affected by the violent regional conflicts – it only reaches 0.2%. Serbia, the biggest country in the region with a population of 7.3 million, in 2009 reached an investment total of about 0.86% of its GDP (Era Watch, 2012).[15]

13 See Eurostat information on R&D expenditure, http://epp.eurostat.ec.europa.eu/statistics_explained/index.php/R_%26_D_expenditure (accessed 4 April 2012).

14 See WBC-INCO.NET, http://wbc-inco.net/object/news/2855 (accessed 17 July 2012).

15 See ERA Watch, Country pages, http://erawatch.jrc.ec.europa.eu/erawatch/opencms/information/country_pages/rs/country?section=Overview (accessed 4 April 2012).

Social Sciences in the Western Balkans: Between Hurdles from the Past and Insufficient Capacity for the Future

The Bologna Process, which was initiated in 1999 and is based on voluntary participation,[16] has had a significant effect on the Western Balkans, bringing additional challenges not only to the changing roles within the higher education systems, but also to how different study cycles are organized and evaluated. By signing the 'Bologna Declaration', the countries of the Western Balkans[17] committed themselves to an effort to create 'A European Higher Education Area (EHEA)' (Marko and Unger, 2010: 5). According to the 'Standards and Guidelines for Quality Assurance in the European Higher Education Area', the relationship between teaching and research is one of the main traits defining quality assurance. Furthermore, EU-funded research under the SSH programme 'is intended to be policy and socially relevant i.e. to be able to inform policy and public debate and to identify and examine key issues and options, while not being driven by short- term policy priorities' (EC, 2009).[18]

Social science research is of a particular importance in postconflict and postcommunist contexts, where political and socio-economic changes often occur without being genuine, transparent and thoroughly thought through. Such changes often lack strategic orientation, are externally designed, or are simply introduced under the

16 The three overarching objectives of the Bologna process have been: (i) Introduction of the three-cycle system (bachelor/master/doctorate); (ii) quality assurance; and (iii) recognition of qualifications and periods of study.

17 Albania, Bosnia-Herzegovina, Macedonia, Montenegro and Serbia are all formal members of the Bologna Process. As for Kosovo, its reforms are in line with the process but 'it is currently not eligible for direct membership to the Bologna Process (...) and is attending Bologna Ministerial meetings on an observer basis', http://eacea.ec.europa.eu/tempus/participating_countries/impact/kosovo.pdf (accessed 6 October 2012).

18 See *FP7 Socio-economic Sciences and Humanities Indicative Strategic Research Roadmap, 2011–2013*, http://ec.europa.eu/research/social-sciences/pdf/roadmap-2011-2013-final_en.pdf, (accessed 03 April, 2012).

leadership of international actors without consideration of the local context and available capacities that would ensure sustainability.

As noted by Ahrens (2000: 51) while discussing reforms of governance structures and economy in postsocialist countries, '[a]t the onset of transition (...) the changes were undertaken in order to rapidly establish market-oriented economies in order to solidify transformation, to prevent a potential reversal, and to avoid an asset-stripping of state-owned enterprises.' Hence, the focus was largely put on economic and political reforms - establishing of market economy and introduction of free elections. Ahrens (2000: 5) notes that reforms took place in a context where 'political leadership and credible commitment to policy reform were lacking.' Therefore, once the sustainability and effectiveness of such reforms became questionable, the need for institution and capacity building was recognized, but 'only after 10 years of the transition', as illustrated by Ahrens (2000: 5). Looking at social sciences and higher education sector in the Western Balkans, the RRPP experience shows that serious institution- and capacity-building reforms are still absent from the top of the reform agendas, especially when it comes to their implementation.

Generally, one can say that 'usefulness' and direct impact on policy making of social science research is often disputed, which is also noted in a UNESCO publication stating that there remains 'usually weak direct influence on political decisions about social policies by social science research' (Lee *et al.*, 2005: 21).[19] However, before social science can open up discussions or inform policy development, competent state-of-the-art research capacity, which can deliver excellent results, must be in place. This equally implies human capital and research infrastructure.

In the case of Eastern Europe, during the communist period, social sciences and social science research were largely ideologically controlled and politically instrumentalized (Kovacs and Kutsar, 2010: 215). Research and education under communism were centrally

19 See UNESCO, Social Science and Social Policy: From National Dilemmas to Global Opportunities, http://unesdoc.unesco.org/images/0014/001402/140246e.pdf (accessed 13 November 2012).

controlled, aiming at the achievement of goals set by the Party. Marko and Unger note that social sciences have continued to be 'ideologically controlled' since the end of communism in Eastern Europe. With the collapse of communism, especially in the former Yugoslavia, this sector not only suffered from severe devastations of infrastructure, brain drain and social capital, but it continued to be ideologically controlled by new political establishments. This especially relates to states that were directly involved in violent conflicts and where the consequences of these conflicts influence state- and nation-building processes.

The violent conflicts in the former Yugoslavia have contributed to ethnic divisions between researchers and institutions, undermining trust and cross-ethnic cooperation. As a consequence, since the early 1990s, networks that are strictly organized along ethnic lines have flourished. In addition, legacies from their socialist past, including high levels of state control over higher education and research institutions, coupled with huge bureaucratic hurdles, have impeded the improvement of research capacities and internationalization. Furthermore, public universities, with their autonomous faculties and research institutes, frequently lack financial autonomy (Marko and Unger, 2010).

Most of the numerous private universities that mushroomed with the transition do not satisfy the necessary quality standards, lack credibility and are perceived as being less interested in science and more interested in money making, '...simply selling diplomas' as Marko and Unger (2010: 92) note. Many of these universities operate despite the fact they failed to acquire official accreditations and were set up by investors whose capital gain often remains unclear. As Bieber in his widely discussed blog contribution from 2011 notes, 'Some of the institutions are certainly on their way to establish themselves as serious places of higher education. Many others have a distinctly dubious ring.'[20] Hence, the influence on social sciences of everyday politics projected through formal institutions and of informal networks and private interests remains a significant challenge.

20 *New Universities in the Balkans: European visions, UFOs and Megatrends*, http://fbieber.wordpress.com/2011/06/26/new-universities-in-the-balkans-european-visions-ufos-and-megatrends/(accessed 13 November 2012).

In general, financial investment in state-of-the art research based on clear and transparent criteria that also takes into account major societal issues is scarce. Policy-making in this field, alongside subsequent budgeting, continues to follow the lines of structures inherited from the communist period. Furthermore, all governments from the Western Balkans continue to finance research related to topics that reinforce dominant national ideologies and identities while at the same time neglecting projects dealing with burning socio-economic issues. These findings confirm the RRPP assessments of social science research capacities in the Western Balkans. For example in Macedonia:

> The Ministry of Education and Science (...) tends to fund projects which are considered to be of national interest. Since, currently the national interest has been placed on issues of national identity, the topics supported are primarily related to the Macedonian history, language and folklore and tend to have theoretical, rather than applicative value. (CRPM, 2008: 30)

On the other hand, the available EU funding mechanisms require high levels of expertise, especially in writing project proposals in English and applying international management tools in projects. This, as a consequence, contributes to poor quality and lack of scientific production in the region, putting social scientific projects on the lowest FP7 success rate scales. There are, however, some differences among the countries of the region. Serbia seems to be performing better than the rest of the region, followed by Macedonia (European Commission, 2011: 29).[21]

21 See the *EU Evaluation and Monitoring Reports*, http://ec.europa.eu/research/evaluations/pdf/archive/fp7_monitoring_reports/fourth_fp7_monitoring_report.pdf#view=fit&pagemode=none (accessed 13 November 2012).

Research, Teaching and Policy Making – the Missing Links

Another legacy from the past that heavily influences the social sciences in the region concerns the rigid division between teaching and research. The legacies of communism are especially visible at public institutions – universities, academies and institutes – where research infrastructure alongside research and project management skills are often completely missing. Under communism teaching and research were deliberately separated, thus creating a huge gap that still needs to be adequately closed. Marko and Unger (2010: 79) note that the 'division of advisory bodies for the entire sector seems to follow the communist legacy of a strict division between universities, which had the almost exclusive task of providing tertiary education, whereas research was concentrated at the Academies of Sciences and/or institutionally directly attached to ministries.' The missing link between teaching and research remains one of the key weaknesses of higher education and research in the Balkans, even though there are initiatives that have been undertaken to solve this problem, such as the RRPP. Pango *et al.* (2011: 10), while referring to Albania, note that much more must be done in order to integrate the two systems '… which so far have been entirely separate from one another, and which should be innovative and efficient for the conditions of a small country with limited financial resources.'

The reasons for this missing link, however, are not only structural, but also relate to human capital. Professors and their assistants (usually MA graduates and PhD candidates) are often underpaid and overburdened with administrative tasks and teach an excessive number of students. In order to improve their socio-economic status, they often serve as experts in internationally funded development projects that are better paid, but also require significant personal investment. Moreover, scholars in the Western Balkans are often engaged in politics, either as members of political parties or as advisors in the government. All these different tasks and engagements are overstretching researchers, but at the same time bringing more visibility, recognition and power in influencing the current situation than teaching could. This is also one of the reasons as to why the completion time of PhD projects is so lengthy. In Serbia, for example, most scholars spend five to eight years completing their PhD, while approximately 5% spend more than 12 years on their project.[22]

Hence, considering the aforementioned time constraints and stresses, it is difficult to fit in research, despite it being one of the central components of the PhD. Many scholars, especially from the younger generation, some of whom were partly or fully educated abroad, therefore choose alternative ways of staying in the research sector; they are engaged by numerous research institutes, think tanks and non-governmental organisations (NGOs). According to an online article published by *Science Insider*, 'University professors in Bosnia and Herzegovina spend only 3% of their work time doing science due to lack of funds (...) and lack of dedicated research funding also prevents them from applying to European research projects and collaborations' (Tatalovic, 2011).[23]

In Serbia, on the other hand, there is a number of self-standing and more-or-less discipline-based research institutes, inherited from the former Yugoslavia. Many of them operate as isolated islands linked neither to teaching nor to policy making. A significant number have not managed to adjust to the new socio-economic and political circumstances that require the building of excellence and acquiring of new skills necessary for international cooperation and competition.[24] Such institutes, including the Academies of Sciences, exist across the region.

Finally, one of the major weaknesses faced by social sciences in the Western Balkans is the poor valorization of research results – even

22 Based on the results of a survey from 2012: 'Capacities and Problems of the Scientific Research Community in Serbia', carried out within the RRPP Policy Dialogue project in Serbia.

23 See *Balkan Countries Pin Hopes on More Science*, http://news.sciencemag.org/scienceinsider/2011/01/balkan-countries-pin-hopes-on.html (accessed 21 March 2012).

24 For more information about the situation in Serbia, read the *RRPP Assessment of Research Capacities in the Social Sciences in Serbia* (2010), www.rrpp-westernbalkans.net/en/library/Country-Assessments.html (accessed 6 October 2012).

when they do exist, they are not properly disseminated to the public and policy-makers who may benefit from them. However, Marko and Unger (2010: 79) suggest that 'Macedonia, Montenegro, (...) and Albania seem to have achieved – beyond the formal establishment of advisory bodies – some "effective" participation of academia in policy planning by influencing the substance of decision-making processes at the level of parliaments and governments.' Still, the influence of research results on policy development remains a field where much more must be done in order to enable informed decision-making. Cooperation between regionally and internationally established researchers and decision-makers is an area where further efforts are needed.

Considering the missing link between research, teaching and policy making mentioned above, the creation of excellent research capacities remains both a great need and a great challenge. In order for research results to be useful for policy development, they need to be trustworthy and produced in accordance with the highest scientific rigour. For this to happen, the evaluation procedures and standards will need to be adjusted and raised, including the engagement of independent experts, domestic and international.

The EU itself must work further on creating a link between education and research if it wants to truly become a 'knowledge society', successfully competing in the global arena. This is also confirmed by the Benelux Bologna Secretariat (2009: 17), which has stated that, 'a closer link between education and research is needed if European higher education is to retain its broad research basis.'

Conclusions: Challenges and Priorities

In order to improve the status of social-science research, to make it useful for policy development whenever possible and reverse the brain drain into a 'brain gain', governments across the region need to make sure that higher education and research are not only in place and linked with each other, but that researchers and their institutions enjoy freedom and autonomy in order to be able to produce excellent and globally relevant results.[25]

Therefore, more attention must be paid to this sector above and beyond the much-needed increase in financial investment into research, especially at public universities. One of the major problems identified in the framework of the RRPP's cooperation with public universities in the Western Balkans relates to the fact that project financing faces immense bureaucratic hurdles and lacks management capacities that follow the principles of good governance. Research institutions should be able to open separate bank accounts for funding coming from international sources, and researchers who acquired the funding should have adequate access to it. At the same time, government accountability can be increased via the introduction of transparent programmes, evaluation schemes and national research agendas. Furthermore, clear evaluation procedures and transparency would facilitate the production of societally relevant research results, which can be used in decision making, covering the needs of different parts of society, including those who are marginalized, such as minorities. Marko and Unger (2010: 130) suggest that 'universities should be a "spring of culture", combining the different needs and interests of society.'

Drawing from experiences acquired throughout work of the RRPP, the highly interrelated weaknesses hindering the linkage of research, teaching practice and policy making and producing poor results on the international research scene can be summarized as follows:[26]

1. Lack of PhD study programmes offering quality methodological training corresponding with international standards.
2. Insufficient national, regional and international mobility.
3. Low level of scientific production and visibility.
4. Bureaucratic hurdles.

25 See also the results of an RRPP-sponsored debate held in Macedonia on the autonomy of universities and the Law on Higher Education: http://soros.org.mk/default.asp?lang=eng&menuid=2179 (accessed 6 October 2012).

26 The problems were identified during numerous RRPP consultative events with stakeholders in the Western Balkans. Those mentioned here are important for building-up excellent and sustainable research capacities.

Lack of PhD Study Programmes Offering Quality Methodological Training Corresponding with International Standards

All Western Balkan countries still lack joint PhD studies offering training in research methods and meeting European standards. Students in the majority of cases are only individually mentored by their professors (Marko and Unger, 2010: 99). Hence they are isolated from a broader national, regional and international research community. This is worrying, especially considering that PhD students are viewed as 'early stage researchers' within the Bologna framework (Benelux Bologna Secretariat, 2009: 9).[27] Considering that quality PhD studies are still in the initial stages of inception, it is essential to invest more into PhD programmes that are 'developed according to common European standards' and provide PhD candidates with methods training, more time and research opportunities (Marko and Unger, 2010: 129). This is especially true if universities wish to achieve successful linking of research and teaching and if the countries in question seriously wish to enhance their research systems and policies. Furthermore, given that the employability of researchers and PhD holders is not purely restricted to an academic career path, the universities need to find ways to develop research capacities that can be employed in different sectors, such as 'industry, non-profit organisations, private companies, private and public independent research centres' (Benelux Bologna Secretariat, 2009: 11).

Insufficient National, Regional and International Mobility

The younger generation of researchers in the Western Balkans, especially those from the former Yugoslavia, are still divided, not only along ethnic lines but also along institutional lines. While institutional cooperation and exchange were encouraged in the former Yugoslavia, the creation of separate states and the now 20-year-old conflicts on different levels have prevented these networks from

27 *Bologna Beyond 2010 Report*, http://www.ehea.info/Uploads/Irina/Bologna%20beyond%202010.pdf (accessed 6 October 2012).

growing, replacing them with those marked by the war and postwar realities. The RRPP is certainly making a contribution to lessening this problem, but such initiatives also need to come from relevant state institutions.

The visa regimes imposed by the Western European countries, which were only recently lifted, except in Kosovo, have also severely impeded mobility and international cooperation. Considering that the visa hurdles for most countries have been removed, investing more into the mobility of students and researchers, and increasing their ability to engage in international networking and cooperation should be a priority. Furthermore, given that EU accession processes are under way in the region and that there is an increase in openness towards cooperation on different levels, attracting international scholars (including those stemming from the region) would help improve research capacities at universities, contributing to the internationalization of locally conducted research. The RRPP experience shows that regionally organized methods seminars conducted by specialists from Switzerland and other European countries were highly appreciated, especially by PhD students. They not only improved their research capacities, but were also exposed to new perspectives, including successful collaborative projects that traverse national and regional borders.

Low Levels of Scientific Production and Visibility (Lack of Good-Quality Publications and Papers)

The vast majority of researchers from the Western Balkans, as well as those from other Central and Eastern European countries, usually publish in national journals, in local languages, thus 'mainly targeting [a] national audience' (Schneider *et al.*, 2012: 21). Evaluations from several RRPP colloquia on academic writing and publishing indicate that there is a great need for improving academic writing skills (including English academic writing) in order to make research results more regionally and internationally visible. Considering that these skills have not been largely thought of as part of the existing curricula, the introduction of academic writing training into PhD studies and programmes would not only improve the writing capacities of researchers from the region, but also open up possibilities for them to publish internationally. This would consequently increase opportunities for international networking through wider participation at international conferences, hence contributing to greater international mobility. Both the RRPP scientific conferences and this joint volume are attempts to move in that direction.

Bureaucratic Hurdles

One of the major impediments for developing better research capacities is the lack of funding. The situation is especially difficult at public universities, where rigid structures and complicated bureaucratic procedures prevent the development of research even when funding is secured. Most importantly, the academic staff is so overburdened with administration and teaching that they lack the time for conducting research and applying for accessible research funding through numerous international programmes, including the EU's FP7 and the Swiss-funded RRPP. A vast number of public universities have not managed to put in place internal structures and human resources that would primarily be dedicated to research management and fundraising. The RRPP experience in providing research grants to private, public and non-governmental research institutions in the Balkans shows that bureaucratic hurdles, in terms of project implementation, are the greatest obstacle at public universities.

This remains the case despite acknowledgement that the relationship between teaching and research is one of the main traits defining quality assurance, according to the Standards and Guidelines for Quality Assurance in the European Higher Education Area.[28] Each university should develop specific quality assurance policies and procedures detailing different standards that would 'help [in] providing public confidence in institutional autonomy' (European Association for Quality Assurance in Higher Education, 2009: 16).

28 See Standards and Guidelines for Quality Assurance in the European Higher Education Area, http://www.enqa.eu/files/ESG_3edition%20(2).pdf (accessed April 25, 2011).

Hence, considering the lack of research capacities at many public universities, even if such policies are formally in place, they do not seem to be implemented effectively. International funding mechanisms, such as the RRPP, require, *inter alia,* transparent management of funds implying separate bank accounts that are accessible by the research team. The policies and structures for funding and enabling research at public universities are often unable to respond to such requirements and therefore need to be adjusted.

In conclusion, in the effort to achieve the 'knowledge triangle of research, education and innovation' and become knowledge-based societies, different actors in the region, especially governments and leaders in the higher education sector, will need to move more quickly to implement reforms and increase investments into higher education, research and development (Marko and Unger, 2010: 135). This implies the improvement of several key interrelated areas:

- expanding existing funding mechanisms dedicated to research promotion and the creation of additional mechanisms that are transparent and related to current socio-economic issues;
- introduction of quality PhD programmes that contain excellent methodological training, research opportunities and better perspectives for younger researchers, women and other marginalized groups;
- openness towards regionalization and internationalization on all levels and relevant budgeting in order to increase mobility of students and access to internationally produced knowledge and networks;
- improvement of scientific production and visibility and internationalization of research results through wider participation at international conferences and training opportunities in academic writing;
- removal of bureaucratic hurdles; and an increase in transparency in terms of management policies, especially at public institutions that are indispensable and can be the first step forward.

In conclusion, even though social science capacities in the Western Balkans remain weak, the RRPP experience over the last five years (2007–2012) proves that there is significant human and social capital in the region, which should be further developed and directed towards facilitating change in the region. During this relatively short period a great number of scholars, researchers and institutions from the Western Balkans have cooperated on more than 50 RRPP research projects tackling political and socio-economic issues of concern for the entire region. These researchers are further expanding their regional and international collaborations and are making their research relevant and visible internationally. Larger, timely and more focused investment into research and higher education would help the region to further develop its human and social capital while at the same time turning the 'brain-drain' into a 'brain-gain'. Such investment in research and higher education would also accelerate and contribute considerably to the necessary changes in the region, not least the EU-accession processes, and the consolidation of stability and sustainable peace.

References

Ahrens, J. (2000) Governance, conditionality and transformation in post-socialist countries. In *Governance Structures in Central and Eastern Europe* (eds H. Hoen, J. Ahrens, D. Bartlett, H.-J. Giessmann, O. Havrylyshyn, K. Henderson, I. Izvorski, I. Jeffries, R. van Rooden), Harmonie Papers Special Issue, Centre of European Security Studies (CESS), Groningen.

Benelux Bologna Secretariat (2009) *Bologna Beyond 2010: Report on the Development of the European Higher Education Area.* Background paper for the Bologna Follow-up group, www.ehea.info/Uploads/Irina/Bologna%20beyond%202010.pdf (accessed 6 October 2012).

Bieber, F. (n.d.) *New Universities in the Balkans: European visions, UFOs and Megatrends,* http://fbieber.wordpress.com/2011/06/26/new-universities-in-the-balkans-european-visions-ufos-and-megatrends/ (accessed 6 October 2012).

CRPM (2008) The assessment of research capacities in social sciences in Macedonia, www.rrpp-westernbalkans.net/en/library/Country-Assessments.html (accessed 6 October 2012).

Daskalovski, Z. (2011) The influence of EU conditionality on Macedonia. In *20 Years after the Collapse of Communism, Expectations, Achievements and Disillusions of 1989,* Interdisciplinary Studies on Central and Eastern Europe, Peter Lang, Bern.

European Association for Quality Assurance in Higher Education (2009) *Standards and Guidelines for Quality Assurance in the European Higher Education Area*, 3rd edn, www.enqa.eu/files/ESG_3edition%20(2).pdf (accessed 6 October 2012).
European Commission (2009) *FP7 Socio-economic Sciences and Humanities Indicative Strategic Research Roadmap, 2011–2013*, http://ec.europa.eu/research/social-sciences/pdf/roadmap-2011-2013-final_en.pdf (accessed 03 April, 2012)
European Commission (2011) *Fourth FP7 Monitoring Report*, http://ec.europa.eu/research/evaluations/pdf/archive/fp7_monitoring_reports/fourth_fp7_monitoring_report.pdf (accessed 6 October 2012).
European Commission (2012) *FP7 Socio-economic Sciences and Humanities Indicative Strategic Research Roadmap, 2011–2013*, http://ec.europa.eu/research/social-sciences/pdf/roadmap-2011-2013-final_en.pdf (accessed 6 October 2012).
Eurostat, European Commission (2012) R & D expenditure, http://epp.eurostat.ec.europa.eu/statistics_explained/index.php/R_%26_D_expenditure (accessed 6 October 2012).
Horvat, V. (2004) Brain Drain. Threat to Successful Transition in South East Europe? Alumni Association of the Center for Interdisciplinary Postgraduate Studies of the University of Sarajevo, in *Southeast European Politics*, Vol. V, No. 1, pp. 76–93, available at: http://www.seep.ceu.hu/archives/issue51/horvat.pdf (accessed 6 October 2012).
Jahic, E. (2011) *Mini Country Report/Montenegro*, http://wbc-inco.net/attach/Bosnia_TC_final_PDF.pdf (accessed 6 October 2012).
Josimovski, S. (2011) *Mini Country Report/former Yugoslav Republic of Macedonia*, www.proinno-europe.eu/inno-policy-trendchart/repository/country-specific-trends (accessed 6 October 2012).
Kacarska, S. (2012) *Twenty Years after 1991: The Tale of Two Generations*, European Fund for the Balkans, Opinion Paper, http://balkanfund.org/spd/wp-content/uploads/2012/03/pp6.pdf (accessed 6 October 2012).
Kovacs, P. and Kutsar, D. (2010) Conclusions: Internationalisation of Central and Eastern European social sciences – is the catching up a myth or reality? In *Internationalisation of Social Sciences in Central and Eastern Europe, The "Catching Up" – A Myth or a Strategy* (eds I. Pálné Kovács and D. Kutsar), Routledge, London, pp. 215–27.
Marko, J. and Unger, H. (2010) *Research and Tertiary Education in Central and South-Eastern Europe, Developments, Structures and Perspectives in the Light of EU Integration*, Nomos, EURAC Research, Bolzano.
Pango, Y., Musai, B., Kamani, P., Muça, M., Kallciu, N., Duraj, A. (2011) *Background Report on Social Sciences and Humanities, Albania*, http://wbc-inco.net/attach/101albania_SSH_Report_final-web.pdf (accessed 13 November, 2012)
Schneider. C.Q., Bochsler, D., Chiru, M. (2012) Comparative Politics in Central and Eastern Europe: Mapping Publications Over the Past Twenty Years, in *European Political Science* advance online publication 22 June 2012.
Lee, R., Martin, W., Sonntag, H., Taylor, P., Wallerstein, I. and Wieviorka, M. (2005) *Social Science and Social Policy: From National Dilemmas to Global Opportunities*, http://unesdoc.unesco.org/images/0014/001402/140246e.pdf (accessed 6 October 2012).

Tatalovic, M. (2011) Balkan Countries Pin Hopes on More Science, http://news.sciencemag.org/scienceinsider/2011/01/balkan-countries-pin-hopes-on.html (accessed 21 March 2012).

Part I

Perspectives on the State of Democracy in the Western Balkans

Ana Stojanova

Defective Democracies: Challenges to Democratic Consolidation in the Western Balkans[1]

Introduction

Since the Third Wave of Democratization[2] spread throughout Eastern Europe at the beginning of the 1990s there has been a growing number of studies concerning the democratization and democratic consolidation of the post-communist countries. Most of these studies acknowledge the different trajectories of transition from authoritarianism to democracy. However there are hardly any empirically grounded assessments explaining the widening gap between the Western Balkans and the rest of Eastern Europe. The aim of this chapter is to identify the economic, political and social factors that delayed the democratic consolidation of the Western Balkans, where consolidation is understood as a 'multifaceted process by which democratic structures, norms, and regime-civil society relationships are firmly established' (Morlino, 1998: 14).

After the fall of the communist regimes at the end of 1980s, all of the newly established states, emerging from the former Czechoslovakia, USSR and Yugoslavia, which were similar in so many aspects (state ideology, institutions, economic structure), faced the challenge of economic transformation and at the same time of political

1 Paper presented at the Third RRPP Annual Scientific Conference, Social, Political and Economic Change in the Western Balkans, 25–26 May 2011, Sveti Stefan, Montenegro.

2 The 'Third Wave of Democratization', as explained by Huntington (1991), began in the mid-1970s with the fall of the dictatorships in Spain and Portugal. By the end of the 1980s this wave of democratization had swept across Eastern Europe transforming virtually all postcommunist European states.

democratization. Nevertheless, when comparing the Western Balkan countries[3] with other Eastern European countries,[4] one cannot help noticing the different records of transition from authoritarianism to democracy. That is to say, the Western Balkan countries were far less successful in building and consolidating liberal democracy than most of the other post-communist European countries. As a result, for a quite long time they were left in a state of 'prolonged transition', and 'the political culture of statism and authoritarianism remained deeply embedded in the region. These negative trends have been particularly evident in several former Yugoslav republics, even though their points of departure in the late 1980s were comparable to that of Central Europe' (Bugajski, 2001: 7). However, the republics that once made up the post-communist bloc in Europe, besides their shared commonalities, varied considerably from each other with respect to their political environment. As a result, some of the countries were better positioned to pursue a democratic course following their disintegration than others. According to Bunce, the most successful transitions to democracy (in the Czech Republic, Estonia, Latvia, Lithuania and Poland) began with mass protests, which 'reduced the uncertainty of the transition – by providing a clear reading of mass sentiments, by strengthening the bargaining power of opposition leaders, and by forcing the communists to give up their defense of the old order …' (Bunce, 2003: 172).

Most of the literature on this region has primarily focused on political change as a direct result of EU's democracy promotion (see Vachudova, 2002, 2006; Mikovic, 2005; Yenigün, 2008; Belloni, 2009) or on the descriptive analysis of the stages of transformation in the Western Balkans (see Jano, 2008; Skuflic, 2010). There is hardly any empirical assessment of the factors that influence the transformation processes in those countries. It is beyond any doubt that the

3 The 'Western Balkans' is a political definition for a region of south-eastern Europe that encompasses the following countries: Croatia, Bosnia-Herzegovina, Serbia, Montenegro, Macedonia, Kosovo and Albania.

4 As it is my intention to conduct a comparative analysis of different trajectories of democratization in Western Balkan countries and other postcommunist European countries that were more successful in consolidating democracy, when I refer to Eastern European countries I will refer to the postcommunist countries that are already members of the EU.

EU's leverage affected domestic politics in Eastern Europe, as well as in the Western Balkans, in a number of ways. However, I argue that the external influences, such as EU's conditionality policy only opened an important opportunity for democratic forces to settle in the region. It is domestic structural conditions that are fundamental for democracy to develop and consolidate in the countries of the Western Balkans. Before proceeding, however, it is important to establish a working definition of democratic consolidation. Based on the postulates of Linz and Stepan (1996: 5), a democratic regime is consolidated when (i) there are no significant actors engaging in secession or regime change; (ii) the majority of the population holds the belief that democracy is the best form of government and (iii) when the governmental and nongovernmental actors of the state become subjects and act according to the democratic institutions. Or put simply, democracy is consolidated when it becomes 'the only game in town'.

The next section of the chapter gives an overview of the literature on this topic. In the third section I review the theoretical background, analytically evaluating the obstacles to democratic consolidation in Eastern Europe and explaining why they are relevant for the Western Balkans. As a conclusion to these theoretical considerations, I draw testable hypotheses that will be elaborated and tested further in the chapter. The fourth section is dedicated to explaining the research methodology and the data used for the analysis. In the fifth section I estimate several time-series cross-sectional models to examine the effect of the previously hypothesized factors on the levels of democracy in both Eastern Europe and the Western Balkans.

The State of the Field

As the third wave of democratization spread throughout the world, the study of democratization processes occupied the central place of the comparative politics field. By the end of the 1980s the wave of democratization reached those countries that had hardly ever experienced democratic rule (as is the case with most of the countries of Eastern Europe). A large body of research has been dedicated to the origins and the sustainability of the new European democracies (see Fishman, 1990; Haggard and Kaufman, 1995; Ekiert, 1996; Linz and Stepan, 1996; Fish, 1998; Sajo, 1998; Kuzio, 2001; Bunce, 2003; Papaioannou and Siourounis, 2005; Levitsky and Way, 2010; Teorell, 2010). All of these scientific works usually study the post-socialist region as a whole and basically agree that 'all new democracies confront the same three issues: breaking with authoritarian rule, building democratic institutions, and devising ways to elicit the cooperation of the former authoritarian elite' (Bunce, 2000: 716). However, I argue that the countries within this region differ significantly in some crucial details. Therefore, dividing the post-socialist region into smaller study units would provide us with a more profound understanding of the transition and democratization process of these countries.

One dividing line regarding the democratization path of the post-communist European countries is suggested by Bunce. She argues that the most successful democracies in the post-socialist world – Poland, Hungary, the Czech Republic, Slovenia and the Baltic states – have used a breaking strategy. That is to say, they have overruled the ex-socialist elites in the first years of their democratic governance. On the other side '… when the electoral strength of the communists versus the opposition forces was roughly equal or tilted to the advantage of the communists, the costs for both democracy and economic reform were high' (Bunce, 2000: 717). The latter, she says, is a bridging strategy. Analysing the post-communist period in the Western Balkan countries where the transformed communist parties won the first elections, we see clear evidence of bridging with the communist past.

However, besides the fact that the Western Balkans is acknowledged as a separate political unit in terms of its specific democratic transition, the literature dedicated to democratization of the region is quite limited. As mentioned previously, most of this literature is focused on EU democracy promotion in the Western Balkans (see Vachudova, 2002; Panebianco and Rossi, 2004; Mikovic, 2005; Vachudova, 2006; Yenigün, 2008; Belloni, 2009). Some of the studies analyse the EU's influence on domestic political change in different countries of the Western Balkans (see Hoffmann, 2005; Cierco, 2006; Papic, 2006; Dolenec, 2008). Nevertheless, some scholars have raised doubts regarding EU conditionality in these countries and suggest that the EU's leverage as a driving force for policy change is quite limited in the Western Balkans (see Djordjevic, 2008; Freyburg and Richter, 2008). Arguing that national identity exerts strong influence on the effectiveness of external democratization driven by political conditionality, Freyburg and Richter (2008: 1) wrote: 'It is questionable whether the EU will be able to repeat the story in South Eastern Europe (SEE), where, again, it made the membership offer conditional on democratic criteria. Recent developments in the remaining candidate countries - Serbia, Albania, Bosnia-Herzegovina, Croatia, and also Turkey - raise doubts about its impact on democratization processes.'

In addition to this literature, there are a number of studies that focus on political and economic conditions and prospects for democratic consolidation in the Western Balkans (see Bugajski, 2001; Balaj *et al.*, 2010; Woodward, 2007; Jano, 2008; Skuflic, 2010). Bugajski offers interesting insights into political and economic developments and prospects in the region. Recognizing the differences between individual states, he claims that 'a political culture of dialogue, tolerance, and compromise has shallow roots in much of the Balkans' and eventually concludes that the process of building of sustainable democratic states remains the major challenge for the entire Balkan peninsula (Bugajski, 2001: 9).

The democratic consolidation of the Western Balkans is the central question in the study by Nyenstad (2006). However, his analysis focused on examining the legacy of the communist past and eventually on identifying the defects in the emerging democracies in the region. Finally, most of the literature covering the democratic transition of the Balkans deals exclusively with the transition and democracy building in one specific country (see Bicanic and Franicevic,

2003; Bieber, 2003; Bolcic, 2003; Hagan and Ivković, 2006; Ramet and Matic, 2007; Pantic, 2008; Edmunds, 2009; Gurdilic, 2010).

This study takes advantage of the political definition of the Western Balkans as a region of south-eastern Europe that is not yet a part of the European Union in order to address the issue of delayed democratic consolidation in the region. Two areas of contribution to the existing literature can be identified in this study. First, it will identify and analyse the economic, political or social obstacles to democratic consolidation in the countries of Western Balkans. Second, after quantifying the expected indicators, it will statistically assess whether there is substantive and significant relationship between democratic consolidation and its determinants in this region. To the best of my knowledge, no one has yet statistically tested this relationship. Eventually, this research will represent a benchmark that might catalyse further research on the subject. And hopefully, it will serve as a tool that will empower policy makers, as well as external democracy promoters, to devise their policies towards Western Balkans so the region can 'catch up' with the rest of the countries of Central and Western Europe.

Theoretical Considerations and Main Hypotheses

Most of the literature on democratic transition is dominated by two types of approaches: the structure-based and the actor-based approach. The structure-based approach, developed by the modernization theorists in the 1950s and 1960s, emphasizes the importance of the structural properties of the society (such as socio-economic development, or social or ethnic divisions) as the factors most conducive to democratization. On the other hand, the actor- or agency-based approaches advocated by O'Donnell and Schmitter (1986), dominated the democratization literature in the 1980s. This approach focuses on the decisions of the political actors as the most important factors for the democratization of a country. Since the beginning of the 1990s, there have been attempts to combine these two approaches. Some of the most prominent scholars who advocate this combined approach are Huntington (1991), Rueschemeyer *et al.* (1992) and Haggard and Kaufman (1995).

Quite recently, with the emergence of the new democracies worldwide, analysts seem to connect the structuralist approaches with democratic consolidation. For example, Gasiorowski and Power (1998: 741) claim that inadequate attention has been paid to the effects of structural factors on democratic consolidation. In their study 'The Structural Determinants of Democratic Consolidation: Evidence from the Third World' they find empirical evidence that certain structural factors (like development-related socioeconomic factors) strongly affect the likelihood of democratic consolidation. Rakner *et al.* (2007: 11) conclude that 'while structural factors were found to matter less with regard to initiating transitions to democracy, they are much more important in the process of consolidating democratic regimes.'

In order to identify and explain the factors that obstructed the process of democratic consolidation in the Western Balkans, I take as a point of departure the structure-based approach initially outlined by Lipset (1959). I argue that structural domestic factors are critical in explaining the defects of the Western Balkan democracies. Below I outline three main hypotheses and the background theory regarding three structural factors of democratic consolidation, at the same time explaining why they are relevant for the democratization process in the Western Balkans.

'Modernization' Theory

The proposition that 'democracy is related to the state of economic development' made by Lipset (1959: 75) has generated probably the largest body of research in the field of political science and has been the subject of extensive qualitative and quantitative empirical examination. In this sense, Lipset (1963: 49) argued that 'the more well-to-do a nation, the greater the chances that it will sustain democracy.' Much evidence has been offered in support of this hypothesis. Przeworski further developed this concept, offering "endogenous" and "exogenous" explanations.[5] He contends that it is beyond doubt that democracies are more likely to be found in the more highly developed countries. Still, he stresses that however democracies emerge '… they are more likely to survive in countries that are already developed' (Przeworski *et al.*, 2000: 106).

After the dissolution of the Yugoslav Federation, all of the new independent states tried to remove the socialist elements from their economies and to transform them into market economies. However, the result was ineffective economic and political reform, clientelism and corruption, which eventually led to a prolonged transition crisis. The privatization process did not achieve the expected results because of this corruption and eventually market competition was restricted. With the exception of Slovenia, all other ex-Yugoslav countries faced a reduction in industrial production, a fall in GDP, a reduction in investment, increasing inflation and very high unemployment rates, problems that most of them are still facing. At the same time, the Albanian economy has undergone a difficult transition from a centrally planned economy to an open-market economy. The country has suffered from high levels of corruption and organized crime, which paralysed political and economic reforms.

The economic problems that these countries faced eventually led them into the trap of partial democratic reform. Therefore my first hypothesis is:

H1: Other things being equal, democracy is more likely to consolidate in economically developed societies.

5 According to Przeworski (2000), a distinction should be made between democracies that result from economic development under authoritarianism (endogenous effect) and democracies that are more likely to survive in developed countries (exogenous effect).

Social Structure Theory

The third wave of democratization that spread throughout Eastern Europe at the end of the 1980s opened a new field for discussion and reconsideration of the relationship between democracy and ethnic identity. The discussion became even more relevant because democratization spread through countries that were historically fragmented along cultural and ethnic lines. The classical view on this issue supported by the eminent theorist of democracy Robert A. Dahl is that a high level of ethno-linguistic and religious fragmentation is a major obstacle for democratization, especially in countries where nationalistic policies are being used in order for one ethnic group to dominate the others.

Very recently, a slightly different explanation of the issue has been presented by Beissinger (2007) who tests the relationship between ethnic diversity and democratization in the countries of the post-Soviet Union. He concludes that 'ethnic diversity does not affect the outcomes of democratization directly, but does so only indirectly, through its interaction with and influence over other processes … that do have a direct effect on democratic outcomes' (Beissinger, 2007: 78). However, his research is focused on post-Soviet states that did not face strong nationalism and ethnic collectivism, as was the case with the countries of ex-Yugoslavia. I argue that ethnic fragmentation exerted a direct influence on the successor countries of ex-Yugoslavia, especially on Bosnia-Herzegovina, Serbia and Croatia where nationalistic sentiments have been manipulated by the leaders of certain political parties looking for popular support. My second hypothesis is therefore:

H2: Other things being equal, democracy is less likely to consolidate in countries with a high degree of ethnic and religious diversity.

'Stateness' Theory

Incorporating 'stateness' into the theory of democratization, Robert Dahl (1989: 207) wrote 'the democratic process presupposes a unit ... If the unit is not considered proper or rightful – if its scope or domain is not justifiable – then it cannot be made rightful simply by democratic procedures.' However, the most prominent scholars supporting and further developing the 'stateness' theory are Linz and Stepan. According to them, 'Democracy is a form of governance of a modern state. Thus without a state no modern democracy is possible' (Linz and Stepan, 1996: 17). When they refer to 'stateness' they presuppose the existence of the following three elements: territorial borders, national identity and the right of citizenship in the state. They claim that the democratic consolidation is hardly possible if the questions of national sovereignty and territorial integrity are unresolved.

Further developing the argument that there is a significant difference between the state and nation Linz and Stepan underline that it is much easier for the political leaders to pursue democratization policies if 'the residents of a state identify with one subjective idea of the nation, and that nation is virtually contiguous with the state' (Linz and Stepan, 1996: 25). But in the case of multinational states, as most of the Western Balkan states are, democratic consolidation is practically impossible if the state leaders neglect the multinational character and different identities residing within the territorial state, simply because that usually leads to political instability and eventually to violence.

For many years, Yugoslavia functioned as a nation-state denying the existence of different national identities and limiting possibilities for self-determination. The dissolution of the multinational communist federation of Yugoslavia raised the issue of statehood building, achieving political sovereignty and international recognition of the new states. I argue that most of the Western Balkan countries (especially Serbia and Bosnia-Herzegovina) failed to successfully incorporate democratic principles as a result of the long period of unsettled and contested statehood matters. Even today, when we speak about

Serbia and Bosnia and Herzegovina (and recently Macedonia),[6] we can rightfully argue that they are still facing the transition process in terms of political stability. Therefore I come to my third hypothesis:

H3: Other things being equal, democracy is less likely to consolidate in countries with unresolved stateness issues.[7]

Methodology and Data

The purpose of this study is to investigate the underlying factors that are challenging and eventually blocking the democratic consolidation in the countries of the Western Balkans. Western Balkan countries shared basically quite similar communist experiences with other countries of Eastern Europe for nearly 50 years and they embraced democratic principles at practically the same time during the third wave of democratization. For that reason I constructed a dataset that comprises almost all Eastern European countries. They can be divided into three groups, depending on their EU membership status. The first group comprises the ten new EU member states: Bulgaria, Czech Republic, Estonia, Hungary, Latvia, Lithuania, Poland, Romania, Slovakia and Slovenia. The second group

6 Macedonian territorial integrity, and therefore its stability, were seriously challenged when the secessionist National Liberation Army – NLA (claiming to represent the Albanian population in Macedonia) launched a guerrilla war in western Macedonia in March, 2001. Even though the conflict was ended with the signing of the Ohrid Framework Agreement several months later, the demand for federalization, which would establish autonomy for ethnic Albanians in the western and northern parts of the country, is still occasionally emphasized by certain political actors in the country.

7 There are several indices that measure the state fragility across countries. Some of them aim at depicting the degree of stateness, whereas others aim at predicting the future risk of state failure. Also, most of these indices are limited to a certain number of years. In my opinion, the best choice for measuring the stateness would be the 'Political Stability and Absence of Violence' indicator developed by the World Bank.

comprises five Western Balkan countries, which are candidates or potential candidates for EU membership. Those are: Albania, Bosnia and Herzegovina, Croatia, Macedonia and Serbia. I purposefully excluded Kosovo and Montenegro from the dataset because they have gained their independence only recently (Montenegro in 2006 and Kosovo in 2008) and there are practically no data for them as separate units before those dates. The third group of countries comprises Belarus, Moldova and Ukraine: countries currently included in the European Neighbourhood Policy (ENP). My sample thus covers 18 countries over a period of 20 years.

To test the three main hypotheses formally I firstly estimated three variants of the following time-series-cross-section model (TSCS):

$$y_{i,t} = \alpha + x_{i,t}\beta + x_{wb,t}\gamma + \varepsilon_{i,t} + \sigma_i; \quad i = 1,\dots,N; \; t = 1,\dots,T.$$

Further on, in order to check the validity of the significant hypothesized factors for democratic consolidation of the Western Balkan countries I estimated the following time-series-cross-section model (TSCS):

$$y_{i,t} = \alpha + x_{i,t}\beta + x_{wb,t}\gamma + (x_{i,t} * x_{wb,t})\delta + \varepsilon_{i,t} + \sigma_i; \quad i = 1,\dots,N; \; t = 1,\dots,T.$$

The subscript *i* denotes a country; *t* denotes a year; while *wb* is the regional dummy that takes a value of 1 for the Western Balkan countries and 0 otherwise. Including the regional dummy for Western Balkans in the regression allowed controlling for the effects caused by the countries that belong to this group, on the dependent variable. The dependent variable of this study is level of democracy. As a measure of democracy I used the unified democracy score (UDS).[8]

I used 1990 as a starting date because that is the year following the democratic revolutions of 1989 in most of the Eastern-bloc European countries, which overthrew the communist regime and started to adopt various forms of market economy and democratic reforms. Albania and ex-Yugoslavian countries abandoned Communism in

8 For more information about the dependent variable, please see the appendix.

the period between 1990 and 1992. However, in order to obtain a rectangular data structure – a balanced panel – I used 1990 as a starting date for these countries as well. The end date is 2009. Assuming that individual specific effects are uncorrelated with the independent variables, I used random-effects multiple logistic regression.

As a first step, three separate statistical investigations were conducted. The intention behind this was to capture the isolated effects of the three main explanatory variables: economic development, ethnic fractionalization and state fragility while controlling for other explanatory factors. The regression results eventually showed which factors exerted an impact on the level of democracy in Eastern Europe. Further on, I included the statistically significant factors from the previous analyses into the same regression model adding at the same time the interaction term for those factors and a regional dummy for Western Balkans. This allowed me to take account of the differences between the Western Balkans and other Eastern European countries with respect to the significant structural factors' effects on the level of democracy. The results for the three main testable hypotheses are presented in Table 3.1 (models 1–3). In the last model (4), I tested jointly the theories that received statisticly significant support controlling simultaneously for the interaction term between these factors and the regional dummy for Western Balkans.

Results

Modernization Theory Variables

To test the modernization theory hypothesis, I used several variables suggested by modernization theorists as main determinants of democratization. As the main explanatory variable I used GDP per capita based on purchasing power parity (PPP), as suggested and used by most scholars working in the field. Another variable outlined by Lipset (1959) as a key prerequisite for democracy is education. Therefore, I used average years of schooling in the population aged 25 and above (dataset constructed by Barro and Lee, 2010). I used the following variables as controls: GDP growth, trade openness, inflation and unemployment. The results of this regression are presented in Table 3.1 (model 1).

After running the regression, I observed that all of the significant factors have the expected signs except for average years of schooling (which did not reach statistical significance anyway) and unemployment. Most importantly, the main development variable supporting the modernization theory, GDP per capita (PPP), is statistically significant at the 1% level, which indicates that it is systematically linked to democratization in Eastern Europe. Trade openness has also reached substantive and statistical significance at a 1% confidence level. Growth in GDP is also positively correlated with democratization and is statistically significant at 5% level. However, its estimated coefficient is almost indistinguishable from zero. The results for education proved not to be supportive of the modernization hypothesis. This contradicts the findings of Papaioannou and Siourounis (2008: 380), according to whom: '… the positive impact of development on democratization mainly works through human capital.' The surprising result, implying that unemployment is positively correlated with democratization, seems counterintuitive and contradicts the findings of most quantitative research on this topic. However, I argue that this result can be expected when related to the post-communist context. A possible explanation behind this result is that one of the economic guarantees which communist regimes were proud of was the full employment. After the fall of communism and especially in the first years of the democratic transition, these countries faced high rates of unemployment.

Social Structure Theory Variables

In model 2 I tested the social structure theory, which suggests that higher levels of ethnic and religious diversity hinder democratic consolidation in a country. I argue that that is occurring in the Western Balkan countries. As a proxy for ethnic diversity I used ethnic fractionalization (as suggested by Alesina *et al.*, 2003), while controlling for the following two variables: religious fractionalization and Muslim share. Even though high levels of ethnic diversity are generally assumed to have a negative impact on democratization, the statistical support for this statement is quite weak when it comes to Eastern Europe. The results in model 2 show that ethnic and religious fractionalization have no significant effect on democratization in Eastern Europe (even though they have the expected signs). This result stands in line with the argument made by Papaioannou and Siourounis (2008), who found no empirical evidence in support of this hypothesis for those countries that democratized during the third wave of democratization. It also supports the conclusion reached by Beissinger who examines the relationship between ethnic diversity and democratization in the countries of the post-Soviet Union – his findings support his argument that 'ethnic diversity is a relatively weak explanation of democratic development on its own, but ethnicity rather exercises its effects on democratization in part through its interaction with other factors that affect democratic development' (Beissinger, 2007: 73).

'Stateness' Theory Variables

To test whether the stateness problem has been one of the fundamental issues for Western Balkan countries' failure to consolidate their democracies, as a first step I examined the effect of political stability conditional on armed conflict on the levels of democracy in Eastern Europe. Following Linz and Stepan (1996: 5) who view democracy as consolidated 'when no significant political groups seriously attempt to overthrow the democratic regime or secede from the state', I use the Political Stability and Absence of Violence index, developed by the World Bank, as a proxy for testing my third hypothesis.

The strong explanatory power of the main variable in model 3 is clearly evident. Political stability exerts a highly significant impact on democratization in postcommunist Eastern Europe. This finding stands in line with my argument that 'Western Balkan states failed to successfully incorporate the democratic principles as a result of the long period of unsettled elements of their statehood.' However, the final conclusion regarding the influence of these factors on democratization in Western Balkans was made after controlling for all significant explanatory variables that are supposed to explain the delayed democratic consolidation of this region.

Combined Analysis

As explained earlier, in model 4 I included only the statistically significant factors of the previous three models, adding, at the same time, interaction terms for those factors and the regional dummy for the Western Balkans. By doing this, I was able to examine if the relationship between the hypothesized structural factors and the level of democracy is different depending on whether the country is in the Western Balkans or not. My expectations were: (i) that the main explanatory variables, GDP per capita (PPP) and political stability and absence of violence, will remain statistically significant for this region as well; and (ii) that their explanatory power will slightly increase.

After running the regression controlling simultaneously for economic development, political stability and region, it is evident (model 4) that three factors: GDP per capita (PPP), trade openness and political stability and absence of violence, have survived the test. The estimate for GDP per capita (PPP) retained its statistical significance at the 1% level, both for the countries of Eastern Europe in general, as well as for the Western Balkans as a separate unit of analysis. While trade openness continued to be a strong explanatory factor for the level of democracy in Eastern Europe, it did not prove to be a significant predictor for the Western Balkan countries. Growth in GDP and unemployment lost their explanatory power when controlled for against the other correlates of democratization, both in Eastern Europe and the Western Balkans.

Turning now to the third hypothesis, which implies that an unresolved stateness issue has been one of the fundamental problems for Western Balkan countries' failure to consolidate their democracies, the estimate for this variable in the joint model suggests that political instability severely impedes democratic consolidation in this region.

Table 3.1: Time-series cross-national regression analysis (1990–2009)

Dependent variable: level of democracy (UDS)	Modernization theory (Model 1)	Social structure theory (Model 2)	'Stateness' theory (Model 3)	Combined analysis (Model 4)
GDP p.c., PPP (USD x 1000)	0.052*** (8.32)	–	–	0.033*** (5.42)
GDP growth (annual %)	0.006** (2.56)	–	–	0.001 (0.30)
Education	-0.037 (-1.42)	–	–	–
Trade openness	0.313*** (2.65)	–	–	0.494** (3.48)
Inflation	-0.00003 (-0.82)	–	–	–
Unemployment	0.016*** (4.09)	–	–	0.006 (1.16)
Ethnic fractionalization	–	-1.006 (-1.06)	–	–
Religious fractionalization	–	-0.250 (-0.26)	–	–
Muslim population	–	-0.001 (-0.19)	–	–
Political stability and absence of violence	–	–	0.277*** (4.55)	-0.026 (-0.34)
Armed conflict	–	–	0.034 (0.14)	–
Western Balkan dummy	-0.365*** (-2.72)	-0.361 (-1.04)	-0.158 (-0.61)	-0.828** (-2.55)
GDP p.c., PPP (USD x 1000) - WB	–	–	–	0.062*** (3.13)
GDP growth (annual %) - WB	–	–	–	-0.005 (-0.46)

Table 3.1 continued

Dependent variable: level of democracy (UDS)	Modernization theory (Model 1)	Social structure theory (Model 2)	'Stateness' theory (Model 3)	Combined analysis (Model 4)
Trade openness – WB	–	–	–	–0.148 (–0.58)
Unemployment – WB	–	–	–	0.013 (1.42)
Political stability and absence of violence – WB	–	–	–	0.241** (2.22)
Overall R-squared	0.6466	0.2823	0.3779	0.5458
Number of observations	259	326	180	178

Note: Absolute z-statistics in parentheses (*Statistically significant at $p<0.1$; ** Statistically significant at $p<0.05$; *** Statistically significant at $p<0.01$).

Concluding Remarks

The striking variation in the democratization trajectories among the ten new EU members and the Western Balkan countries clearly shows that the Western Balkan countries are slow-pace reformers. The primary aim of this paper has been to identify the main factors that delayed the democratic consolidation of the Western Balkans. The discussion and the analysis regarding the democratization of the Western Balkans were conducted with comparative references to the other postcommunist European countries that recently joined the EU. Arguing that domestic structural factors are critical in explaining the democratization path in Western Balkans, I have taken the structure-based approach as the underlying theoretical perspective.

By employing a time-series-cross-section statistical model on a dataset comprising 18 Eastern European countries in the period 1990–2009, I first identified the significant correlates of successful democratization in Eastern Europe as a whole. Subsequently, with the aim of controlling for the effects caused by the Western Balkan countries on the dependant variable, I included a regional dummy for this region. The results indicated that economic backwardness and political instability are the crucial factors that blocked and challenge democratic consolidation in the Western Balkans region. Certain efforts to strengthen democratic rule in these states have already been made, but they are far from enough to overcome the status quo of not-yet-completed democratization. This implies that the ruling elites of the Western Balkan states have to dedicate further efforts to creating policies that will reform their economies and help avert nationalistic sentiments and ethnic tensions. However, there is a worrisome trend that the political leaders of this region, unable to cope with dramatically falling living standards, are turning to populist measures that seek to reaffirm the ethno-nationalistic sentiments. This eventually leads to episodes of authoritarian reversion, which remains one of the major risks that the Western Balkans countries face today.

In summary, besides the main factors identified in this analysis, democratization in each separate country of the Western Balkan region is a consequence of a combination of different economic, social and political causes. Therefore, a more in-depth investigation of the democratization process in each of the Western Balkan states would probably provide better understanding of the political reality in this part of the world.

Appendix

Armed conflict: dummy variable that codes whether an armed conflict has occurred in a given country for a specified period. An armed conflict is defined as 'a contested incompatibility that concerns government and/or territory where the use of armed force between two parties, of which at least one is the government of a state, results in at least 25 battle-related deaths.' Source: Gleditsch *et al.* (2002).

GDP growth: percentage of annual growth of the real GDP. Source: World Bank (2010).

GDP p.c., PPP: real GDP per capita based on purchasing power parity (PPP). Source: World Bank (2010).

Education: average years of total schooling in the population aged 25 and above. Source: Barro and Lee (2010).

Ethnic/religious fractionalization: index of ethnic/linguistic heterogeneity. It measures the probability that two randomly selected individuals from a given country will not belong to the same ethnic/religious group. Source: Alesina *et al.* (2003).

Inflation: Percentage of annual inflation based on consumer prices. Source: International Monetary Fund (2010).

Level of democracy: Unified Democracy Score (UDS) is a measure of democracy, which is synthetized from ten existing measures of democracy: Arat (1991); Bowman, Lehoucq and Mahoney (2005) (BLM); Bollen and Jackman (1989); Freedom House (2007); Hadenius (1992); Przeworski *et al.* (2000) (PACL); Polity scores by Marshall, Jaggers and Gurr (2006); Polyarchy scale by Coppedge and Reinicke (1991); Gasiorowski's (1996) Political Regime Change measure (PRC); and Vanhanen (2003). The score ranges from –2.5 to 3.5 with higher values corresponding to higher levels of democracy. Source: Pemstein *et al.* (2010).

Muslim population: percentage of Muslim population in a given country. Source: Pew Research Center (2009).

Political stability and absence of violence: index that measures the perceptions of the likelihood that the government will be destabilized or overthrown by unconstitutional or violent means, including domestic violence and terrorism. The index ranges from about -2.5 to 2.5, with higher values corresponding to more political stability. Source: World Bank (2010).

Trade openness: dummy variable indicating trade openness based on five different indicators for specific trade-related policies. A country was classified as closed if it displayed at least one of the following characteristics: (i) Average tariff rates of 40% or more; (ii) nontariff barriers covering 40% or more of trade; (iii) a black market exchange rate that is depreciated by 20% or more relative to the official exchange rate, on average, during the 1970s or 1980s; (iv) a state monopoly on major export; (v) a socialist economic system. Source: Wacziarg and Welch (2008).

Unemployment: annual unemployment rate, percent of total labour force. Source: International Monetary Fund (2010).

References

Alesina, A., Devleeschauer, A., Easterly, W., Kurlat, S. and Wacziarg, R. (2003) Fractionalization. *Journal of Economic Growth* 8 (2), pp. 155–94.

Arat, Z. F. (1991) Democracy and human rights in developing countries. Lynne Rienner, Boulder, CO.

Balaj B., Biberaj E., Bugajski J., Conley H. A., Ignjatovic D., Joseph E. P., Teleki, I. (2010) *Western Balkans Policy Review 2010,* A Report of the CSIS Lavrentis Lavrentiadis Chair in Southeast European Studies, ed. Janusz Bugajski. Center for Strategic and International Studies, Washington, DC, pp. 1–126.

Barro, R. and Lee, J.-W. (2010) *A New Data Set of Educational Attainment in the World, 1950–2010,* Working Paper 15902, National Bureau of Economic Research, Cambridge, MA, pp. 1–47.

Beissinger, M. (2007) Ethnic identity and democratization: lessons from the post-Soviet region. *Taiwan Journal of Democracy* 3 (2), pp. 73–99.

Belloni, R. (2009) European integration and the Western Balkans: lessons, prospects and limits. *Journal of Balkan and Near East Studies* 11 (3), pp. 313–31.

Bicanic, I. and Franicevic, V. (2003) *Understanding Reform: the Case of Croatia,* Working Paper 33 The WIIW Balkan Observatory, Vienna, pp. 1–43.

Bieber, F. (ed.) (2003) *Montenegro in Transition: Problems of Identity and Statehood,* Nomos Verlagsgesellschaft, Baden-Baden.

Bolcic, S. (2003) Blocked transition and post-socialist transformation: Serbia in the nineties *Review of Sociology* 9 (2), pp. 27–49.

Bollen, K. A., and Jackman R. W. (1989) Democracy, stability, and dichotomies. *American Sociological Review* 54, pp. 612–21.

Bowman, K., Lehoucq F., and James M. (2005) Measuring political democracy: case expertise, data adequacy, and Central America. *Comparative Political Studies* 38, pp. 939–70.

Bugajski, J. (2001) Facing the future: the Balkans to the year 2010. *ZEI Discussion Papers*, pp. 3–66.

Bunce, V. (2000) Comparative democratization: big and bounded generalizations. *Comparative Political Studies* 33 (6/7), pp. 703–34.

Bunce, V. (2003) Rethinking recent democratization: lessons from the postcommunist experience *World Politics* 55 (2), pp. 167–92.

Cierco, T. (2006) Stabilizing Macedonia: The Key Role of the European Union, paper presented at the annual meeting of the International Studies Association, Town and Country Resort and Convention Center, San Diego, CA, 22 March 2006.

Coppedge, M. and Reinicke W. H. (1991) Measuring polyarchy, in *On measuring democracy: Its consequences and concomitants*, ed. Alex Inkeles, pp. 47–68. NJ: Transaction, New Brunswick.

Dahl, R. (1989) *Democracy and Its Critics,* Yale University Press, New Haven, CT.

Dahl, R. (2000) *On Democracy,* Yale University Press, New Haven, CT.

Djordjevic, O. (2008) *The Limits of Europeanization 'From Without': Is There an EU-Driven Democratization Process in Serbia?* Discussion Paper 18, UNISCI, pp. 77–93.

Dolenec, D. (2008) Europeanization as a democratizing force in postcommunist Europe: Croatia in comparative perspective. *Politička Misao* 45 (5), pp. 23–46.

Edmunds, T. (2009) Illiberal resilience in Serbia. *Journal of Democracy* 20 (1), pp. 128–42.

Ekiert, G. (1996) *The State Against Society: Political Crisis and Their Aftermath in East Central Europe,* Princeton University Press, Princeton, NJ.

European Bank for Reconstruction and Development, *Transition Report 2009,* European Bank for Reconstruction and Development, London.

Fish, S. (1998) Reversal and erosion of democracy in the postcommunist world. *East European Politics and Societies* 12, pp. 31–78.

Fishman, R. (1990) Rethinking state and regime: Southern Europe's transition to democracy. *World Politics* 42, pp. 422–40.

Freedom House 2007. Freedom in the World, at http://www.freedomhouse.org (accessed 7 November 2012).

Freyburg, T. and Richter, S. (2008) National Identity Matters: The Limited Impact of EU Political Conditionality in the Western Balkans. Working Paper No. 19, National Centre of Competence in Research: *Challenges to Democracy in the 21st Century,* pp. 1–18.

Gasiorowski, M. and Power, T. (1998) The structural determinants of democratic consolidation: evidence from the Third World. *Comparative Political Studies* 31, pp. 740–71.

Gasiorowski, M. J. (1996) An overview of the political regime change data set. *Comparative Political Studies* 29, pp. 469–83.

Gleditsch, N. P., Wallensteen P., Eriksson M., Sollenberg M. and Strand H. (2002) Armed Conflict 1946–2001: A New Dataset, *Journal of Peace Research* 39(5), pp. 615–637.
Gurdilic, J. (2010) *Transformation of Democracy in Croatia: Europeanization*, LAP LAMBERT Academic Publishing,, Saarbrücken.
Hadenius, A. (1992) Democracy and development. Cambridge University Press, Cambridge.
Hagan, J. and Ivković, S. (2006) War crimes, democracy, and the rule of law in Belgrade, the former Yugoslavia, and beyond. *Annals of the American Academy of Political and Social Science* 605, pp. 130–51.
Haggard, S. and Kaufman, R. (1995) *The Political Economy of Democratic Transitions*, Princeton University Press, Princeton, NJ.
Hoffmann, J (2005) Integrating Albania: the role of the European Union in the democratization process. *Albanian Journal of Politics* 1 (1), pp. 55–74.
Huntington, S. (1991) *The Third Wave: Democratization in the Late Twentieth Century*, University of Oklahoma Press, Norman.
International Monetary Fund (2010) *World Economic Outlook Database 2010*, World Economic Outlook Report, IMF, Washington, DC.
Jano, D. (2008) From Balkanization to Europeanization: the stages of Western Balkans complex transformations. *L'Europe en formation* 349–50, pp. 55–68.
Kuzio, T. (2001) Transition in post-communist states: triple or quadruple? *Politics* 21 (3), pp. 168–77.
Levitsky, S. and Way, L. (2010) *Competitive Authoritarianism: Hybrid Regimes After the Cold War*, Cambridge University Press, Cambridge.
Linz, J. and Stepan, A. (1996) *Problems of Democratic Transition and Consolidation: Southern Europe, South America and Post-Communist Europe*, The Johns Hopkins University Press Baltimore, MD.
Lipset, S. (1959) Some social requisites of democracy: economic development and political legitimacy. *American Political Science Review* 53 (1), pp. 69–105.
Lipset, S. (1963) *Political Man: The Social Bases of Politics*, 2nd edn, Anchor Books, New York, NY.
Marshall, M. G., Jaggers, K. and Gurr, T. R. (2006) Polity IV: Political regime characteristics and transitions, pp. 1800–2004, at http://www.systemicpeace.org/polity/polity4.htm (accessed 7 November 2012).
Mikovic, D. (2005) The EU as a Normative Power: Attempts of Exporting Regional Co-operation to the Western Balkans. Master's thesis. Lund University, Department of Political Science.
Morlino, L. (1998) *Democracy between Consolidation and Crisis: Parties, Groups, and Citizens in Southern Europe*, Oxford University Press, Oxford.
Nyenstad, J. (2006) Democratic Consolidation of the Western Balkans: Democratization Theory, Regional Analysis, and Policy Recommendations. Ph.D. thesis. University of Southern Denmark Institute of Political Science.
O'Donnell, G. and Schmitter, P. (1986) *Transitions from Authoritarian Rule: Tentative Conclusions about Uncertain Democracies*, The Johns Hopkins University Press, Baltimore, MD.

Panebianco, S. and Rossi, R. (2004) *EU Attempts to Export Norms of Good Governance to the Mediterranean and Western Balkan Countries,* JMWP n° 53, Jean Monnet Centre EuroMed, Department of Political Studies - University of Catania, pp. 1–25.

Pantic, V. (2008) National Integration, Media and Democracy in Post-Milosevic Serbia: Socialist Legacies, Neoliberal Strategies. Ph.D. thesis. Simon Fraser University.

Papaioannou, E. and Siourounis, G. (2008) Economic and social factors driving the third wave of democratization. *Journal of Comparative Economics* 36, pp. 365–87.

Papic, M. (2006) Rolling up the sleeves: how EU policy towards Serbia and Montenegro acts as the glue that holds the State Union together? *Review of European and Russian Affairs* 2 (2), pp. 56–80.

Pemstein, D., Meserve, S. and Melton, J. (2010) Democratic compromise: a latent variable analysis of ten measures of regime type. *Political Analysis* 18 (4), pp. 426–49..

Pew Research Centre (2009) *'Mapping the Global Muslim Population', A Report on the Size and Distribution of the World's Muslim Population,* The Pew Forum on Religion and Public Life, October 2009, Washington D.C.

Przeworski, A. (1995) *The Sustainability of Democracy,* Cambridge.

Przeworski, A., Alvarez, M., Cheibub, J. and Limongi, F. (1996) What makes democracies endure? *Journal of Democracy* 7, pp. 39–55.

Przeworski, A., Alvarez, M., Cheibub, J. and Limongi, F. (2000) *Democracy and Development: Political Institutions and Well-Being in the World, 1950–1990,* Cambridge University Press, Cambridge.

Rakner, L., Fritz, V. and Menocal, A. (2007) *Democratization's Third Wave and the Challenges of Democratic Deepening: Assessing International Democracy Assistance and Lessons Learned,* Working Paper 1, The Advisory Board for Irish Aid, London, pp. 1–57.

Ramet, S. and Matic, D. (eds) (2007) *Democratic Transition in Croatia: Value Transformation, Education, and Media,* Texas A&M University Press, College Station.

Rueschemeyer, D., Stephens, E. and Stephens, J. (1992) *Capitalist Development and Democracy,* University of Chicago Press, Chicago.

Sajo, A. (1998) Corruption, clientilism, and the future of the constitutional state in Eastern Europe. *East European Constitutional Review* 7, pp. 37–46.

Skuflic L. (2010) Transition Process in the Western Balkans: How Much Successful Is This Story?. *Intelligent Information Management* 2(4), pp. 243–252.

Teorell, J. (2010) *Determinants of Democratization: Explaining Regime Change in the World, 1972–2006,* Cambridge University Press, Cambridge.

World Bank (2010) *World Development Indicators,* World Bank, Washington, DC.

Vachudova, M. (2002) The Leverage of the European Union on Reform in Postcommunist Europe, paper presented at the European Consortium for Political Research, Torino, 22–27 March 2002.

Vachudova, M. (2006) *Democratization in the Western Balkans: Illiberal Regimes and the Leverage of International Actors,* The National Council for Eurasian and East European Research, www.ucis.pitt.edu/nceeer/2007_820-19g_Vachudova1.pdf (accessed 8 October 2012).

Vanhanen, T. (2003) Democratization: A comparative analysis of 170 countries. Routledge, New York.

Wacziarg, R. and Welch, K. (2008) Trade liberalization and growth: new evidence. *World Bank Economic Review* 22 (2), pp. 187–231.

Woodward, S. (2007) *Is Democracy Possible in the Balkans? On Preconditions and Conditions in Bosnia, Kosovo and Serbia,* The National Council for Eurasian and East European Research, www.ucis.pitt.edu/nceeer/2007_820-20g_Woodward.pdf (accessed 8 October 2012).

Yenigün, C. (2008) EU's Role on the Western Balkan Democratization, paper presented at the International Conference on Balkan Studies, Tirana, 7–8 November 2008.

Snjezana Milivojevic

High Tech Low Pay: Journalism and Journalists in Serbia

This chapter addresses media transition as an aspect of democratization in the Western Balkans. The issue of the media and democracy is examined with particular attention to the quality of journalism and its capacity to respond to a changing media environment. This issue is important as Western Balkan countries are going through difficult and long transitions, which are complicated by the global economic crisis and technological changes in the media industry.

The analysis focuses on Serbia but most of the general trends may be recognized throughout the region. The chapter starts by identifying changes in journalism as a global process. Unlike consolidated democracies, where changes are triggered by technological revolution, in this region, changes are mostly connected to political and economic restructuring of media systems. The way in which these general trends affect Serbian journalism is presented through a discussion of the professional identity of journalists, their economic conditions, political autonomy and the technological challenges that they face. Empirical evidence is provided by the research project 'Profession at the Crossroads – Journalism at the Threshold of the Information Society', conducted by the University of Belgrade team during 2010–2011.[1]

The chapter concludes with a general assessment of the capacity of journalism to respond to a combination of global media changes and domestic transitional processes.

1 Prepared in the framework of the Regional Research Promotion Programme in the Western Balkans (RRPP), which is run by the University of Fribourg on a mandate of the Swiss Agency for Development and Cooperation, SDC, Federal Department of Foreign Affairs. The views expressed in this report are those of the authors and do not necessarily represent opinions of the SDC and the University of Fribourg.

Journalism at the Crossroads

Journalism is at the most serious crossroads in its history. Its decline is troubling as it is among the most important institutions for a vibrant democracy. The position of journalism contrasts with the celebratory tone and high expectations associated with the information society. While information technology is receiving praise and there is unprecedented penetration of ICT and the media into everyday life, journalism, as a way of 'publishing accounts of contemporary events, conditions or persons of possible significance or interest to the public, based on information believed to be reliable,' may easily become obsolete (McQuail, 2008: 48). This is because journalism is simultaneously facing technological, economic and social challenges that require serious reconsideration of the profession.

The first set of challenges, comes from technological development. The 'new media ecology' comes with a variety of platforms, delivery and service choices, which journalism still needs to adjust to. The ways of doing journalism are being questioned as never before because *professionalism* and *objectivity* have become contemporary standards. Of course, all media were once new and technology has always brought challenges to journalism but never on the scale that has occurred since the Internet became a member of the media family. With the 'Industrial Age' giving way to the 'Information Age', the complexity of technological changes presents a unique new environment for practising journalism.

The second major challenge comes from the economics of the information society. In its most obvious form it endangers a century-old business model of journalism, putting forward the question *'who will pay for the news?'* With the money migrating from content producers to content providers, the old advertising-based business model falls apart and its first casualty may be the news (Currah, 2009: 11–17). New ways of financing news production are needed to overcome the 'free information' culture that comes with the information society. The Internet economy has opened new horizons for the media but it has also transformed media economics, damaging the traditional business model of journalism beyond repair. The present economic crisis only intensifies the problem by downsizing media operations and leaving journalists without work.

Finally, the information society is also bringing fundamental changes in the wider social and cultural environment. The new media are not only offering new ways of delivering information; they also enable new actors, cause traditional actors to converge, and create new forms of public communication. The Fourth Estate is being transformed by interactivity, mobility, a culture of free and easy access to information, and civic activism. The traditional roles of the media - to inform, entertain and educate - are being modified as the media are expected to inform, entertain and *connect*. This new role is transforming the media into a 'Fifth Estate', which includes civic journalists and content providers/generators as well as users (Dutton, 2009:1–15). Media audiences are melting into a multiplicity of interactive, mobile and individualized actors. Media policies, economics and practices are evolving, bringing our understanding and very notion of media into question (Jakubowicz, 2009: 19).

Media face these three sets of challenges simultaneously, but some of them are unique (technological), some cyclical (economic), and some long-term in character (social) (Levy and Nielsen, 2010: 4). There are differences between regions, but across the democratic world journalism is in a state of flux. Academic and professional discourses concerned with the *future of journalism* are overwhelmingly loud. In most democratic societies with a long tradition of media freedom, they focus on the technological changes set in motion by new media developments and the present economic crisis. In Central and East European countries they are about locating a democratic 'place on the map' (Jakubowicz and Sukosd, 2008: 102). Media problems there resemble those in other EU countries, although restrictive policies bring political concerns onto the media agenda (Hume, 2011: 11).

In the Western Balkans these challenges are emphasized by the delayed transition and a weak tradition of journalistic professionalism. As recent comparative studies have documented, the media in the region share major pan-European tendencies, such as technological convergence, ownership concentration and audience fragmentation (Television Across Europe: More Channels, Less Independence, 2008:18), but they also face additional problems associated with transitional and postconflict societies and a lasting focus on political and ideological issues. In many of them, major changes within the professional culture of journalism have not been properly addressed yet.

In Serbia, a slow and complicated transition has put additional pressure on both the media and journalism. The first wave of transition has not been completed and most of the initial transitional goals are still on the policy agenda. (Television Across Europe: regulation, policy and independence, 2005: 1315–1383.) Privatization, ownership concentration, the development of media markets and the economic crisis are all simultaneously shaping the media world. The information society is at an early stage of development. According to official statistics 39% of households have access to the internet, while individual usage figures show that 3.7% of the population has never used the Internet. (Statistical Office of the Republic of Serbia, 2010: 14–19) But, according to the International Telecommunication Union (ITU, Serbia ranked 50 out of 152 countries according to the Information and Communication Technology Development Index (IDI) in 2010. Social and cultural changes such as the rapid feminization of media professions and 'new gender relations' are creating new issues within the professional community. This combination of old and new challenges is marked by social and cultural circumstances connected to wider issues associated with the Serbian transition to democracy.

The initial post-1989 momentum to professionalize journalism and liberate it from political control was very strong (Milivojevic, 1993: 87–9). Its strength diminished during the conflict, while war propaganda and hate speech dominated the 1990s, and later, when system transformation became a priority during the 2000s. Also, at this early stage, professional claims were made reflecting 'high modernism' of journalism, when it seemed unquestionably clear that the goals were professional autonomy, public service duty, right to report and objectivity (Hallin, 1992: 15). Unfortunately, the conflict in ex-Yugoslavia and other transitions have shown that the media were not always promoters of democracy and that it is difficult for journalism to evolve free from political pressure and commercial priorities. (Splichal. S. and Sparks, C., 1994; Dobek-Ostrowska, B. and Glowacki. M., 2008.) Recent academic studies of media development are therefore taking a different approach to understanding media in unconsolidated and weak democracies. Instead of asking 'how can the media contribute to democratization?' the question is shifting to 'what kind of democracy is needed for media to be able to perform its democratic role?' (Zielonka and Mancini, 2011: 1). In both cases, quality journalism is essential for democratic media performance.

Methodology

The goal of the 'Profession at the Crossroads – Journalism at the Threshold of the Information Society' project was to determine how the contemporary Serbian journalistic community identifies, prioritizes and responds to all those changes. The main working hypothesis was *that it has modest resources to respond to simultaneous technological, economic and social challenges, which are currently changing the professional culture of journalism*. This was divided into three further hypotheses:

(H1) Journalists perceive their present socio-economic status and conditions of the media industry as a major impediment to professional development.
(H2) Despite long-term social changes, political pressure is still the most frequent threat to media autonomy and journalistic independence.
(H3) Unique and overwhelming technological changes in the media world are not acknowledged as a major challenge to the profession of journalism.

The research was carried out across the media community and, due to its complex goals, it included a combination of qualitative and quantitative methods. Quantitative research was based on two separate but complementary surveys. The first was a survey of journalists/editors with a sample of 260 respondents. The second survey was conducted on a smaller sample of owners/managers, with a total of 51 respondents. This chapter only refers to the main findings for journalists/editors, as they are treated as the initial survey population. The survey was conducted primarily by a web-based questionnaire among members of the largest professional database, *novinar.rs*, developed by the Independent Association of Journalists during 2009.

Qualitative research was conducted as a series of four focus-group interviews with journalists/editors selected using the same criteria as the survey sample. A total of 30 journalists were interviewed in four sessions: two in Belgrade, one in Vojvodina (Novi Sad) and one in central Serbia (Kragujevac). There were equal numbers of male and female interviewees and an equal number of younger and older professionals, two-thirds from the broadcast media and one-third from the printed press, half from national/Belgrade-based media and the other half equally divided among two regions. Ownership structure, editorial differences and circulation/ratings were also considered in selecting the participants. Focus-group interviews generated material necessary to clarify and interpret the findings of the main survey.

The Professional Identity of Journalists

Although journalism is a very 'public' occupation, it is not easy to determine who are journalists in Serbia today. Due to a long period of intense devastation of the media sector, even the size of journalistic community is quite a riddle. The last official data refer to the 2002 census and to a loosely defined publishing industry, with 6148 employed 'journalists and other publishers' (Strategic Marketing Research (SMR), 2007). There are no precise criteria to identify 'journalists' or 'news media producers' within such a broadly defined sector. The media industry has changed significantly since then, especially due to foreign investment into the media, starting in 2002, and since the allocation of the first broadcasting licenses from 2006 onwards. Recent reports of the economic crisis indicate that up to 20% of jobs were lost in the sector during 2009/2010. All the indicators combined would put the number of journalists at close to 4000 at the time of research. A more strict definition of journalists as those involved in the 'news media' would probably lower the number to around 3200 journalists/editors, with the remainder employed in other media occupations. This was 'the population' for our web-based survey, which included almost 10% of it (total number 315).

The unknown number, however, is very significant for assessing the power of the media industry at the threshold of the information society. The official number of media outlets at the same time was around 1000 (between 937 and 1072 in our three-month survey period), which testifies to a highly diversified sector with disproportionately small media operations. The size of the advertising market was 175 million euro in 2010, completing a bleak picture of a highly saturated and fragmented market full of unsustainable media (Media Sustainability Index, 2012: 140). In terms of professional opportunities, the majority of journalists are working in broadcasting. According to the Pew Project for Excellence in Journalism's *The State of The News Media 2010*

> diversity of platforms aside, the majority of professionally produced news journalism is still primarily underwritten by newspapers, or what we should today probably call something like 'multi-news organizations with the particular emphasis on print' ... Newspapers are particularly central in the United States where the three national networks employed only 500 journalists and the number of journalists ... even after often brutal staff cuts in 2007 and 2008 employed more than 40 000 full time journalists. It is also true in the UK, where the largest public broadcaster employs about 7000 journalists, while the press employs more than 12 000. (Levy and Nielsen, 2010: 3)

This ratio in Serbia appears to be different but without exact numbers it is difficult to examine two important things. Firstly, the particular history and explosion of media after the 1990s, with an increasing number of radio and television channels, and two large public service broadcasters (Radio televizija Srbije (RTS) and Radio televizija Vojvodine (RTV)), contributed to more journalists working in broadcasting than in the printed press. This is in contradiction with the conclusion from the liberal media model that the 'private news industry is of central importance for the future of journalism'. Secondly, the investigation of the future of journalism should consider the economic downturn in the media industry differently in countries with heavily advertising-based media and in countries where the state/public sector is still significant in both size and influence. The economic base of quality journalism in the latter case is still very dependent on public funding and vulnerable to political pressure or control.

Paradoxically, one of the first research findings is that little is known about the profession that makes it its duty to help others know. Even the recent media study prepared by a team of specially commissioned EU experts for the Ministry of Culture in Serbia was strategizing media development without exact data. In the absence of reliable demographics it is difficult to generalize research results to the entire journalistic community, although the sample approximates its structure. Journalists in our project were mostly employed in broadcasting (almost 60%), the rest in print journalism (30%) or various other media (news agencies, online media, freelance journalists). More than half worked in Belgrade and the other half were distributed evenly in two regions. There were more female (51.5%) than male respondents (43.6%) although gender differences seem to be increasing as younger female journalists, as well as students of journalism, are entering the professional field (the remaining 4.9% did not respond). The gender structure also reflects positions of authority within the profession – women made up less than 33% of the owners/managers sample, with only one of them as an owner and all the others as managers. This is confirmed in most of the focus group interviews, where the image of a contemporary journalist was mostly associated with 'a woman in her thirties, and journalism [was] recognized as … a typically female profession like any other low paid occupation' (Milivojevic, 2011: 147).

In terms of education, journalists are a highly educated group, 73% of them having a university-level education and the remaining quarter with a high-school degree. This is even higher than in the 2002 census when 56% of journalists had a university degree. The common belief that one of the causes of low-quality journalism and sensationalism is a reduction in the quality of education of journalists is obviously not supported by evidence. There is also a widespread view that a formal education is not enough to make a good journalist, but there is still need for an explanation about why both the public perception and self- image of journalists so often assume that they have not received sufficient education. The educational background of the surveyed group is more than ten times higher than that of the general population, where only 6,5% has a university level degree, which is among the lowest percentages in Europe (http://www.politika.rs/rubrike/tema-dana/Svaki-peti-u-Srbiji-bez-zavrshene-osnovne-shkole.lt.html).

In terms of professional profile there are also signs of dynamism. According to our research, almost one-third of journalists have already been affected by media convergence as one-third work for more platforms or have more than just journalistic responsibilities. A high percentage of editors (37%) implies that, in small production units, journalists usually perform more professional roles. The same applies to owners and managers, with many of them being both (or members of governing boards), while only 22% of them self-identified in a single role. Almost 75% of journalists are full-time employees, with 16% part time and only 3.8% freelancers. The majority of them work in privately owned media (55.7%), 37.5 in public/state-owned media and 3.56% do not know the type of ownership of the media they work for.

Media and Socio-economic Conditions

Serbian journalists regard socio-economic conditions as a major impediment to their professional development. The economic situation can be regarded as having two distinct but interrelated aspects – the condition of the media industry and the state of the profession. The media industry is emerging under extremely difficult conditions. Privatization has been delayed and postponed several times is primarily an issue of media freedom as a large number of media outlets are still under the political control of the state. But, its second and less debated consequence is that not enough new capital has been injected into the sector. The long transition period has exhausted media resources and has slowed down development as they survived on low-quality/low-cost production in a highly unregulated environment. The media market in the meantime became dominated by highly concentrated advertising industry making the advertising revenue an important instrument of media control. Finally, the delayed transition has exhausted media outlets, leaving them extremely weak at the moment when the economic crisis hit the media in 2009.

In terms of economic restructuring, the media industry is becoming corporatized: 37% of journalists already work in domestic or international corporations. The state/public sector is approximately the same size and the remaining journalists work either in smaller private media or some form of nonprivatized outlets. Almost 75% of media owners/managers are from media outlets established since 1990 and their managing and business experience has been shaped mostly during authoritarian or difficult transitional times.

Journalists identified economic difficulties in the media industry as the third major problem at the moment (17.23%) after low quality of journalism and the domination of tabloid content (22.13%) and strong political pressure (20.59%). But they singled out low pay (20.36%) as the main problem of journalism. When identifying the main forms of external pressure on the media they recognized state budget cuts, nontransparent criteria for state or international funding, cutting off commercial revenue and impediments to media distribution. These amounted to almost 40% of the most frequent forms of pressure. When asked how to improve economic conditions and increase independence, journalists most often proposed state aid (29.4%) or international donations (25.08%); less than a quarter thought that a better credit policy would be a solution.

The economic challenges recognized by Serbian journalists were not necessarily associated with the global economic crisis and even less with technological changes in the media world. Most of the constraining economic circumstances were seen as a financial and investment crisis that was attributed to the delayed transition, the state's indifference to the future of the media and the absence of media autonomy (47% combined).

The economic impediments experienced by the media industry are those of a transitional country with a particular political culture and additionally intensified by the global economic crisis. Unfortunately, the dominant view of socio-economic conditions is still almost exclusively focused on a lack of funding. From a journalistic perspective this challenges the profession not because it requires novel models of economic organization but because existing resources are scarce. In that sense, economic circumstances are a double impediment to professional development. First, they constrain working conditions for the majority of low paid, overworked, exploited and underunionized journalists but they also prevent journalists from considering changes in the business of journalism and creating new professional practices. The difficulty of obtaining journalistic resources, arising from unfinished transitional issues, also prevents them from preparing for the economic challenges of the future.

Questionable Political Autonomy

Serbian journalists regard external political pressures as a major threat to their professionalism. Media autonomy and journalistic independence are still the main goals behind most professional and regulatory activities throughout the Western Balkans. Their formulation reflects transitional goals almost in the same way as when they were first defined at the beginning of the transition. In fact, dismantling the state monopoly and liberation from political control has been the major goal of media transformation in many postcommunist countries since the 1990s.

Quality journalism remained a cornerstone of successful media transition and of the democratic performance of the media. Its underlying ideals of media freedom and professional autonomy were part of the liberal media tradition, which guided international assistance throughout postcommunist Europe. But media conditions in Western Balkan countries resemble much more a model that Hallin and Mancini identified as polarized pluralist or Mediterranean, where 'media developed as an institution of the political and literary worlds more than of the market …' and where

> the media are still relatively strongly politicized and political parallelism is relatively high. Newspapers tend to represent distinct political tendencies, and

> it is reflected in the different political attitudes of the readership. At times, newspapers play an active role, mobilizing those readers to support political causes. Public broadcasting tends to be party-politicized. Both journalists and media owners often have political ties or alliances, and it remains fairly common for journalists to become politicians and vice versa. (Hallin and Mancini, 2004: 98)

This political parallelism, the important role of the state and the role of political culture, contributed to an understanding of professionalism that is different from that in the liberal or North Atlantic model. During the first wave of transition in the Western Balkans, the notion of objective, neutral journalism, ideas of media autonomy, self-regulation, internal and external pluralism were combined with a different tradition of politically engaged journalism, sometimes producing clashes within the professional community itself – especially where the professional legitimacy of journalism during authoritarian regimes was derived from its critical watchdog role both in institutional (media outlets) and professional (journalism) terms. It was also assumed that privatization is crucial for media autonomy and journalists became highly sensitive to political pressures and attacks on independence without developing the same sensitivity to commercial pressures from media owners and advertisers. In this respect, the situation in Serbia had a specific trajectory because of the long authoritarian period during the 1990s and a very late start to the transition, only after the regime changed in 2000. Journalists are therefore still highly sensitive to political interference, although the political and professional culture provided for an easy continuation of a high level of media-political parallelism.

From this perspective the results indicate continuity with the normative goals of the 1990s resulting in strong concern over political independence and weak media autonomy (20.59%). Although they rank third on the list of major problems, when combined with the incomplete transition (13.59%) and inadequate media policy (14.85%) they form a kind of *political knot* regarding relations between the state, politics and the media. This situation does not significantly differ throughout the region, where political parallelism is embraced by new political elites and is almost an expected benefit of every election victory.

Among those exercising pressure upon media are mostly political parties (governing parties 25.59%, opposition parties 3.68%) but also local authorities (13.09%) and government (4.26%). There is no doubt that, in the view of journalists, the main threat to media freedom and autonomy comes from the political field. It is still the most important source of pressure, even compared to obviously growing forms of economic pressures. Due to political parallelism, a high level of clientelism and systemic corruption, many economic instruments are still institutionally or otherwise connected to political power.

Technological Challenges to Journalism

Technological challenges to journalism rank very low on the list of problems, as a technological gap is perceived as a major problem for media development only by 4.34% of journalists. Part of it probably comes from a reductionist understanding of technological changes as just adding new media to the existing mass-media family. From that perspective the research results look like an unexpected wave of optimism with professionals welcoming and easily accepting new technology-based practices.

In practical terms, the technological gap with the more advanced European societies is not seen as a major problem by survey respondents. Statistical data shows a serious lagging behind and focus group interviews confirmed that there are all sorts of digital divides within the media community: between national media and those in other parts of the country, between journalists who still refuse to accept new technology and those who are completely online-based in their work, and between generations.

The second important aspect of technological changes is the challenge it poses to the cognitive basis of journalism. What kind of knowledge, skills and new practices will journalism have to develop for professionals to master the changes? In terms of educational demands there is more openness and self-criticism on the part of journalists – only 11% of them said they did not have any training/

education in the new media but 66% still think that journalists need significant additional education.

In structural terms, there is hardly any discussion within the professional community about the changes and challenges that new technology poses for the profession. Most of the journalists surveyed have mixed feelings about new media demands: when asked how they obtain information in everyday work they already put the Internet in the first place (20.28%), ahead of personal interviews, press conferences, or expert sources. But, they still use the Internet very conventionally, mostly turning to reliable sites – almost 65% of their sources are either official web sites (governments, parties, companies) large media (Reuters, BBC, CNN) and Google News. Other content providers and aggregators, including social media, mostly complement these sites. It was repeatedly stated at the focus groups that the question of credibility comes first when the future of journalism is considered. It is because of this *credibility defence* that journalists do not see citizen journalists, or other nonprofessional information providers, as competition. They very confidently believe that the profession will change but will survive, unlike some other media occupations. Even in a multimedia context, journalism will not change essentially.

Conclusion

In conclusion, Serbian journalists do not perceive the present radical changes in journalism as a major challenge to their profession. Like their colleagues in other Western Balkan countries they do find quality journalism vital for democratic media performance. Their views are also shaped by very specific professional and political circumstances: a transition that started ten years later than in other postcommunist countries, the largest media market in the region both in terms of production and audiences, a highly impoverished yet pluralized media industry and a deeply scared postconflict culture.

Professional identity is only slowly emerging as there is weak consensus over professional and ethical standards and, most importantly, over the media's role in a democratic society. Major dividing lines from the authoritarian past still antagonize the journalistic community, which therefore focuses more on *institutional* than *occupational* aspects of professionalism.

The economic difficulties of the emerging media industry, typical for a transitional society and this kind of political culture, are intensified by a global economic crisis. Unfortunately, economic problems are mostly reduced to insufficient funding, while serious economic restructuring of the media world is still not an issue.

A major threat to professional autonomy still comes from the political field. The profession has a long history of political instrumentalization; significant state ownership still provides for easy state control over the media, and political parties preserve clientelistic and corrupt relations with the main media outlets.

At the same time, the technological revolution and the spread of information and communication technologies are not perceived as fundamentally altering the working environment. Journalists believe that the combined practical, cognitive and structural effects of technological changes are less demanding and threatening for their future. They also do not consider citizen journalists or other content generators as serious rivals for the audience's attention. Despite strong self-criticism about the state of professional education and ethical standards, they still find journalism vital for public communication.

At the threshold of the information society, the culture of professional journalism in Serbia is shaped by a particular combination of economic exhaustion, political pressures and technological oblivion. Some of the public debates surrounding journalism still sound as if they refer to the media situation in the 1990s. There is lot of evidence that journalism in Serbia is in a state of limbo, caught somewhere between delayed transition and the information society. The professional community, therefore, is slowly mobilizing its resources to respond to the forthcoming challenges.

References

Currah, A. (2009) *What's Happening to Our News: An Investigation into the Likely Impact of the Digital Revolution on the Economics of News Publishing in the UK,* Reuters Institute for the Study of Journalism, Oxford.

Dobek-Ostrowska, B. and Glowacki, M. (eds) (2008) *Comparing Media Systems in Central Europe: Between Commercialization and Politicization,* University of Wroclaw Press, Wroclaw.

Dutton W. (2009) The Fifth Estate emerging through the network of networks. *Prometheus* 27 (1), pp. 1–15.

Fenton, N. (ed.) (2000) *New Media, Old News: Journalism and Democracy in the Digital Age,* Sage, London.

Hallin, D. (1992) The passing of the 'high modernism' of American journalism. *Journal of Communication* 42 (3), pp. 14–25.

Hallin, D. and Mancini, P. (2004) *Comparing Media Systems. Three Models of Media and Politics,* Cambridge University Press, Cambridge.

Hume, E. (2011) *Caught in the Middle: Central and Eastern European Journalism at a Crossroads,* Center for International Media Assistance and National Endowment for Democracy, Washington D.C.

Jakubowicz, K. (2009) A new notion of media? First Council of Europe Conference of Ministers responsible for Media and New Communication Services, Reykjavik, Iceland, 28–29 May.

Jakubowicz, K. and Sukosd, M. (2008) *Finding the Right Place on the Map,* Intelect, Bristol.

Kepplinger, H. and Koecher, R. (1990) Professionalism in the media world? *European Journal of Communication* 5 (2–3), pp. 285–311.

Levy, D.and Nielsen, R. (2010) *The Changing Business of Journalism and its Implications for Democracy,* Reuters Institute for the Study of Journalism, Oxford.

Mancini, P. (2005) Is there a European model of journalism? In *Making Journalists* (ed. H. de Burgh), Routledge, London.

McQuail, D. (2008) Journalism as a public occupation: alternative images. In *Democracy, Journalism and Technology: New Developments in an Enlarged Europe* (eds. Carpentier, Pruulmann-Vengerfeldt, P., Nordenstreng, K., Hartmann, M., Vihalemm, P., Cammaerts, B., Nieminen, H., Tobias, O.), Tartu University Press, Tartu.

Milivojevic, S. (1993) Novinarski profesionalizam: Granice medijske autonomje, *Gledista* 1–6, pp. 87–95.

Television Across Europe: regulation, policy and independence, Monitoring Reports- Serbia, Vol. 3 (2005), EU Monitoring and Advocacy Program and Network Media Program, Open Society Institute, Budapest, pp. 1315–83. http://www.opensocietyfoundations.org/sites/default/files/volthree_20051011_0.pdf (accessed 10 October 2012).

Measuring the Information Society (2011) Executive Summary, International Telecommunication Union, Geneve.

Media Sustainability Index 2012, IREX, Washington, DC. http://www.irex.org/system/files/u105/EE_MSI_2012_Serbia.pdf. (accessed 10 October 2012).

Milivojevic, S.(ur) (2011) *Profesija na raskrscu: novinarstvo na pragu infromacionog drustva,*Centar za medije i medijska istrazivanja Fakulteta politickih nauka, Beograd. http://www.fpn.bg.ac.rs/wp-content/uploads/2011/07/Profesija-na-Raskr%C5%A1%C4% 87u.pdf (accessed 10 October 2012).

Schudson, M. and Downie, L. Jr. (2009) Reconstruction of American journalism. *Columbia Journalism Review* http://www.cjr.org/reconstruction/the_reconstruction_of_american.php?page=all (accessed 10 October 2012).

State of the News Media (2010) Annual report on American journalism by Pew Project for Excellence in Journalism, www.stateofthemedia.org/2010/index.php (accessed 10 October 2012).

Svaki peti u Srbiji bez zavrsene osnovne skole, Politika, 25.04.2008. http://www.politika.rs/rubrike/tema-dana/Svaki-peti-u-Srbiji-bez-zavrshene-osnovne-shkole.lt.html (accessed 10 October 2012).

Usage of information and communication technologies in the Republic of Serbia,(2010) Statistical Office of the Republic of Serbia, http://webrzs.stat.gov.rs/WebSite/public/PublicationView.aspx?pKey=41&pLevel=1&pubType=2&pubKey=164 (accessed 10 October 2012).

Novinari i novinarstvo u očima građana i novinara Srbije(2007) Strategic Marketing Research, http:// www.anem.rs/sr/medijskaScena/istrazivanja/story/8808/ISTRA%C5%BDIVANJE+%E2%80%9CNOVINARI+I+NOVINARSTVO+U+O%C4%8CIMA+GRA%C4%90ANA+I+NOVINARA+SRBIJE%E2%80%9D.html (accessed 10 October 2012).

Television Across Europe: More Chnnels, Less Independence. (2008) Follow-up Reports. EU Monitoring and Advocacy Program and Media Program, Open Society Institute, Budapest.

Zielonka, J. and Mancini, P. (2011) A Media Map of Central and Eastern Europe: Executive Summary, http://mde.politics.ox.ac.uk/images/stories/summary_mdcee_2011.pdf (accessed 10 October 2012).

Mina Petrovic and Jelisaveta Vukelic

The Transformation of the Governance Regime in Serbia: Public Participation in Environmental Decision Making

Introduction

This chapter focuses on the civil sector's participation in environmental decision making as a key issue in environmental governance in Serbia. A partnership between civil society and the public sector is regarded as an important precondition for the new environmental governance that should be developing with the country's accession to the EU. This analysis researches the links needed between civil and state actors as well as among civil actors themselves. It is conceptually framed by regulation theory, concepts of social capital and participative and transactional civic activism. It starts from the hypothesis that there is a weak state, with low trust in institutions and low social capital among civil actors, which diminish public participation and the potential for environmental (transactional) activism in Serbia. This hypothesis stems from aspects of Serbia's current situation linked both to the enduring economic crisis and closed political opportunities. The chapter is informed by data from the RRPP Project 'Public Participation in Environment Decision Making – the Case of Bor and Pancevo', carried out in late 2010 and early 2011.

It is useful to analyse the conditions for new environmental governance from the perspective of *regulation theory* because this postulates a shift from government to governance regimes (in terms of ideal types) as a general phenomenon of late modern societies. The shift refers to the increased engagement or participation of other nonstate actors – private and civic sectors – in the governance process (Jessop, 1994). The concept of social capital is therefore closely connected to the phenomenon of a new governance regime.

Although there are many definitions of *social capital*, we rely upon the Putnamian approach, which conceptualizes social capital as consisting of social trust (based on the norms of reciprocity) and social networks (Putnam, 2000). Social trust is a belief that people are generally trustworthy and that they share the same basic norms of reciprocity and act accordingly. Relations of trust make cooperation much easier because, instead of having to monitor others, individuals are able to trust them to act as expected. On the other hand, social networks are considered to be a crucial aspect of social capital. Their function is to channel the provision of information and to act as means of mobilization, participation and cooperation (Putnam, 2000: 19).

Woolcock, further developing the concept of social capital, distinguishes several types of social capital/relations: bonding capital refers to relations developed only among actors of the same (social/power) position and in close physical proximity; bridging capital refers to relations between actors of the same (social/power) position but with significant physical distance and therefore different social contexts, and linking capital refers to relations developed between actors of different social/power positions and/or social/spatial contexts (Keyes, 2001). In our analysis we understand governance as an extremely complex web of relationships among actors, which presupposes developed communication between various levels of social networks in both directions – top down and bottom up – and between actors from the key social sectors (public, private/market and the third sector). In circumstances where these linkages are weak, incidences of weak state, corruption and anomie are much more evident than in efficient and flexible development systems (Woolcock, 1998).

The *new governance regime* might be seen as a turn to the 'partnership' interpretation of civil society, which reflects a neoliberal transformation of state power and freeing of capital (Brenner, 2000; Mayer, 2003; Fagan, 2005). However, in developed democratic and market systems it follows a long tradition of state regulative capacities and civil society participative activism that constantly pose new requirements to the power-holders. In postsocialist societies, on the other hand, such a shift presumes institutional path breaking in all sectors, state, civil society and market economy, due to the lack of market pluralism, cooperative state and autonomous civic society during the socialist period. The overall level of *civic activism and political participation* remained quite low throughout Central and Eastern Europe (Howard, 2003) in comparison to Western Europe. There are many possible reasons, from those related to the complex legacy of both presocialist and socialist periods as well as to newly created institutional settings. These include closed political structures (centralized state), lack of resources for participation, poverty and economic concerns, a sense of powerlessness, underdeveloped social capital and a nonparticipative political culture.

Consequently, a Western-type governance model, particularly regarding public participation, cannot simply be reproduced in post-socialist societies (although it has been largely externally initiated, generally through the process of accession to the EU), due to a lack of institutional or cultural infrastructure on which such a model should rely. In other words, most postsocialist states lack cooperative culture due to an authoritarian legacy and no sustained tradition of institutionalized state-society relations (Borzel, 2008). State actors are therefore weak as they lack important resources (expertise, information, personnel and support) and are consequently reluctant to seek cooperation with nonstate actors, as they perceive this to involve a loss of autonomy. Moreover, weak states face weak societies, as nonstate actors also face capacity problems and lack the necessary resources to serve as reliable partners cooperating in public policy-making. For that reason, their relations with state actors are often characterized by mutual distrust (Borzel, 2009: 21–4).

Environmental policy is one of the areas that promote new governance regimes in postsocialist countries, primarily due to the fact that it develops mainly under the influence of EU policy making. The EU strongly encourages accession countries to involve nonstate actors in policy formulation, although new political opportunities hardly empower citizens and civil society actors if they are not effectively implemented (Borzel, 2006, 2008). Public participation in environmental decision making is therefore a good example of governance transformation in general and of the opening of political opportunities for public participation in particular.

Following the same logic, Petrova and Tarrow (2007) made a distinction between *participative and transactional environmental activism* in their attempt to understand the puzzling phenomenon of civic activism in Eastern Europe. Participative activism assumes large-scale citizen involvement in collective (political) action, referring to direct, grassroots involvement of citizens in decision-making processes. Transactional activism means 'the ties – enduring and temporary – among organized non-state actors and between them and political parties, power holders, and other institutions' (Petrova and Tarrow, 2007: 79). This type of activism – which is almost the opposite of Western experiences of mass mobilization and challenging governmental decisions and actions – is characterized by the dominance of loosely linked (and frequently internally competing) environmental NGOs involved in partnerships with governing structures and foreign donors while barely engaged in public mobilization for environmental causes.

Although Petrova and Tarrow claim that transactional activism has been more typical of postsocialist countries, as a result of their institutional legacy, it has also largely been stimulated by the international donor programs aimed at the NGO sector (Howard, 2003; Fagan, 2005; Cisar, 2008, 2010). Such support was motivated by the expectation that NGOs could engage collaboratively in the new governance regime and, in the process, build and extend the capacity of government agencies to seek cooperation with nonstate actors. However, much research has indicated that international donor programs pushed NGOs toward adopting the norms and practices of professional organizations (Carmin, 2010) with agendas determined primarily by the funding priorities of their donors, rather than establishing a commitment to a particular issue tied to the priorities of domestic constituencies (Fagan, 2006; Carmin, 2008). Thus they mainly act as implementation agencies rather than autonomous agencies of civil society (Fagan, 2006). It could also be said that, unlike Central and Eastern Europe (CEE), where building civil society was an objective in its own right (perceived as an important part of the democratic consolidation process), the main objective of EU support in the Western Balkans and Serbia was more directed to state capacity-building and emergency relief, with the emphasis on economic reconstruction (Fagan, 2010). So it could be hypothesized that NGOs in CEE have developed a certain activist (mostly transactional) potential, while in the Western Balkans NGO work has been limited (with rare exceptions) to the third sector/state surrogate/assistant role.

Our research aim is to illustrate the main obstacles to developing the environmental governance regime in Serbia, primarily focusing on civil sector participation in decision making. We argue that the linkages needed among state and civil actors as well as among civil actors themselves are weak in Serbia, not only due to the socialist legacy but also because of postsocialist administrative structures and regulatory styles, which reproduce the centralization of decision making. This is particularly evident in Serbia, as well as in the whole Western Balkan region, because of the delayed process of accession to the EU. We argue, therefore, that the Serbian political elite sticks to traditional command-and-control approaches to decision making and lacks interest in introducing and efficiently implementing new laws and institutions that support public participation, although this has been promoted at the normative level in Serbia. We also hypothesize that transaction activism emerges in a deficient form in Serbia, as an elitist type of NGO activism not based on advocacy and lobbying that would lead to cooperation of civil society organizations between themselves (horizontal alliances) and with political and economic elites (vertical relations) (Baldassari and Diani, 2007; Cisar, 2010).

Our research analysis addresses both the national level (adopted laws and institutions) and the local level (implementation practices). However, if we consider the transition from an authoritarian sytem to a democratic one and from government to governance regimes in postsocialist countries as aspects of their (re)integration in a global (or European) system, we might take the changes at both analytical levels as expressions of local adaptation to this reintegration process. In that sense, we want to emphasize the specifics of the transition in Serbian society. Regarding public participation, we also want to check if environmental problems that are perceived as important and jeopardizing citizens' health can instigate environmental activism (and what type of activism) in circumstances where there is prevailing low trust and economic problems which generally diminish environmental concerns (Inglehart, 1995; Rootes, 1997). For that reason we have chosen two localities marked as ecological hot spots in Serbia for our field research. A local community's economic performance and its closeness to the capital city (both spatially and politically as these determine the visibility of environmental problems and their discursive construction) have been perceived as conceptually important variables to compare.

In the following sections we identify the legislative and institutional (structural) capacities for, and obstacles to, the establishment of an environmental governance regime and public participation in Serbia. Then we analyse public participation and civil society activism using empirical data on the mutual perceptions of local authorities, NGOs and citizens as actors in environmental governance at the local level. Empirical research was conducted in two cities: Bor and Pancevo. The citizens' opinions were obtained through questionnaire research on representative samples (N = 450 and N = 350), while the opinions of NGOs and local authorities (LAs) were collected through qualitative methods (interviews, in both cities the sample size of each actor was the same, N = 10). Finally, we summarize the main findings.

Serbian Case Study

The Institutional and Legislative Context: Impediments to Environmental Governance Regime and Public Participation

Due to conflicts and delayed socio-economic transformation it could be said that Serbia entered the first phase of institutional transition to a market society only after 2000 and transition has again been slowed by the 2008 global economic crisis. During the 1990s, the political elite's 'adaptive' strategy (Lazic, 2000: 28–33) was marked by political capitalism and corruption. Even after the political change of 2000, the authorities maintained strong control over economic resources, which slowed the privatization process and limited FDI. The Serbian government envisaged that the privatization process would end in 2010 but it has not yet been completed. Moreover, privatization has not had the expected effects on employment and industrial production, particularly on restructuring and revitalizing inherited industrial giants (Arandarenko, 2010).

Complex legal and institutional transformations have proven particularly difficult as they required the dissolution of informal connections between Serbian political and economic elites who were hesitant to support policy changes that would diminish their power (Vujovic and Petrovic, 2007). This weakened the development of the civil sector's capacity to challenge political decisions and had a negative impact on private investments. Newly formed NGOs that relied mostly on foreign donations were in a particularly difficult position during Milošević's regime, as they were perceived by that government as foreign/hostile agents – as actors over which the state had no control. Political decentralization and state devolution were thwarted by a central government-level political elite not keen on allowing local government to develop as a powerful political entity or on bestowing it with any substantial financial autonomy (Djordjevic, 2008; Komsic, 2009).

Ecological issues emerged recently on the Serbian political agenda mainly through the process of Serbia's accession to the EU. Given that neither the Serbian political elite nor the public in general have an unquestionably positive attitude towards the EU, the process is evolving rather gradually. New regulative mechanisms are developing extremely slowly, particularly in the sense that environmental laws[1] have been feebly implemented or put into practice (*National Environment Strategy*, 2007). Established institutional bodies at the national level, like the Agency for Environmental Protection (founded in 2001) and the Serbian Fund for Environmental Protection (founded in 2005), have mostly been inactive while local environmental protection departments, required by the Law on Environmental Protection, have rarely been established in practice.

Bearing in mind Serbia's economic difficulties and the need for reindustrialization, it is of no surprise that the 'polluter pays' principle, introduced by a set of environmental laws in 2004, has not been

1 In 1991, the Law on Environmental Protection replaced all the laws in this field adopted mainly through the 1970s and 1980s. It was replaced again in 2004 by the following laws: The Law on Environmental Protection, The Law on Strategic Environmental Assessment (SEA law), The Law on Environmental Impact Assessment and the Law on Integrated Pollution Prevention and Control (Law on IPCC) (Official Gazette RS, No. 135/2004). Five years later, a new set of environmental laws was passed, the so called 'set of green laws'.

implemented appropriately (UNECE, 2007). Serbia has not reached the level of GDP recorded in 1989 yet.[2] The share of industry in GDP fluctuates around 20%, which, at the Serbia's level of economic development, is very unfavourable and indicates the need for reindustrialization (Arandarenko, 2010).

Access to information is quite poor, despite extensive and rather progressive legislation that stipulates its dissemination. The Environmental Protection Agency has been established with the intention that it should manage environmental information as an instrument for good governance and decision making, but its work has been insignificant. The implementation of environmental law has been particularly unsuccessful with respect to public participation, although the Law on Local Self-Governance and the Law on Environmental Protection both introduce public participation. According to research findings (Vujovic, 2004), citizens saw political party structures as the most important channels of influence (32%) at the local level, followed by the municipal council (26%) and personal connections and corruption (22%). Local communities (7%), NGOs (1%), and citizen petitions (0.8%) were ranked as the least influential decision-making channels (Vujovic, 2004: 173). The low level of citizen participation has been associated with a lack of trust in political institutions, limited availability of information, as well as the negative impact of widespread unemployment (around 20%) and poverty (with more than 20% of the population in financial risk of poverty) (Vujovic, 2004: 173).[3]

Unlike other CEE countries, the law that regulates the NGO sector was repeatedly delayed in Serbia. It was only in 2009 that the new Law on Civic Associations, in compliance with EU regulations was enacted. The 2009 Law on Civic Associations allowed

2 In 1993 it was only at 42%, in 2000 at 50%, and in 2008 at 78% of GDP in 1989 (Serbian Statistical Office). Industrial production in 2008 reached only 45% of its level in 1989. During the 2000s growth in industrial output was only about 0.6% annually, or 7% for 10 years period.

3 The unemployment rate of around 20% at the beginning of the 2000s was reduced to 14% in 2008, but increased again to 19% in 2010. Poverty levels have remained constantly high; in 2008, 20.6% of population were at financial risk of poverty, while in 2010 that percentage rose to 22.5% (Republican Statistical Office).

international nongovernmental organizations to register and work in Serbia for the first time. Before 2000, foreign donors helped the NGO sector more through strengthening their service-provision function than supporting their advocacy role in the political arena. However, tax regulations are still unfavourable as they treat NGOs in the same way as small and medium enterprises.

According to the NGO Sustainability Index in Serbia (USAID, 2009) the sector has just entered into a mid-transition phase characterized by increasing mutual respect between state and nonstate agents, and the very beginning of information sharing and networking within the NGO sector, with embryonic alternative policy analysis primarily in universities and think thanks, but still without generating alternative political claims or coalitions to pursue issues of common interest and to monitor or lobby political parties, the legislature or executive bodies. Permanent economic crisis stimulates the opportunistic behaviour of the 'donor-driven' NGOs, which are motivated primarily to secure regular incomes for their employees. Generally, NGOs in Serbia are largely dependent on foreign donations, while the role of membership contributions is rather negligible (REC, 2006; USAID, 2009). They are therefore forced to concentrate on the donor's priorities, rather than on the needs of their own organizations or communities. This tendency is especially apparent among NGOs at the local level, which also claim that both mutual cooperation and the exchange of information are lacking (USAID, 2009).

The general characteristics of the NGO sector are reflected in the environmental NGOs (ENGOs). Environmental NGOs in Serbia seem to be in a less favourable position than those in other south-eastern European countries regarding the availability of resources for necessary equipment, training programmes and for obtaining public support (REC, 2006). Research on NGOs conducted in 2011 suggested that environmental organizations are, compared to the average results for the whole NGO sector, more frequently involved in practical activities (for example, cleaning) in the local communities (57% compared to the average 49%). On the other hand, their involvement in informal education activities (34% compared to the average 51%), networking (22% versus 29%), laws monitoring (4% versus 9%) and advocacy (12% versus 16%) is below the measured average for the whole sample (Gradjanske inicijative, 2011). The biggest and most prominent ENGOs in Serbia have close links both with international donors and national government and appear to be leaders of transactional activism in Serbia. However, the transactional character of these organizations is questionable as their founders are most often members of the ruling elite (for example, leaders of the organizations that include former Ministers for the environment and people closely linked with the ruling Democratic Party) than autonomous civil society actors.

In the light of these insights both participative and transactional activism types seem underdeveloped in Serbia. In the following section we illustrate this statement, relying on our empirical research findings.

Local Actors' Perspectives on Environmental Governance and Public Participation: Two Case Studies

As we have mentioned, our case studies were conducted in two cities known as ecological hot spots in Serbia: Pancevo and Bor.[4] In both cities, citizens' opinions were obtained through questionnaire research on representative samples (N = 450 and N = 350), while the opinions of NGOs and LAs were collected through qualitative methods (interviews – in both cities the sample size of each actor was the same: N = 10). Nongovernmental organizations in Serbia are rarely specialized as their existence depends mostly on foreign donation funds and this causes them to shift their orientation according to changes in donor funding policies. We therefore interviewed local NGOs that dealt at least occasionally with environmental issues.

Pancevo is an economically more developed city than Bor (less mono-functional), with industries that are more prosperous and

4 The research was conducted by Institute for Sociological Research, Faculty of Philosophy University of Belgrade within the Regional Research Program Promotion, funded by University of Friburg, Switzerland. The field research was conducted in Pancevo by the end of 2010 and at the beginning of 2011 in Bor.

strategically more important for the Serbian economy. It is close to the capital city (less than 20 km away), so it is more important to the national state authorities (in the context of a centralized state on the one hand and a higher environmental threat for the population of Belgrade on the other). Ecological issues have been more politicized in this city in comparison to Bor. In both cities polluters are in close proximity to the city centre and residential areas. The main ecological problems in Pancevo stem from the huge petro-chemical complex, founded in the 1960s, which consists of three giant enterprises.[5] Their share in municipal GDP could be estimated at 70%, and the share of jobs at the local labour market at 45% (Analysis of local economy development in Pancevo, 2005). Only one of these companies has been privatized, but the whole complex has recently been modernized.

Bor is a peripheral city, located in eastern Serbia, with very poor transport infrastructure that connects it with other parts of Serbia and with corridor E10. It has a mining industry which dates back more than a century.[6] The metallurgy complex (RTB Bor) was established during socialism and has not been privatized yet (despite several attempts in 2007 and 2008). Its technology, which has not been modernized since 1971, is obsolete and thus produces considerable air, water and soil pollution (high emissions of SO_2). Due to an economic crisis, in 2002 its production was only 19% of the level in 1990, while the number employed there decreased to 8800. In 2010, the number employed fell to 4800, which affected the unemployment level in Bor considerably. In order to improve production technology, to increase the chances for RTB's privatization and to reduce pollution, the national government took a loan of 42 million euros from the World Bank in 2011.

5 *Study on local economic development of Pančevo Municipality* underlines the paradoxical situation of Pancevo that according to GDP level and average wages is among the most developed municipalities in Serbia, while other indicators, like high unemployment rates, refer to its less favourable position.

6 The mining started in 1903 and up to the Second World War was a French concession. Even in that period, the mining technology was rather undeveloped with serious environmental degradation, which caused huge protests in 1935. In 1990, 24 000 people were employed in the metallurgy complex in city of about 50 000 inhabitants.

As ecological hot spots, both municipalities are among the rare ones in Serbia that have founded local institutions, adopted laws and created financial mechanisms linked to environmental governance. However, they are rather inactive or ineffective. According to LA representatives, significant local environmental governance problems are linked to the lack of state power decentralization and the fact that the industrial complexes in both cities are under the auspices of the national government. Therefore: 'local authorities have inadequate responsibilities, the transparency of decision making process is extremely low and there is no chance for citizens to participate in environment decision making' (LA representative, Pancevo). The economic significance of the industrial plants for local employment is also frequently mentioned by LA representatives as an impediment to proper environmental intervention: 'Even when the prosecutor initiates a charge for a hazardous situation everything goes without sanctions as RTB Bor cannot be closed' (LA representative, Bor).

Our research confirmed a high level of party-political interference in local level environmental governance, which was most frequently underlined by NGO sector respondents:

> mobilization of the public emerged in Pancevo only when it was initiated by political actors and inter party struggles for power … In 2004 the city of Pancevo got a new system for monitoring pollution [as a donation from the city of Ravenna], when the Mayor [of the local government which was run by the Democratic Party (DP), which was in opposition to the Serbian Democratic Party (SDP) at national level] decided to introduce a parallel and independent monitoring system to the one run by the Institute for Public Health [under the auspices of the national government]. Driven by political considerations, the Mayor decided to use any data showing the enhanced emission of hazardous substances to mobilize the public … this led more to politicized public alarm in Serbia about the irresponsible national government than to a reduction in pollution in Pancevo, where citizens felt panic without any additional information about what they should do in alarming situations. (NGO, Pancevo)

Since 2008, the same political parties have been in power at the local and national levels and, even though the system of parallel monitoring still exists, there is no public alarm at increased emissions in Pancevo. Political party affiliation also proves crucial in Bor as

> environmental concerns of the Republican government started to increase only when the Mayor and Director of RTB Bor came from the same party [which participates in the ruling coalition at the national level] … which is directly

> associated with the recent increase in the Government's engagement in getting a WB loan for improving RTB's technology. (NGO, Bor)

Local governments in both cities occasionally organize public competitions for ecological projects financed by EU funds or other donations. From the NGOs' perspective these competitions are 'nontransparent and unfair' and highly dependent on political parties: 'people in power create their own NGOs just to get funds for bigger projects or control certain fields' (NGO, Bor); '... each party has its satellite NGO,[7] there are no neutral NGOs and as such they are very weak for any action' (NGO, Pancevo). In Pancevo, the predominance of party politics caused some NGOs to transform into a local branch of the Green Party (formed as a national party in 1990) in order to enhance the influence of environmental ideas in the new multiparty system, but they have never had any significant authority.[8]

In both of the cities that we researched, the NGO representatives interviewed almost universally claimed that local authorities have no interest in including the civil sector in the governance regime and expressed little trust in their capabilities to deal with the environment issue in general: 'LAs have no continuity in environmental policy ... they are proactive just before the elections and do nothing afterwards' (NGO, Bor). They also referred to the huge gap between accepted laws and real local practices: 'Since the beginning of the 2000s, there has been an increase in ecological declarations, but nothing has ever been implemented' (NGO, Pancevo). The existing cooperation between NGOs and local authorities has been described as 'formal and insignificant' (NGO, Pancevo), which is in accordance with the little support given by LA respondents in both cities to potential NGO involvement in environmental governance, although they describe NGOs as 'potentially significant partners'. The (vertical) linkages between NGOs and power holders and institutions are weak

7 According to the respondent, NGOs are particularly inclined to DS and G17+, the most European-oriented parties in Serbia in power at the moment.

8 Ecological parties are active in both cities but have little political influence. For instance, in Pancevo, until 2000, the Green Party had one or two members in the municipal parliament, and since then the local branch of newly organized national party, Zeleni Srbije, has replaced it with a few representatives in the local assembly.

while their position with regard to strong political actors diminishes their potential role in advocacy, lobbying, environmental campaigns and other political activities characteristic of transactional activism. Interviewed NGOs declared that they were not familiar with advocacy roles, which confirmed previous research (REC, 2006).

Our research findings also show that NGOs lack mutual (horizontal) cooperation and adequate functional relations. They are isolated, competitive and linked to each other only if this is required for a specific project. This is particularly true in Pancevo, where NGO representatives complained about a lack of international ecological organizations that they could rely on in their activities, like Greenpeace, in Serbia. In Bor, NGOs complained more about inequalities within the NGO sector in Serbia, and perceive organizations in and around Belgrade 'as in a favourable position regarding financing'.

Finally, although most of the NGOs interviewed stated that they actively engage citizens in their programmes, citizens are rarely mobilized as activists but rather as service recipients. Therefore, NGOs do not work on promoting participative activism. This follows logically from their weakness in lobbying and advocacy work. Nongovernmental organizations in Bor were particularly against initiating public protests: '… fighting against the RTB is hopeless, therefore, we [the NGOs] do not want to become public enemy number one.' Bor's peripheral position was also used in arguments against protesting 'even if citizens do protest, their voices are less influential than the voices of Pancevo's citizens, who are closer to Belgrade and thus "better heard"' (NGO, Bor). Without reflecting on their possible role in increasing citizens' participative activism, NGOs in both cities were more concerned with citizens' indifference towards the environment: 'Citizens are preoccupied with their narrow personal interests … they do nothing that might be in their power to take care about the environment' (NGO Pancevo). Interestingly, the local authority representatives interviewed shared almost the same attitudes towards citizens whom they saw as well informed but not interested in participating in decision making.

The citizens confirmed that existing ties between them and NGOs as civic partners are very weak or nonexistent. Our research shows that citizens are not familiar with the work of NGOs and generally do not trust these organizations (in both cities 50% of citizens had no confidence in them and around 30% had just limited trust). Only 10% of respondents in Pancevo and 5% in Bor had heard about any local ENGOs, with less than 30% believing they had achieved positive effects on the environment.

In Pancevo as well as in Bor, the majority of the citizens also have low confidence in LAs. For example, 44% and 46% (respectively) of respondents stated that their LA addresses environmental protection issues according to its political interests, whereas 39% and 38% (respectively) declared that local authorities protect polluters. There is almost no difference between the two samples regarding citizens' claims that they are badly informed about environmental issues because information is unreliable (around 40%) or unavailable (around 20%). Citizens in both cities have little faith in environmental activism. Thus 71% of respondents in Pancevo and 75% in Bor believed that the petitions they had heard of had had no effects (refused - 18%/5%; not even answered - 27%/17.5%; officially accepted but with no real effect - 36%/53%). According to our research findings, relations between citizens and both LAs and NGOs are not well developed and thus citizens have almost no social capital for participating in environmental governance. Moreover, citizens in both cities do not trust each other and usually do not belong to wider interpersonal networks related to environmental activism.

According to an index of *environmental social capital* (ESC), which is calculated taking into account citizens' relations with public authorities and NGOs with regard to environmental protection (experience with programmes and contacts), their membership in ENGOs and participation in environmental networks (for example, personal ties with people active in the field of environmental protection), citizens generally have low ESC in both cities. It is slightly higher in Pancevo (where 50% of citizens have low ESC, 33% have moderate ESC and 17% have high ESC in comparison to 64%, 27% and 9%, respectively in Bor). We also calculated an index of *citizens' trust* (CT) as a separate dimension of social capital, by taking into account citizens' evaluation of the trust they have in the work of local authorities (in terms of environmental protection, information, inclusion of citizens in decision making and acceptance of civic initiatives), and NGOs (in terms of environmental protection, information, inclusion of citizens in NGOs programs). The level of CT is particularly low: 83% of citizens in Pancevo and 94% in Bor have low levels.

In both cities citizens are preoccupied with economic hardships, which is, as expected, more pronounced in Bor than Pancevo (75% in comparison to 57%). Ecological issues are perceived as the biggest city problem in both samples, but, due to its higher politicization, more often in Pancevo, than in Bor (56% in comparison to 47%). However, the great majority of citizens (85%) in both cities share concerns that environmental problems have negative effects on their health. The majority of Pancevo citizens prioritize environmental protection over economic growth: 58.2% would be against opening new heavy industry sites in Pancevo, even if it would help create a significant number of new jobs, which reflects the more diversified economic options in Pancevo. On the other hand, the majority of citizens in Bor (61%) would welcome such industry because of new employment opportunities.

The index of *civic environmental activism* (CEA) is rather low in both cities (Table 5.1). The index is based not only on the actual CEA (which is extremely low, as less than 5% of citizens participated in any kind of activism in the three-year period studied, in either city) but also on potential activism.[9] We opt for this kind of index in order to be able to use it in further statistical analysis, which would not be possible if we concentrated only on actual activism, given the low percentage of those who are active.

Citizens in Bor have a slightly higher (but statistically significant) level of CEA despite the more serious economic problems, and limited NGO willingness to initiate public protest. However this is in accordance with the fact that little has been done to solve the serious environmental problems and livelihood difficulties there.

Low levels of CEA are consistent with a predominance of economic concerns, inadequate information and the low trust and environmental social capital of the citizens. Civic environmental activism is significantly correlated with the level of citizens' trust

9 The index of civic environmental activism is calculated taking into account citizens' participation in listed activities (like participation in public meetings, protests, boycotts, signing petitions, etc.) in the last three years, as well as their readiness to take part in these activities in the near future and their interest in participating in local governance and decision making.

Table 5.1: Index of civic environmental activism (CEA) in Pancevo and Bor

City	Index			Total (%)
	No Activism (%)	Lower Activism (%)	Higher Activism (%)	
Pancevo	2.9	63.4	33.7	100.0
Bor	1.6	48.9	49.5	100.0
Total	2.3	57.1	40.6	100.0

Note: Contingency coefficient 0.159 , $p<0.001$

Table 5.2: Correlations of basic variables with CEA

		CEI	CT	ESC	C
CEI	Pearson correlation	1	0.161**	0.326**	0.148**
	Sig. (2-tailed)		0.001	0.000	0.000
	N	734	422	340	734

Notes: ** Correlation is significant at the 0.01 level (two-tailed), * Correlation is significant at the 0.05 level (two-tailed); CEA – civic environmental activism, CT – citizens'trust, ESC – environmental social capital, C – city.

(CT) (Table 5.2). The correlation is low because CEA is not only rare in a situation where there is widespread low CT but even active citizens have low trust and are often motivated to change the institutional environment and thus contribute to increasing general trust levels. Civic environmental activism appears significantly and more intensively correlated with environmental social capital (ESC). The weakest, but still significant, correlation is found with the *city* (C) taken as a contextual variable that reflects differences in economic conditions and the introduction of technology for reducing pollution. Individual economic position did not appear as a significant variable. The variable was based on a subjective perception of an individual's material position that proved an unreliable indicator, particularly in circumstances of generally low living standards.

Finally, the interaction of various levels of environmental social capital (ESC) and place of living (Figure 5.1), and various levels of citizens' trust (CT) and place of living (Figure 5.2) with civic environmental activism (CEA) have been analysed using a univariate general linear model.[10] In both cases, the results confirm a significant correlation between the independent and dependent variables but do not show a significant interaction between independent variables and the dependent one. Higher environmental social capital and higher levels of citizens' trust generate a higher level of civic environmental activism in both cities. However, it appears that citizens in Bor have a somewhat higher level of civic environmental activism at the same level of environmental social capital, and rather higher civic environmental activism CEA at the same level of citizens' trust in comparison to citizens in Pancevo. This suggests that a higher level of either economic or ecological immediate uncertainty provokes higher readiness for environmental activism among citizens in Bor, although they have less faith or functional connections. It could be concluded that such activism from the citizens in Bor reflects their desperation rather than effective or well established civic activism.

Concluding Remarks

Low trust in institutions and the low social capital of the actors impede the shift from government to governance regimes and, in addition to the economic hardships that force people to focus more on their livelihoods, diminish the level of participation of citizens and other civil society actors in environmental decision making in Serbia. As in many postsocialist countries, political actors do not have the important resources and capabilities that would enable them to engage in new modes of governance or to cooperate with

10 In both cases, the index of civic environmental activism is taken as a (continuous) dependent variable, while the index of environmental social capital and the index of trust are taken as independent variable (both are categorical variables).

Figure 5.1: Civic environmental activism with different levels of environmental social capital in Pancevo and Bor

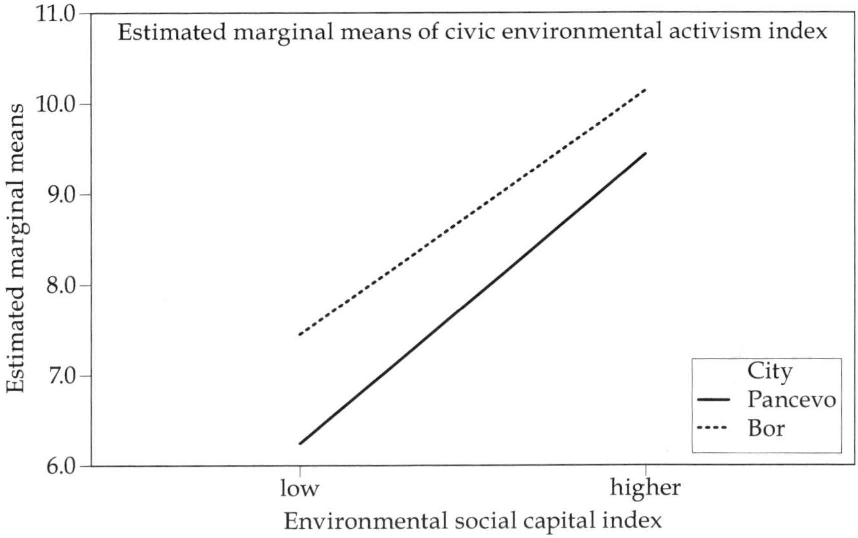

Figure 5.2: Civic environmental activism with different levels of citizens' trust in Pancevo and Bor

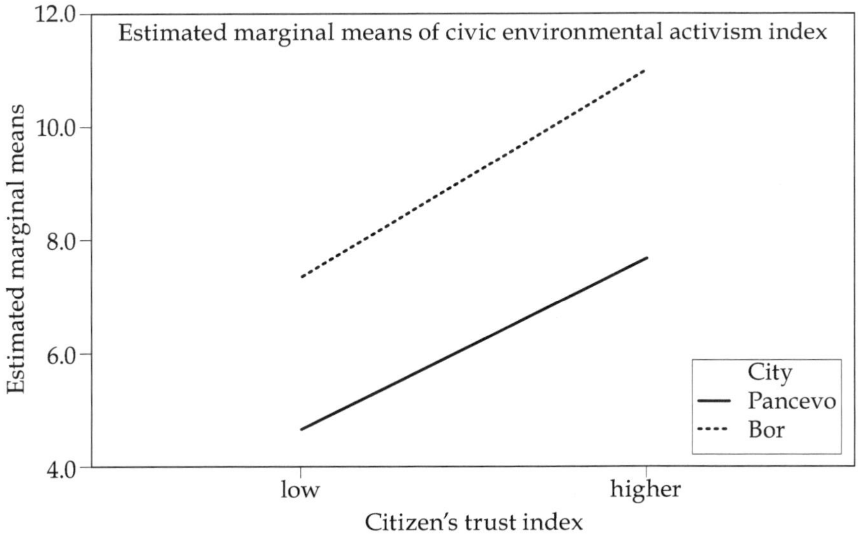

civil society actors without fear of losing their autonomy and power. Consequently, the political elite slows down the capacity-building process of local state institutions by preserving the centralized executive patterns, with political parties as the most important decision-making authorities. This diminishes the political opportunities of other actors and leads to a situation in which environmental laws are not enforced. These laws can hardly empower citizens and civil society actors without effective implementation. Postsocialist administrative structures and regulatory styles therefore still reproduce centralized decision-making patterns – a process that is exacerbated by enduring economic hardships and the delayed process of accession to the EU. According to our research findings LAs do not support any kind of civic activism, and have no links with civil society actors; thus they do not support any kind of civic activism.

On the other hand, civil society actors also lack the autonomy and the capacity for collective action to engage in a new mode of governance. Our research findings show that ENGOs lack both horizontal and vertical functional relations and thus have rather low social capital. Their vertical linkages with representatives of local authorities do not exist or are such that they place NGOs in a satellite position with regard to strong political actors, which confirms our hypothesis that transaction activism has emerged in a deficient form in Serbia, as an elitist type of NGO activism that is not based on advocacy or lobbying by NGOs as autonomous agencies of civil society. The relations among the NGOs are more competitive than cooperative, and their activities are mainly short term and are focused on immediate benefits for their members (employment). Nongovernmental organizations also fail to cooperate with each other. They rarely support public participation in decision making or develop enduring activities that include local citizens and they are therefore rather disconnected from local communities, lacking accountability and legitimacy. This leads to a situation in which there is a civil society without citizens in Serbia.

The mobilization of citizens has been reduced mainly to immediate and mostly ineffective reactions. Citizens are alienated from both the (local) state and the NGO sector. Without the necessary trust in institutions and in other civil society actors, citizens have few opportunities for developing environmental activism or participating in decision-making processes. Besides that, citizens generally lack impartial information about the environment, which limits their ability for bottom up activities. Our field research in two ecological hot spots in Serbia confirmed the local community's economic situation and its closeness to the capital city as important variables. An unfavourable economic situation and the importance of the polluters for the local economy and in providing employment generally reduce civic activism (not only of citizens but also of NGOs, as in the case of Bor) and even decrease environmental concerns (as in the case of citizens in Bor supporting heavy industry for employment). However, increases in pollution and in citizens' health fears might provoke sporadic public mobilization (as was the case in Pancevo when the pollution issue was misused by politicians), or when they are related to a somewhat higher index of civic environmental activism, as seen among citizens in Bor. Nevertheless, without responsive institutional actors leading to increased trust in institutions, and without developing more functional relations both horizontally and vertically among different actors (social capital relations), such public mobilization will be reduced to immediate and mostly ineffective reactions.

Our research on public participation in environmental decision making reflects the key obstacles to the transformation of governance and the opening of political opportunities for public participation in postsocialist Serbia. Firstly, it points to the traditional command-and-control approach of political actors who lack interest in introducing and efficiently implementing new laws and institutions that support public participation. Secondly, from local actors' reflections on the transformation of social institutions, and their perceptions of the norms and behavioural patterns that guide their everyday practices, our research documents that legislative and institutional changes are rather superficial, which, in particular, excludes actors distanced from 'traditional' political power (citizens, NGOs and remote local communities).

References

Arandarenko Mihajlo (eds) (2010) *Ekonomsko-socijalna struktura Srbije – Učinak prve decenije tranzicije,* Ekonomski fakultet, Beograd, p. 259.

Baldassarri, D. and Diani, M. (2007) The integrative power of civic networks. *American Journal of Sociology* 113 (3), pp. 735–80.

Borzel, T. (2006) Participation through law enforcement: the case of the European Union. *Comparative Political Studies* 39 (1), pp. 128–52.

Borzel T. (2008) Environmental policy. In: *Europeanization, New Research Agenda* (eds P. Graziano and M. Vink), New York, NY, pp. 226–38.

Borzel, T. (2009) New modes of governance and accession: the paradox of double weakness. In: *Coping with Accession to the European Union, New Modes of Environmental Governance* (ed. T. Borzel), Palgrave MacMillan, New York, NY, pp. 7–31, at 21–4.

Brenner, N. (2000) Building Euro-regions: location politics and the political geography of neoliberalism in post-unification Germany. *European Urban and Regional Research* 7 (4), pp. 319–45.

Carmin, J. (2008) Investing in civil society: the diversification of environmental NGOs in Central and Eastern Europe. *Development and Transition* 9 (1), pp. 11–14.

Carmin, J. (2010) Civic engagement in environmental governance in Central and Eastern Europe. In: *The International Handbook of Environmental Sociology* (eds M. Redclift and G. Woodgate), Edward Elgar, Cheltenham, pp. 394–407.

Carter, F.W. and Turnock, D. (2002) *Environmental Problems of East Central Europe,* 2nd edn, Routledge, London.

Cisar, O. (2008) Political Activism in the Czech Republic. Paper presented at the Workshop on Contentious Politics, Columbia University, New York, NY, 28 April 2008.

Cisar, O. (2010) Externally sponsored contention: The channeling of environmental movement organizations in the Czech Republic after the fall of communism. *Environmental Politics* 19 (5), pp. 736–55.

Djordjevic, S. (2008) Lokalna sampouprava u Srbiji. *Pregled* 52 (1), pp. 43–68.

Fagan, A. (2005) Taking stock of civil-society development in post-communist Europe: evidence from the Czech Republic. *Democratization* 12 (4), pp. 528–47.

Fagan, A. (2006) Transnational aid for civil society development in post-socialist Europe: democratic consolidation or a new imperialism? *Journal of Communist Studies and Transition Politics* 22 (1), pp. 115–34.

Fagan A. (2010) *Europe's Balkan Dilemma: Paths to Civil Society or State- Building*? I.B. Tauris, London and New York.

Gradjanske inicijative (2011) Nevladin sektor u Srbiji, Beograd,. www.gradjanske.org (accessed 11 October 2012).

Hannigan, J.A. (2006) *Environmental Sociology,* second edition, Routledge, London.

Howard, M. (2003) *The Weakness of Civil Society in Post-Communist Europe,* Cambridge University Press, Cambridge, p. 206.

Jessop, B. (1994) The transition to post-Fordism and the Schumpeterian workfare state. In: Burrows, B. and Loader, R. (eds) *Towards a Post-Fordist Welfare State,* Routledge, New York, NY, pp. 13–37.
Inglehart, R. (1995) Public support for environmental protection: objective problems and subjective values in 43 societies. *Political Science and Politics* 28, pp. 57–72.
Keyes, L. (2001) Housing, social capital and poor communities. In: *Social Capital and Poor Communities* (eds S. Saegert, P. Thompson and M. Warren), New York, NY, pp. 136–64.
Komsic, J. (2009) Politicko institucionalni aspekti regionalnog razvoja Srbije u svetlu evropskih standarda. *Izazovi evropskih integracija* 6, pp. 73–101.
Lazić, M. (2000) Elite u postsocijalistickoj transformaciji srpskog drustva. In *Racji hod* (ed. M. Lazic), Filip Visnjic, Beograd, pp. 21–65, at pp. 28–33.
Mayer, M. (2003) The onward sweep of social capital: causes and consequences for understanding cities, communities and urban movements. *International Journal of Urban and Regional Research* 27 (1), pp. 10–32.
National Environment Strategy (2007) Government of the Republic of Serbia, Belgrade, p. 140.
Petrova, T. and Tarrow, S. (2007) Transactional and participatory activism in the emerging European polity: the puzzle of East-Central Europe. *Comparative Political Studies* 40 (1), pp. 74–94, at p. 79.
Putnam, R. (2000) *Bowling Alone: the collapse and revival of American community,* Simon & Schuster, New York, NY, p. 515, at p. 19.
REC (2006) Registar NVO Srbije iz oblasti zaštite životne sredine - Registar i rezultati procene organizacija civilnog društva iz oblasti *životne* sredine u Srbiji, Regional Environmental Center, Szentendre,.
Rootes, C. (1997) Environmental movements and green parties in western and eastern Europe. In *The International Handbook of Environmental Sociology* (eds M. Redclift and G.Woodgate), Edward Elgar, Cheltenham UK/Northampton, MA, USA, pp. 319–49.
UNECE (2007) *Environmental Performance Review, Republic of Serbia, Second Review,* United Nations, New York and Geneva, p. 169.
USAID (2009) The 2008 NGO Sustainability Index for Central and Eastern Europe and Eurasia,. http://transition.usaid.gov/locations/europe_eurasia/dem_gov/ngoindex/reports/2011/2008complete_document.pdf (accessed 11 October 2012)
Vujovic, S. (2004) Akteri urbanih promena u Srbiji. In *Društvena transformacija i strategije društvenih grupa – Svakodnevnica Srbije na početku milenijuma* (ed. A. Milic), Beograd, pp. 151–93, at p. 173.
Vujovic, S. and Petrovic, M. (2007) Belgrade post-socialist urban evolution: reflections by the authors in the development process. In *Cities in Transition: The Restructuring of Urban Space in Post-socialist Central and Eastern Europe* (ed. K. Stanilov), Springer, Dordrecht, pp. 360–84.
Woolcock, M. (1998) Social capital and economic development: towards a theoretical synthesis and policy framework. *Theory and Society* 27 (2), pp. 151–208.

Predrag Cvetičanin, Jasmina Nedeljković
and Nemanja Krstić

Social Space in Serbia

In this chapter, following a discussion of Bourdieu's conception of social space, we will present two maps of social space in Serbia based on data from the Cultural Needs, Habits and Taste of Citizens of Serbia and Macedonia (2007) and Social and Cultural Capital in Serbia (2012) research studies. We point to some differences that emerge in these maps in relation to Bourdieu's conception and between the maps themselves. Despite these differences, the results of both studies indicate that social capital in Serbian society plays an important role in generating structures of social inequality. Membership of political parties, informal clans and ownership of extended social networks for the exchange of 'services' are revealed to be important social resources in post-socialist Serbia, in particular when it comes to finding employment and for career advancement, as well as for attempts to ensure access to goods and services in short supply, to influence official decisions, or to bypass formal procedures. We therefore included indicators of social capital in the construction of social space. Analyses of social space in Serbia indicate that the practices of social actors are not random but are socially structured – certain types of life-strategies and everyday practices are more likely in some parts of social space than in others. Furthermore, and also in line with Bourdieu's conception, our results indicate that strategies and everyday practices are shaped by the interplay between the actual combination of resources (capitals) at agents' disposal and their embodied habituses. Finally, they show that social strategies and practices are relational – that they are established and defined in relations of struggle with Others – those that they oppose in 'the field of social classes' and in other fields.

Social Space

The conception of social space that Bourdieu (1984: 191) also refers to as 'the field of social classes', is characteristic of the mature phase of his sociology. Social space represents a model of spatial conception of the social structure that, as is the case with other fields, stands for 'quasi-reality', which exists independently of those who are positioned within it. This structure of objective positions results from the combination of the most important powers and resources – economic capital, cultural capital and social capital – and their evolution through time.

As is well known, Bourdieu (e.g. 1984, 1986) expands the concept of capital to refer to several types of resources – economic, social, cultural and symbolic – and indicates that individuals and groups, in attempting to maintain or improve their positions in the social order, use all of these resources (not only economic ones). Moreover, he emphasizes that it is not possible to understand the structure and functioning of the social world if the concept of capital in all of its forms is not introduced into the analysis, not only in the form that is known to economic theory.

According to Bourdieu, the social world is 'accumulated history' (Bourdieu, 1986) and precisely because accumulated resources (capitals) in their objective and embodied forms show a tendency to act as objective forces, not everything is equally possible or impossible in the social world. The structure and distribution of different types and subtypes of capital at a given moment in time represent, for Bourdieu, the immanent structure of the social world inscribed into the reality of the world itself, determining chances of success for social practices.

The study of social space in Serbia represents an analysis of the social structure in Serbia (conceived of in a particular way) and the most general framework of social practices and social groupings in Serbia. As any account of socio-economic change, transition and development in Serbian society must begin with a conception of its current social structure, this type of analysis represents a framework for understanding the results of all other (economic, political, cultural) analyses.

In the 'Social and Cultural Capital in Serbia' project this analysis enabled us to ascertain how social groups in Serbia differ in terms of resources (economic and, in particular, social and cultural capital), to reconstruct the strategies that the citizens of Serbia use in everyday life (relying on a combination of resources available to them) and to analyse the social and symbolic struggles of the holders of different types of capital in everyday life in Serbian society.

Three Dimensions of Social Space

Social space itself is constructed along three orthogonal axes. In this three-dimensional space, according to Bourdieu (1984, 1992, 1996), occupational groups are positioned in relation to three parameters – total volume of capital, composition of capital and changes in these two characteristics over time, which he refers to as 'social trajectory'.

Along the first and most important axis, occupational groups are positioned on the basis of the total volume of (different types of) capital they possess. According to Bourdieu, someone's class position is determined by the position that person takes on this axis (which he represents vertically on maps of social space). In research that he undertook in France, industrialists, managers in the private sector and university professors were concentrated in this upper part of the social space. Bourdieu labels them the 'dominant class' or 'bourgeoisie'.[1] At the opposite pole of this axis we find grouped manual labourers and farmers whose overall volume of capital is relatively small. Bourdieu marks them as the 'working classes'. Between them – in relation to total volume of capital – in the middle of social space we find small entrepreneurs, clerks, teachers in elementary schools, which Bourdieu refers to as the 'petty bourgeoisie'.

1 In his late work, Bourdieu uses the term 'field of power' instead of dominant class to emphasize the relational character of this construct.

The second axis - the composition of capital - which is represented horizontally in Bourdieu's maps of social space, defines the difference between class fractions. According to Bourdieu, classes differ internally depending on the dominance of economic or cultural capital in the overall volume of capital they control. For example, in the dominant class we can differentiate the class fraction that relies primarily on its cultural capital but which is not rich in economic capital (university professors and artists). On the other side, we find industrialists and other large employers who control large economic capital, but whose cultural capital is of lesser scope. Between these two poles we find members of the 'professions' (lawyers, physicians, managers) whose structure of capital (economic and cultural) is balanced. Similarly, among the petty bourgeoisie it is possible to differentiate small entrepreneurs, who primarily control economic capital and, on the other hand, teachers whose main resource is cultural capital. The position between them is occupied by clerks and technicians.

Representatives of different occupational groups are also differentiated along a third axis - social trajectory - which represents the introduction of a temporal dimension into an otherwise synchronic analysis. Social trajectory is constructed on the basis of data about changes in the volume and composition of capital over time - usually through three generations of a single family. It thus becomes possible to study several different types of social mobility. In addition to upward and downward social mobility, it is also possible to follow horizontal or 'transversal' mobility, which involves a change in the type of resources that social groups rely on in social struggles. Bourdieu terms this type of mobility, in which social groups change the composition of capital available to them, 'conversion of capital'. However, even within vertical mobility, it is possible to distinguish between *intra-class social mobility*, which takes place within the same fields and on the basis of the accumulation of the same types of capital (such as when children of teachers become university professors) or *inter-class social mobility*, which involves changes in both the scope and composition of capital (such as when small entrepreneurs invest in their children's higher education, instead of directing them toward the family business).

Social Space in Serbia (in 2005)

In Cvetičanin and Popescu (2011) we presented the construction of social space in Serbia based on data from the survey Cultural Needs, Habits and Taste of Citizens of Serbia and Macedonia (2005). We suggested that, bearing in mind the role that social capital has in socialist and post-socialist societies, it should be taken into consideration in the construction of social space in these societies.

The domination of social capital in socialist societies was enacted by the use of personal networks and informal contacts for a variety of purposes. This use of informal networks did not have a special name in Serbia, although in other socialist countries the terms such as *blat* in the USSR (Ledeneva, 1998, 2006), *guanxi* in China (Smart, 1993; Yang, 1994) or *załatwić sprawy* in Poland (Wedel, 1986) were invented. These informal practices represent a specific form of nonmonetary exchange, an intermediate type between commodity exchange and gift giving. Such types of informal exchange of favours and the use of 'connections and acquaintances' are based both on personal relationships and on positions of control over access to public resources.

Our research shows that in the post-socialist society in Serbia, social capital has not lost its power. Moreover, we argue that in Serbian society there are two distinct types of social capital, *political social capital* and *social capital of solidarity*.

We contend that the existence of two types of cultural capital (*local* and *global*) should be taken into account for the construction of social space in Serbia. We postulate that in societies (including Serbia) that were at some point of history 'Westernized' - either through colonization or though the activities of their own elites - there is a constant tension and struggle between global and local culture for the status of legitimate culture. In these societies, this tension is more important than the tension between high culture and popular culture.

Types of Social Capital in Serbia

We identified two types of social networks in Serbia that may be used as social capital. We differentiate between *political social capital* (mainly impersonal and instrumental) and *social capital of solidarity* (which, in addition to being instrumental, has an important expressive and emotional function). Social networks represent *political social capital* when they link people whose control over access to public resources (goods and services) enables them to use these resources to satisfy the private needs of other members of these networks and in this way accumulate power (and acquire access to the resources they do not control). The sum of these networks represents the parallel, informal structure of power in Serbian society. These positions of control over access to public resources are located in the political sphere proper (politicians, representatives of the local, regional and national governments) but they can also be positions of authority in firms and public institutions (for example, CEOs, deans or military generals), or hold positions as experts in public institutions (for example, doctors, judges or university professors). In principle, anyone who has control over access to public resources, no matter how small the advantage conferred, possesses political social capital in some amount.

In contrast, the *social capital of solidarity* is based on the existence of 'primary ties', social networks of solidarity among neighbours, friends, relatives, or 'countrymen'[2] who can pitch in to help with money, goods, services or emotional support. The emotional and expressive function of these social networks is as crucial as the instrumental one. Importantly, however, these social networks can also be used as capital. Unlike political social capital, which requires a trade-off in the form of access to previously unavailable resources, the basis for requesting favours by virtue of social capital of solidarity rests precisely in claiming 'primary ties' – that is, being a relative, friend, or a neighbour.

2 'Countryman' (Serbian *zemljak*) is a term used to refer to persons who come from the same village or part of the country

Types of Cultural Capital in Serbia

A second important group of resources that shape social space in Serbia is cultural capital. In Cvetičanin and Popescu (2009), we demonstrated that two main oppositions structure the field of cultural practices in Serbia: the opposition between local and global culture, and the opposition between traditional culture and contemporary, popular culture.

These forces are active in the field of cultural practices in Serbia and produce seven types of distinct cultural practices (see Figure 6.1). There are four types of 'pure' cultural practices: (i) *traditional folklore cultural practices* (instances of traditional local culture); (ii) *neofolk cultural practices* (examples of contemporary popular local culture); (iii) *contemporary global cultural practices* or *urban cultural practices* (cases of contemporary popular global culture); and (iv) *traditional elite cultural practices* (instances of traditional global culture). There are also three types of omnivorous cultural practices, where by 'omnivores' we understand those who cross important cultural boundaries in one (in this case, Serbian) society: (v) *rurban omnivores* (who in their cultural practices cross the boundary between contemporary popular global and contemporary popular local culture); (vi) *elite omnivores* (who cross the boundary which separates traditional global elite culture and contemporary popular global culture; and finally (vii) *conformist omnivores* (who cross both important symbolic boundaries in the field of cultural styles in Serbia: the boundary between local and global culture and the boundary between traditional and contemporary popular culture) (Cvetičanin, 2007).

In contrast to the French society, described in Bourdieu's works, highbrow culture in Serbia does not automatically entail a claim to legitimate culture. In Serbia, the main opposition between global and local culture enables the formation of two types of cultural capital – local cultural capital and global cultural capital – whose proponents struggle to promote their cultural resources as legitimate.

Figure 6.1: Field of cultural practices in Serbia

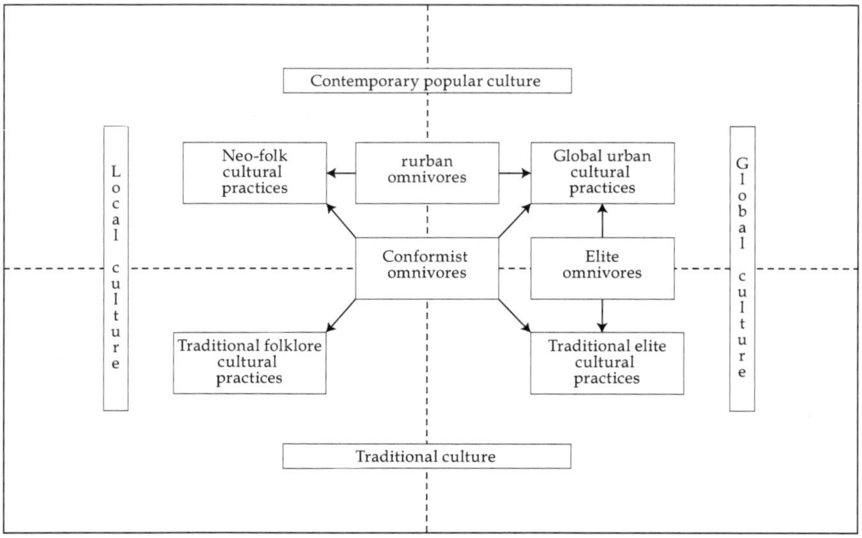

Constructing Social Space in Serbia (2005)

Constructing social space is undertaken using the statistical technique known as multiple correspondence analysis (MCA), which was developed by a group of French mathematicians and statisticians led by Jean-Paul Benzécri (Benzécri, 1973). The standpoint of this school, known as geometrical data analysis, is that it is not allowed to make *a priori* assumptions about the nature of the data that are being analysed (for example, their division into independent and dependent variables). The idea is that data should be given the opportunity to 'speak for themselves'. Multiple correspondence analysis is therefore conceived as an inductive, exploratory technique, the main goal of which is to identify hidden structures within the data. In this way it is similar to factor analysis – especially the method of extraction known as principal component analysis. However, with the introduction of so-called 'passive' or 'supplementary' variables, MCA can also be used for explanatory purposes.

In the analysis performed by MCA two types of variables are used: 'active' variables, whose interrelations constitute the map, and 'supplementary' variables, which are projected onto them without changing relations within the map. It should also be noted that MCA displays its results in two types of outputs: so-called 'clouds of modalities', which indicate spatial relations between variables, and so-called 'clouds of individuals' in which the positioning of individuals on these maps can be seen in relation to certain features (gender, age, education, occupational group, etc.).

In the construction of social space in Serbia we used indicators of economic capital and two types of cultural and social capital as active variables. We operationalized economic capital with five indicators, cultural capital with four and social capital with three indicators (see Cvetičanin and Popescu, 2011: 451–2).

Multiple correspondent analysis has identified five axes, which together explain 85.24% of the variance. Axis 1, which explains the greatest part of the total variance (62.11%), as in Bourdieu's model, expresses the total volume of capital. In Figure 6.2 (in which only two main axes are presented), axis 1 distinguishes between high total volume of capital (marked TVC ++) and low total volume of capital (marked TVC--). Axis 2, which explains 10.34% of the variance, represents the dimension of the composition of capital. In our analysis it is conceived differently from Bourdieu's work. It was revealed that, on the one hand, the basic opposition that we identified in the field of cultural practices in Serbia – that between global and local culture – plays an important role in the constitution of social space. On the other hand, indicators of two types of social capital have been dispersed along the same axis that divides large volume of economic capital (accompanied by indicators of political social capital) and small volume of economic capital (accompanied by indicators of possession of social capital of solidarity).

When the angle bisector through the origin at 45 degrees in relation to both Axis 1 and 2 is drawn, it is possible to see that mainly indicators of social capital are plotted along bisector I. In the first quadrant of the map of social space in Serbia (top right corner) we find a concentration of both low values of indicators of economic capital and lack of indicators of political social capital (such as party membership and party leadership membership or ties in public institutions),

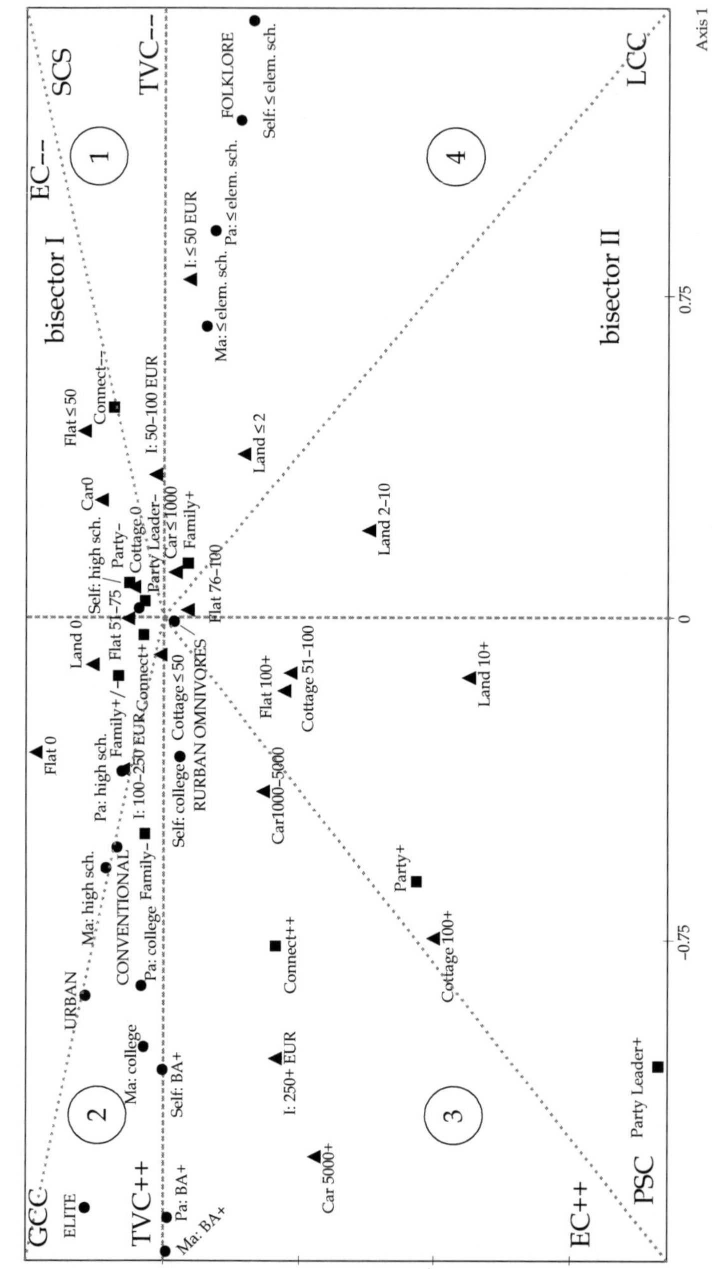

Figure 6.2: Social space in Serbia (2005)

but also positive indicators of the social capital of solidarity (Family+). Conversely, in the third quadrant of the map (the lower left corner), plotted along the origin bisector I, are indicators of political social capital (membership in political parties, membership in party leadership, and a large number of 'connections and acquaintances' in public institutions). Also located in the vicinity of this axis are high values of economic capital indicators (such as a large apartment or summer/ weekend house/cottage, an expensive car and high family income).

On the other hand, the angle bisector axis stretching from quadrant 4 (lower right corner) to quadrant 2 (top left corner) is the axis that discriminates between local cultural capital (bottom right corner, marked LCC) and global cultural capital (top left corner, marked GCC).

The results of the above analyses suggest that these different types (qualities) of capitals can be used in the construction of social space. This transforms composition of capital into a complex jigsaw puzzle, the elements of which are, in addition to the range of economic capital, 'local cultural capital', 'global cultural capital', 'social capital of solidarity' and 'political social capital'. Our map of social space thus constructed indicates the existence of different bases (resources) for social groupings in Serbia and different strategies available to these groups.

In the next step of the analysis, in the social space thus constructed, we projected as supplementary variables indicators of material and cultural consumption, indicators of identity, worldviews and political preferences. The results unequivocally indicate a strong 'gravitational pull' of social space. In the maps it is easy to see that the endless variety of social and cultural practices, although they cannot be reduced to social conditioning, are not at all random – the result of coincidence or the will and wilful self-shaping of the individual; instead, certain cultural styles, tastes, types of material consumption, certain identities and political preferences are simply more likely in certain parts of the social space than in others (see Cvetičanin and Popescu, 2011: 459–60).

Finally, in the map of social space we projected indicators of four social classes: farmers, workers, middle class and upper classes.[3] In

3 Previously the original scale with 27 occupational groups was grouped into nine basic groups of occupations, taking care to ensure participants who

clouds of individuals, the statistical program[4] drew concentration ellipses in which 88% of individuals are positioned who belong to these groups (Le Roux *et al.*, 2008; Le Roux and Rouanet, 2010). The ordering of dimensions on the map remained the same – the left pole of the horizontal axis (Axis 1) is the pole of the large total volume of capital, the right pole of small total volume of capital. In the upper left quadrant there are indicators of global cultural capital, in the lower right quadrant indicators of local cultural capital. Indicators of high values of economic capital and indicators of political social capital are found in the lower right quadrant, while in the upper left quadrant are modalities of low economic capital and indicators of social capital of solidarity.

As can be seen in Figure 6.3, farmers take up a part of social space characterized by a low overall volume of capital, a low level of economic capital, social capital of solidarity and local cultural capital (these are also the resources that are available to them in conceiving their strategies). Workers are grouped in the area characterized by similar dimensions as farmers. The only difference is that the class of workers is divided on the basis of whether they hold local or global cultural capital. The middle classes are located in the centre of social space, which is characterized by average level of overall volume of capital, average level of economic capital and the division between owning political social capital and social capital of solidarity, that is, between global and local cultural capital.[5] Finally, the upper classes are mainly grouped on the left side of social space characterized

belong to them had approximately identical educational levels, income, similar working conditions, and basic resources that they rely on in their work and life strategies. The nine groups are: (i) farmers; (ii) unskilled and semi-skilled workers; (iii) skilled workers; (iv) lower level experts; (v) clerks and lower managers; (vi) small entrepreneurs and the self-employed; (vii) experts; (viii) large employers; (ix) professional politicians, managers of state companies, high ranking police and army officers. The analyses showed that these occupational groups "inhabit" different parts of social space and that based on proximity in social space they can be grouped into four 'theoretical' social classes (see Cvetičanin and Popescu, 2011: 463–5).

4 For MCA we used SPAD 7.3.

5 This division is also a possible source of the ambivalent attitudes of the middle classes in the full list of questions (related to political attitudes, worldview and identity determinants).

by high overall volume of capital, high volume of economic capital, political social capital and global cultural capital (these are the resources on which they base their strategies).

Figure 6.3: Four theoretical classes in Serbia: central points and concentration ellipses in clouds of individuals in social space (2005)

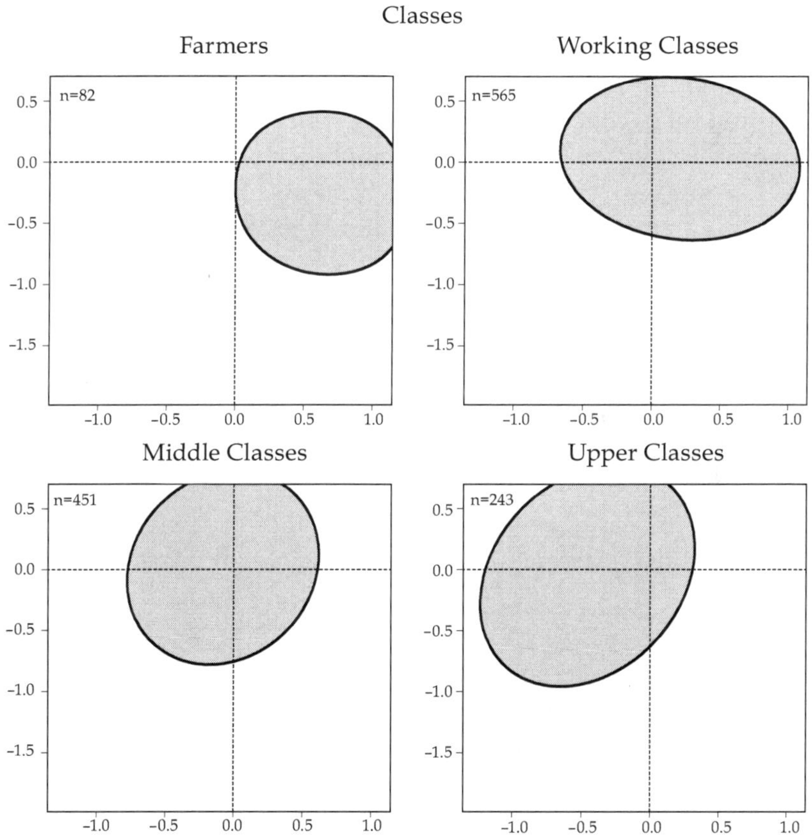

Social Space in Serbia (in 2010)

Research in the 'Social and Cultural Capital in Serbia' project was designed as a telephone survey on a national proportional sample of 2000 respondents. The survey took place in two waves (October to December 2010 and February to March 2011). The number of respondents who took part was 889, which is in accordance with the usual response rate for telephone surveys (44.5%). A standardized questionnaire with 31 questions was used in the survey and required about 15 minutes to complete. The questionnaire included nine questions intended to identify embodied, institutionalized and objectified cultural capital, six questions on economic capital and three questions for establishing social capital available to respondents. The remaining 13 questions were used to gather standard socio-demographic data such as gender, ages, place of birth, parents' occupations, and respondents' occupation.

In order to construct Serbian social space, as in the previous case, we employed multiple correspondence analysis, or MCA (Lebart *et al.*, 1984, Greenacre, 2007; Le Roux *et al.*, 2008; Le Roux and Rouanet, 2010). We used specific MCA (Le Roux and Rouanet, 2010), with the 'missing' categories as passive categories of the active variables. Table 6.1 shows the eigenvalues and variances explained by the first five axes.

Table 6.1: Eigenvalues, raw and modified inertia for the first five axes

Axes	1	2	3	4	5
Eigenvalues (λ)	0.2810	0.1869	0.1589	0.1535	0.1484
Raw inertia	10.69%	7.11%	6.04%	5.84%	5.65%
Modified inertia	57.59%	13.70%	6.46%	5.38%	4.45%

Considering the limitations imposed by the telephone survey, we had at our disposal a smaller range of variables in constructing social space and a smaller number of modalities for them compared to the research from 2005.

We operationalized economic capital with four indicators: (i) average monthly income of the respondent's family per family member; (ii) size of respondent's dwelling (if the respondent was the owner); (iii) size of respondent's summer house/cottage (if any); (iv) the value of the respondent's car (if any). Cultural capital was operationalized using three indicators: (i) respondent's education; (ii) respondent's mother's education; (iii) respondent's father's education. We relied on two indicators of social capital. The first represents political-social capital in the narrow sense: (i) respondent's membership in a political party; and the second one was showing (ii) whether the respondent had access to informal networks for the exchange of favours in public institutions. In total, we used 17 modalities of economic capital, 12 modalities of cultural and five modalities of social capital as active variables.

From constructed social space (see Figure 6.4) it can be seen that Axis 1, which explains 58% of the variance stretches between maximum capital values on the left (per capita household income of over 250 EUR (I > 250 EUR); ownership of an automobile the value of which exceeds 5000 EUR (CAR > 5000 EUR); ownership of a cottage house larger than 50 m^2 (COTTAGE 50+); highest educational level of the father (EduP BA+) and of the respondent (EduS BA+) and a large number of informal ties in public institutions (CONN 5–10)). The only maximal modality of capital that is not positioned on this pole, although it is on the left side of the map, is ownership of a house/apartment larger than 100 m^2 (HOUSE >100 m^2); instead, it is located close to the centre of the map. On the right side of the map there are mainly minimal modalities of the indicators employed) per capita household income of less than 50 EUR (I < 50 EUR); no automobile (CAR0); apartment/house smaller than 50 m^2 (HOUSE < 50 m^2); elementary or lower education of the father and the respondent (EduP-elem.) and (EduS-elemen.) and lack of ties in public institutions (Conn 0)). On the basis of these indices we can conclude that, as in other maps of social space, Axis 1 represents the total volume of capital and therefore, as in Bourdieu's model, the axis along which social classes are differentiated.

Axis 2, which explains 14% of the variance, according to Bourdieu, represents the dimension of capital composition. What is different from the map of social space based on the 2005 survey

Figure 6.4: Map of social space 2010 (Axes 1 and 2)

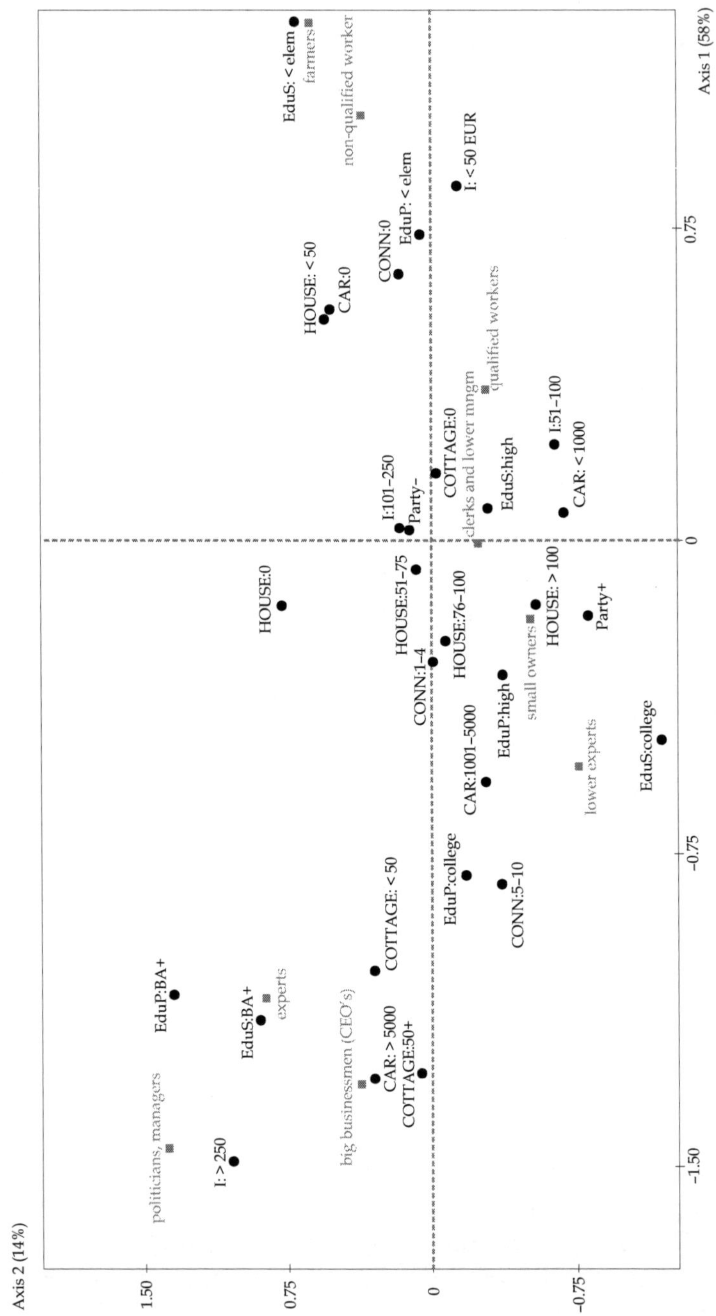

data and what is probably one of the most interesting results of this analysis is that in the map of social space (in 2010) Axis 2 separates the indicators of cultural capital (in the upper regions of the map) and of social capital (in the lower regions). The second difference in comparison with the 2005 research is bifurcation of the indicators of economic capital. Instead of high values of indicators of economic capital (income and ownership) appearing together – as is usually the case, maximum values of income (together with high modalities of cultural capital) appear in the upper left quadrant of this map of social space. On the other hand, high indicators of ownership, in particular, ownership of large apartments/houses, are concentrated in the lower part of the map among high values of indicators of social capital.

When we projected indicators of nine occupational groups as supplementary variables, it emerged that, at the left end of the map, where the highest values of capital are concentrated, there are also indices of professional politicians, managers in public companies, high-ranking army and police officers, owners of large companies and experts. Farmers and manual labourers are located on the other side of the map, which is characterized by a low total volume of capital. At the bottom of the left side of the map, where social capital appears as dominant (close to the map origin), there is a concentration of the points of lower ranking experts, clerks and representatives of lower management and small entrepreneurs. On the right side, very close by, one finds marks of skilled workers. This gives us an overview of the composition of resources on which representatives of particular occupational groups rely.

When the distribution of occupational groups is viewed in the other main output of the MCA – in the 'cloud of individuals' – then it becomes even clearer that occupations are linked into three groupings: farmers and unskilled workers (light gray ellipse), skilled workers, lower experts, clerks and small entrepreneurs (dark gray ellipse), and mainly experts, members of the cultural fraction of the dominant class (medium gray ellipse). In other words, unlike the differentiation between four social classes, which was based on the results of analyses from 2005, the results of the analysis of the data from the 2010 survey indicate the differentiation between three theoretical classes in Serbia.

Figure 6.5: Three social classes in cloud of individuals

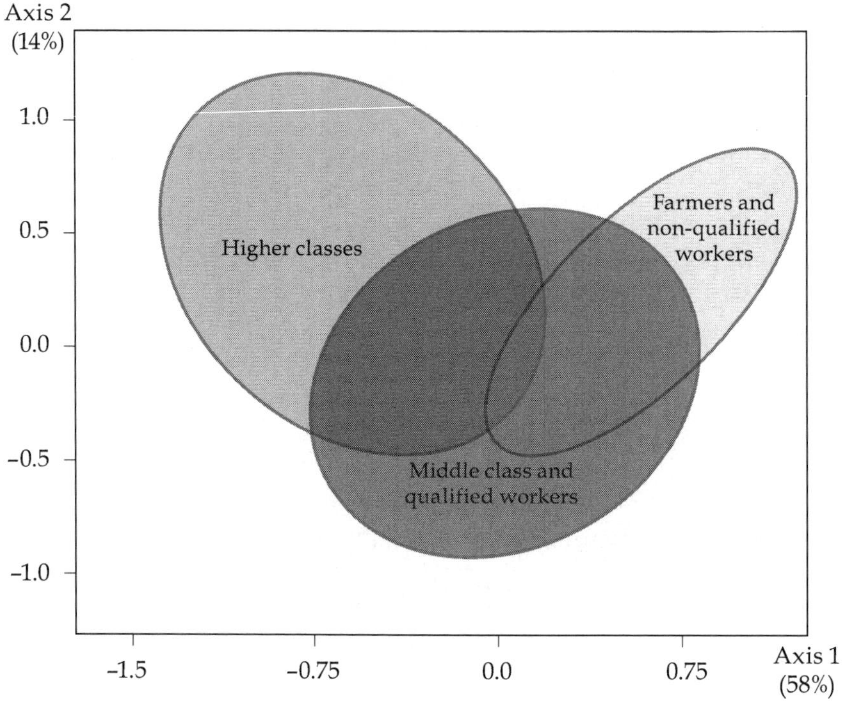

In the final step of our analysis, we projected onto social space constructed in the above manner, as supplementary variables, indicators of cultural practices and additional variables on social capital. We used 22 variables as indicators of cultural practices: thirteen indicators of taste, eight indicators of cultural participation and one indicator of ownership of cultural goods. For indicators of social capital we used answers to the questions 'do people approach respondents asking for help and who asks them for help' (with 11 predefined options)

Figure 6.6 shows the projection of indicators of cultural practices in social space. The diagonal that crosscuts the upper left-hand corner, passes through the centre of the map and ends in the lower right-hand corner is the same diagonal that we also noted

Figure 6.6: Projection of indicators of cultural practices in social space (2010)

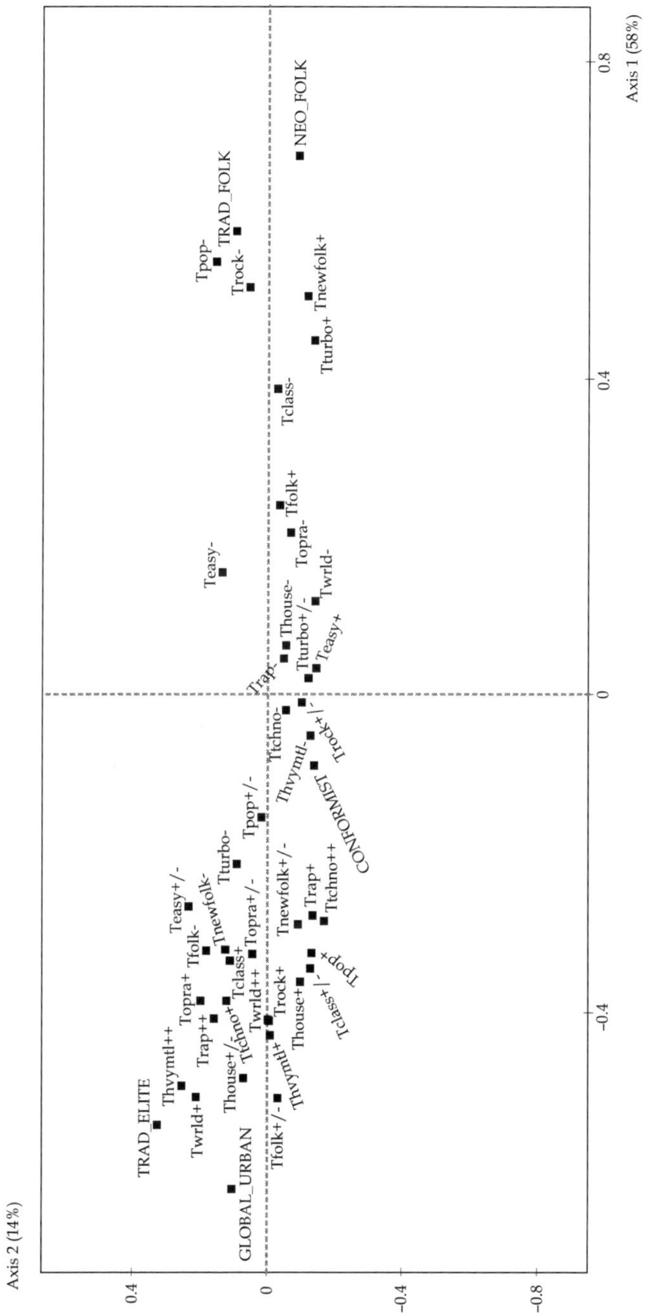

on Figure 6.2. It stretches between poles of global cultural capital and local cultural capital. In the upper left-hand corner of social space – where the high classes are located – there are also indices of traditional elite taste, a liking of opera and classical music ((Topera+), (Tclass+)) and global urban taste linked to rap, techno and heavy metal ((Trap+), (Ttchno+), (Thvymtl+)). In the central section of social space, where the middle classes are positioned, we find indicators of conformist taste – easy listening and pop music ((Teasy+), (Tpop+)) and an ambivalent relationship with global cultural forms on the one hand ((Tclass+/–), (Trock+/–)) and local cultural forms on the other ((Tnewfolk+/–), (Tturbo+/–)). Finally, in the upper right-hand corner of social space, the rejection of traditional and contemporary global forms ((Tclass-), (Trock-), (Tpop-)) is accompanied by indices of traditional folklore taste and neo-folklore taste ((Tnewfolk+), (Tturbo+)).

Figure 6.7 shows the projection of supplementary indicators of social capital across social space. The modalities we used are respondents' answers to the two questions relating to giving mutual aid in everyday life. The first question was whether respondents are asked for help[6] and the second was whether particular profiles of people with whom they are in contact request their assistance.[7]

Responses to the first question are positioned from left to right – from the modality 'yes, always' (MHELP+++), through the modality 'yes, sometimes' (MHELP++) and 'yes, but rarely' (MHELP+), to the final point 'never' (MHELP0). What surprised us is that the results of the analysis point to the conclusion that the poorest (in all types of capital) rarely ask others for help. Likewise, those with the highest total volume of capital also rarely request assistance from others. From the results of our preliminary analysis we can conclude that

6 With the modalities: 1) yes, always; 2) yes, sometimes; 3) yes, but rarely; 4) never.

7 The respondents were asked whether they receive requests for assistance from: 1) cousins; 2) *"kumovi"* (godfathers/godsons); 3) countrymen; 4) neighbors; 5) neighborhood friends; 6) friends from school; 7) colleagues from work; 8) business friends (outside their company/institution); 9) members of the party to which they belong; 10) members of their religious community; 11) acquaintances who have done them a favor. The final option was left open, so that respondents could provide answers themselves as to who else requested help from them. The offered modalities were (1) often; (2) sometimes; (3) never.

Figure 6.7: Projection of indicators of social capital in social space (2010)

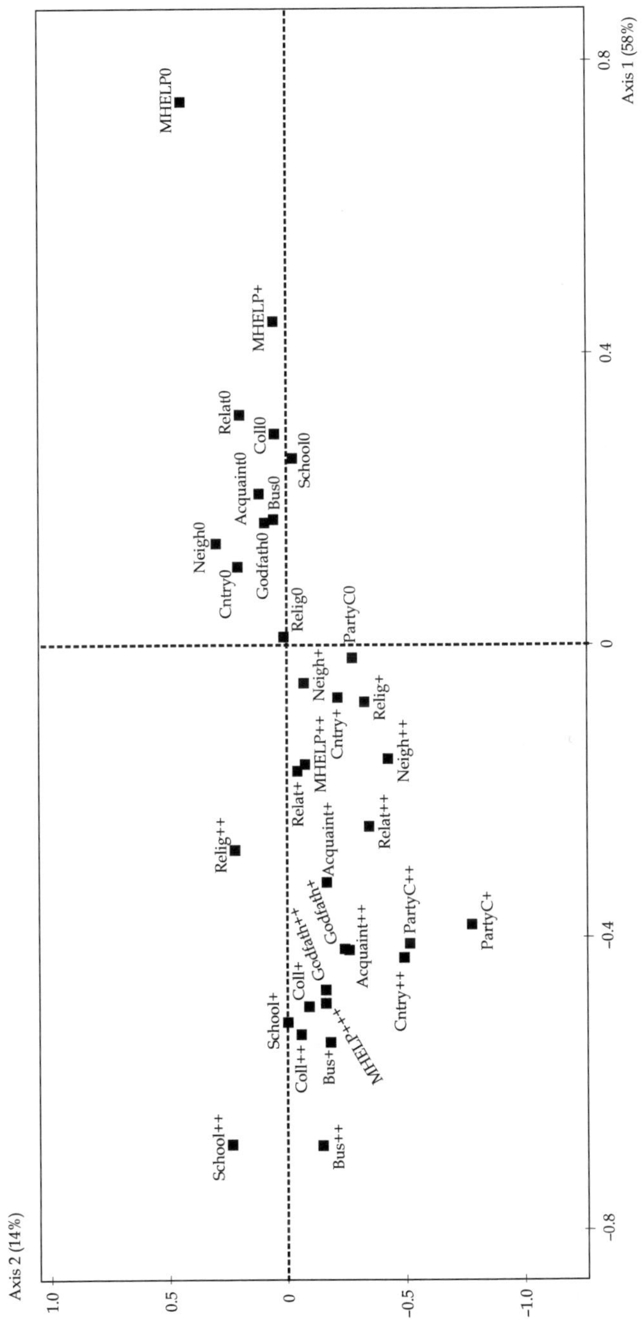

mutual assistance is a practice most common among the members of the middle classes. It should be noted that, in accordance with the composition of capital that we have noted in this constructed social space, indicators of social capital are almost entirely concentrated in the upper regions of the map (the social capital pole).

In accordance with what could have been expected, respondents in the part of the map closer to the pole of the low total volume of capital receive more requests for assistance from relatives (Relat++), neighbours (Neigh++) and members of their religious communities (Relig++). On the other hand, respondents who are closer to the pole with high total volume of capital, are more frequently approached by colleagues (Coll++), business friends (Bus++) and friends from school (School++). Somewhere in the middle are acquaintances (Acquint++) and their party colleagues (PartyC++).

Although it was not possible to obtain enough indices to enable us to identify domains of the action of 'political social capital' and 'social capital of solidarity', traces of these specific types of social capital can be glimpsed in these findings.

Discussion and Conclusion

We would like to point out some basic differences and similarities in the results of the analyses of social space based on data from 2005 and 2010 and to point to the role of these analyses in our wider project.

Key differences in the construction of social space in Serbia (in 2005 and 2010) are reflected in different ways of conceiving the dimension of the composition of capital. In both cases, the main dimension (Axis 1) represents the total volume of capital of respondents, with the highest values of all types of capital grouped in the left part of the map, and minimal values on the right. On the other hand, the results of the 2010 analysis indicate that Axis 2 does not separate indicators of economic capital and cultural capital (as in Bourdieu's conception), but does not clearly make a distinction between different types of social capital and cultural capital either (as in the 2005 study). Instead, the map of social space from 2010 shows a differentiation of indicators of cultural capital (in the upper regions of the map) and of social capital (in the lower regions of the map). Further, the analysis of the 2010 data points to a bifurcation of indicators of economic capital in the map. High values of indicators of cultural capital are followed by high indicators of respondent income (in the upper part of the map), and high indicators of affluence/ownership of respondents (house/apartment) are also located in that part of the map where high values of social capital indices are located.

The difference in the results of the two studies is also reflected in the division of occupational groups into social classes. Unlike the four-class model that we constructed in our research in 2005, the data from this study indicate a threefold division between social classes in Serbia.

When indicators of cultural practices and indicators of the existence and use of social networks were projected into social space (based on the 2010 data), it was revealed that cultural and economic capital represent key resources of two fractions of the upper social classes, while the middle class in particular makes use of social capital in its strategies.

On the other hand, the basic similarities and also the basic results of our analyses of social space in Serbia suggest that practices of social actors are not random but are socially structured - certain types of life-strategies and everyday practices are more likely in some parts of social space than in others. Furthermore, and also in line with Bourdieu's conception, our results indicate that strategies and everyday practices are shaped by the interplay between the actual combination of resources (capitals) at agents' disposal and their embodied habituses. Finally, they show that social strategies and practices are relational - that they are established and defined in relations of struggle with Others - those that they oppose in the field of social classes and in other fields.

This chapter is part of the larger Social and Cultural Capital in Serbia research project. It presented the results of the analyses of social structure in Serbia at two points in time. The current analysis is significant in three ways in relation to the rest of the analyses. First, they have shown which resources social groups in Serbia rely on. For example, farmers have at their disposal a small overall volume of capital, a low level of economic capital, local cultural capital and they mainly rely on their own individual resources, and sometimes on family and neighbourhood social networks (social capital of solidarity). The situation of unskilled workers is very similar. On the other hand, skilled workers in Serbia have at their disposal resources comparable to those available to representatives of the middle classes (lower-lever experts, clerks, small owners). They all use social capital as their main resource, while possessing an average overall volume of capital and an average level of economic capital. The differentiation between these groups is based on whether they have at their disposal global or local cultural capital. Among the representatives of the upper classes the main distinction appears between members of social groups that rely on informal networks for exchange of favours (political social capital) and those who use global cultural capital (and, in particular, education) as their main resource.

Secondly, on the basis of these analyses, we were able to formulate hypotheses about which life strategies would be used by members of different social groups. On the basis of analyses of data obtained from semi-structured interviews, life strategies in Serbia have been classified as (i) individualistic reactive (used mainly by farmers, unqualified workers and the unemployed); (ii) collectivistic reactive (qualified workers and members of the middle classes); (iii) individualistic pro-active (which are used by members of the upper classes who rely on global cultural capital, in particular, education); and (iv) collectivistic pro-active (used by members of the dominant classes, who rely on political social capital and the ownership of economic capital).

The third goal of our project was to analyse the social and symbolic struggles of the holders of different types of capital in everyday life in Serbian society. Analyses of social space in Serbia have revealed that the two main resources in Serbian society are social capital and cultural capital and that it is to be expected that classification struggles should be waged between their proponents for the 'definition of the dominant principle of domination', the basic principle on the basis of which domination and social hierarchy are established in a society.

Reference

Benzécri, J.-P. (1973) *L'Analyse des Données. Volume II. L'Analyse des Correspondances*, Dunod, Paris.

Bourdieu, P. (1984) *Distinction: a social critique of the judgement of taste*, Harvard University Press, Cambridge, MA.

Bourdieu, P. (1986) The forms of capital. In *Handbook of Theory and Research for the Sociology of Education* (ed. J. Richardson), Greenwood, New York, NY, pp. 241–58.

Bouridieu, P. and Wacquant J.L.D. (1992) *An Invitation to Reflexive Sociology*, The University of Chicago Press, Chicago IL

Bourdieu, P. (1996) *The State Nobility: Elite Schools in the Field of Power*, Stanford University Press, Stanford, CA.

Cvetičanin, P. (2007) *Cultural Needs, Habits and Taste of Citizens of Serbia and Macedonia*, OGI, Niš.

Cvetičanin, P. and Popescu, M. (2009) Struggles on Symbolic Boundaries, paper presented at the SCUD network seminar: Cultural Legitimacy and Class Domination, Manchester, UK, November 2009.

Cvetičanin, P. and Popescu, M (2011) "The Art of Making Classes in Serbia – Another Particular Case of the Possible", *Poetics* 39: pp. 444–468.

Cvetičanin, P. (ed.) Social and Cultural Capital in Serbia (2012), Centre for Empirical Cultural Studies of South-East Europe, Niš

Greenacre, M. (2007) *Correspondence Analysis in Practice*, Interdisciplinary statistics, 2nd ed. Chapman & Hall/CRC, Boca Raton:

Lebart, L., Morineau, A. and Warwick, K. (1984) *Multivariate Descriptive Statistical Analysis: Correspondence Analysis and Related Techniques for Large Matrices*, John Wiley & Sons, New York, NY.

Ledeneva, A. (1998) *Russia's Economy of Favours: Blat, Networking, and Informal Exchange*, Cambride University Press, Cambridge.

Ledeneva, A. (2006) *How Russia Really Works: The Informal Practices that Shaped Post-Soviet Politics and Business*, Cornell University Press, Ithaca, NY.

Le Roux, B. and Rouanet, H. (2010) *Multiple Correspondence Analysis*, Sage Publications, Thousand Oaks, CA.

Le Roux, B., Rouanet, H., Savage, M. and Warde, A. (2008) Class and cultural division in the UK. *Sociology* 42, pp. 1049–71.

Smart, A. (1993) Gifts, bribes, and Guanxi: a reconsideration of Bourdieu's social capital. *Cultural Anthropology*, 8, pp. 388–408.

Wedel, J. (1986) *The Private Poland*, Facts on File, New York, NY.

Yang, M. (1994) *Gifts, Favors, and Banquets: The Art of Social Relationships in China*, Cornell University Press, Ithaca, NY.

Part II

The Challenges of State-Building in the Western Balkans

Marius Calu

What Makes Kosovo A 'Weak' State?

Introduction

Kosovo has undoubtedly been the focal point of many international controversies and debates over the politics of interventionism, international law, ethnic cleansing, peace-building, state-building, the role of international administrators, the right to self-determination and, more recently, the problems arising from the 2008 unilateral declaration of independence. Kosovo declared independence almost ten years after the 1999 war and, under increasing influence from the European Union, it aims not only to foster its international recognition and defend its status but also to continue build its domestic sovereignty in tandem with the Europeanization of the Western Balkans. In other words, in its post-2008 quest to meet European standards and construct stable democratic governance, Kosovo continues to have a highly contested statehood and even lacks the support of five EU member states, while also facing the challenges of perennial state weakness.

The overall aim of this chapter is to investigate the process of postconflict state-building in Kosovo from the perspective of exogenous and endogenous factors that can perpetuate state weakness by undermining the character of domestic sovereignty. I investigate this by considering a literature that starts with a critique of liberal interventionism, which emphasizes the changing character of sovereignty and the society–state rift so as to explain why contemporary state-building has a paradoxical effect of state weakening and state failure. I argue that a competing literature has been emerging with the aim of stimulating more consistent explanations of state weakness by highlighting the perennial legacy of the past in relation to the absence of state-society interdependence.

Firstly, I briefly examine some of the core conceptions on state formation and point out the contemporary model of democratic legal authority so as to understand what type of state-building has become necessary in Kosovo and why. Secondly, this analysis will suggest the meanings of state weakness and state failure in contrast to the proposed tasks and responsibilities that make a state functional. I will establish the meaning of these categories while looking at arguments that challenge the causes behind these state-building problems in the context of postconflict Kosovo.

Thirdly, by examining the impact of interventionism (exogenous cause) versus the impact of the dual legacy of communism and conflict from the past (endogenous cause), this chapter will highlight the gap between local and international conceptions of authority. The legitimacy of democratization, which has been prioritized in postconflict societies, has generally been considered to be undermined by the influence and control of external administrators. However, legitimacy is also indicated by the capacity of the political authority to provide essential public goods.

Overall, I suggest that different understandings of authority encourage external administrators to provide external legitimacy (suprastate authority) while local population are seeking substate actors (local legitimacy) that can simulate the duties of state authority. By introducing Migdal's 'state-in-society' approach and the notion of social control, I indicate the integrated/disintegrated characters of domestic sovereignty and political authority vis-à-vis state-building practices in Kosovo. The relevance of such arguments for the case of Kosovo will be explained by comparing the classical liberal state-building rationale and the EU-inspired logic of state-building in southeastern Europe that promotes a 'postliberal' model of governance. The last section of this chapter is dedicated to role of the EU in Kosovo and the endogenous challenges for its dual mission: state-building in concomitance with Europeanization.

If we identify external imposition/control as the key problem of postconflict state-building missions (external source of legitimacy) then encouraging local autonomy for self-governing capacity should give positive results (developing domestic legitimization). However, in practice this may not work given that the problem of postconflict societies to develop a democratic legal authority has more significant and complex origins (local context, legacy of conflict; society–state gap). Furthermore, liberal-democratic measures and standards that define contemporary state-building are implemented improperly not necessarily because they are imposed and given a different character but because they are in conflict with the internal pre-established fracture between the state and its population.

This chapter discusses how, in the case of Kosovo, the post-1999 state-building efforts starting with UNMIK, the role of NATO and afterwards the primary influence of the EU and thus the external administration of the province (*cause A*), have been criticized for creating a certain degree of dependency on legitimacy from outside, in the detriment of democratization and domestic legitimacy (Ignatieff, 2003; Chandler, 2004, 2010; Tansey, 2007; Zaum, 2007; Lemay-Hebert, 2008; Weller, 2008). As a consequence, the progress of state-building in Kosovo has started to encourage and implement local autonomy (EULEX, declaration of independence) (*solution a*). However, the more significant and perhaps the real cause is the dual legacy of conflict and communism (*cause B*), which has been manifested in several ways including ethnic, social and political division, the absence of national cohesion, economic dependency and security issues. Once statebuilders begin to understand better the causes behind Kosovo's permanent state weakness and the limits that work in the detriment of sustaining a functional model of governance, the focus will turn to finding solutions to step forward from the legacy of the past.

Rationale of State Formation

In order to understand the logic behind characterizing a state as 'strong', 'failed', 'limited' or 'weak', it is important to consider different views on what a state is. There are several conceptions of the state including the social contract theory, the Weberian view of the state as a 'corporate group' (Von Einsiedel, 2005: 15) and the theory that focuses on the juridical statehood of a state. Consequently, there is no agreement on the definition of state failure either.

As regards the formation of the modern state, finding a solution for the issue of political order can firstly be identified with Charles Tilly's representation of 'war-making and state-making as organized crime' based on the idea that security is essentially offered in return for extraction (Tilly, 1990). Secondly, the liberal tradition of political thought developed the idea of 'the social contract' between rulers and subjects and made legitimacy a key concept for state-building. Thirdly, the political economy tradition describes the emergence of the modern state 'as an efficient mechanism for ensuring property rights and securing markets that allowed capitalism (and imperialism) to flourish' (Milliken and Krause, 2002: 755).

Altogether, these conceptions on the modern state formation process highlight three core functions and responsibilities of the state as a provider of security, representation and welfare (Milliken and Krause, 2002: 756). As a result, a very simple way of identifying state weakness or failure is in relation to the state's capacity and will to perform these main functions of governance. The conceptions of what a state is and how a state should work can be put together to analyse the rationale behind contemporary efforts for state-building materialized by the model of *democratic legal authority*. This model is 'based on a belief, by the people in a geographically defined polity, in the legality of democratically enacted rules and the right of democratic authorities to issue commands under such rules' (Ponzio, 2010: 35). If this is the objective of postconflict state-building missions, then the understanding of authority is essential for the functionality of state-building processes. As Ponzio (2010) argues, the 'gap in conception of authority' between international officials and the local population could represent the key challenge to all contemporary attempts to implement democratic legal authority in post-conflict societies. This is nevertheless related to the concern over the character of underconstructed domestic sovereignty.

State Weakness

In a thorough analysis of the contemporary world states, Rotberg (2007) has categorized them in the following order: strong, weak, failing and collapsed. The criteria for such classification are mainly derived from the states' ability or inability to deliver 'essential political goods – the critical ingredients of good governance' (Rotberg, 2007: 85). The concept of 'essential political goods' is another source of debate but, generally, the key political goods can be identified as: security, good governance, effective rule of law, freedom and rights, functional economy and infrastructure. My focus is nonetheless on domestic sovereignty when evaluating whether 'the state has the capacity to govern and is able to exercise its powers and use its resources for the benefit of its people' (Kumar, 2008: 253). From the perspective of the European Union and its exported model of governance through enlargement and state-building practice, the conditions to develop a functional and strong state are mainly political (stable institutions, guarantee of democracy, rule of law, human rights and minority issues) and economic (functional market economy).

While failure indicates the total collapse of central authority and governance capacity, *weak states* are those that do not have the capacity to provide or are not willing to provide *some* of the fundamental goods associated with stability: physical security, legitimate political institutions, economic management and social welfare (Ayoob, 2007; Rotberg, 2007).

State in Society

As regards the success and failure of the modern state and its capacity to gain obedience, the fundamental factor is the relationship of the state to those it claims to rule. In consequence, the impact of economic interdependence, the global information system, the challenge of supranational governance, 'the disintegrative effects of virulent ethnic and tribal forces, all have deeply affected the relationship between states and their populations' (Migdal, 2001: 236).

For these reasons, before analysing the contemporary international context of state failure it is useful to introduce the concept of *social control*. State control over its own society is a key element for evaluating domestic sovereignty as reflected by three indicators: compliance, participation and legitimacy (Migdal, 2001: 52). The first tells who is in control of what and illustrates obedience. Participation integrates people/citizens by giving them specialized tasks in the institutional apparatus of the state (public services) and the third and most inclusive indicator of social control is legitimacy as it confirms that people accept the state's 'rules of the game' and its social control as true and right.

It is therefore the exercise of social control through these three elements that indicates the strength or weakness of a state, both domestically and internationally. Convincing or coercing other societal entities to accept *official* state authority is an attribute of *strong states*. In contrast, weak states are less efficient when they negotiate their claims for authority.

Exogenous Impact of Liberal Interventionism

With the end of the Cold War the external restraints of the United States and of the Soviet Union have been lifted but, in return, the new situation revealed, more than ever, the weak domestic structure of ex-colonial and ex-socialist states. Various factors like 'resurgent identity politics, the weakening of intergroup reciprocities and linkages, the determination to thwart state repressiveness, the flow of refugees across borders, have resulted in a revised view of the legitimate claims of the state upon society' (Lake and Rothchild, 1996: 230). In the new international context, the profound administrative weaknesses in many *developing* countries could not be obscured anymore by the 'legal form of state sovereignty' (Bickerton, 2007: 101).

The majority of states that were born after the end of World War Two could not ask for legitimacy from their own societies as they lacked a sense of nationhood. As a result, they had to seek for legitimacy somewhere else, outside their own boundaries, thus going back to the international community. The postcolonial critique (Clapham, 1996; Gong, 1984; Grovogui, 2007; Herbst, 1996; Krishna, 1993; Mayall,1996; Mazrui, 1995) argues that the Western-centric norms of sovereignty must have predicted the difficulties for political self-creation in the absence of positive sovereignty: 'This idea that states can fail is obviously the precursor to the idea that states need to be rebuilt' (Bickerton, 2007: 102). This statement can nonetheless be related to the rationale behind justifying liberal interventionism. Based on the dual character reinforced by the post-1945 settlements, the norms of full sovereignty generate responsibilities of the state towards other states, such as the duty not to intervene but they also generate responsibilities of states 'towards their own population, a point made in arguments about "standard of civilization" in the nineteenth and early twentieth century' (Zaum, 2007).

The changing character of sovereignty is therefore at the core of understanding the development of the idea of perpetual state weakness: the result has been that many of the new states have *de jure* features of sovereignty that include international recognition and UN membership, but lack the capacity needed to develop an integrative and functioning political system. For instance, the non-Western world has had to catch up with the West in a rather paradoxical manner: to develop domestic positive sovereignty it had to first give up its right to popular sovereignty and self-governance and then continue under the supervision of the international community. Moreover, the legacy of colonialism has exacerbated division along ethnic, cultural or religious lines and has undermined state authority right from the start: 'identity groups, cut off from their brethren in other states, were sometimes left too weak to provide for their security, too small to be economically viable, and incomplete in their identity, and they had strong incentives to change the status quo' (Levy, 2007: 29).

In the analysis of state-building and state-weakness the element where the exogenous and the endogenous theoretical perspectives meet is the *legitimacy of the political authority under the impact of the society–state fracture.* This intersection of arguments also indicates the role of non-state actors in keeping political authority away from the state: 'both forces originating outside the boundaries that the state claims for itself and those within its borders have contested state efforts to monopolize the exercising of authority. The result has been the *limited* state' (Migdal, 2001: 263). In the context of the liberal state-building framework, the problems of identifying collective will, implementing popular democracy or developing domestic sovereignty are related to the causes behind the absence of the society-state interdependence. The next section will take on the endogenous elements that are considered to contribute to state weakness in relation to legitimacy.

What is the Local Context? Endogenous Elements of State Weakness

The analysis of the local context will look at the impact of the historical legacy of communism and conflict on the evolution of state-building. The focus of state-building missions is generally on finding ways to consolidate societies emerging out of conflicts. However, over time international state-building may begin to neglect the original causes of the conflict and becomes incapable of explaining what maintains state weakness or state failure. This theoretical evaluation will aim to show that even though there is little danger of state collapse, postconflict societies such as Kosovo have a perpetual state weakness that is fuelled by the same social, political, economic and cultural legacies: 'if we are to understand the inherent limitations of states we must develop a focus on *process*, one that starts with the web of relationships between them and their societies' (Migdal, 2001: 235).

A key aspect of state-building in ex-colonial or ex-communist societies is that they have a heterogeneous character with cultural, ethnic, racial, religious, social and political factions. I argue that, in Kosovo, alternative substate forms of authority are an impediment to establishing a pluralistic society in the postconflict period 'compounded by the post-communist culture of distrust of central government, breeding tradition of non-communication and non-cooperation with central government structures' (Richmond and Franks, 2009: 133). The first issue I analyse in this section is the evolution of the state-society relationship in post-communist societies like Yugoslavia and the former Soviet Bloc.

Impact of the (Post-) Communist/Conflict Legacy

The development of state-building in the twentieth century has shown that the Weberian theory had only partially touched on the problem of legitimacy crisis and of the disintegration of political systems. Following on from the arguments of Max Weber, analysts of the communist system have shown that the right to use violent force does not represent a sufficient condition to secure domination in accordance with the conditions of a particular regime (Medvev, 1989; Tucker, 1999; Khazanov, 2004; Price, 2007). All political systems, regardless of their nature - democratic, authoritarian or totalitarian - manipulate a set of social and cultural values. In the case of ex-socialist countries, political authorities represented by the single state-party have exercised the monopoly over power on the basis of the universal principles of the Marxist-communist doctrine. The communist system was initially imposed in the countries of Central and Eastern Europe through the military intervention of the Soviet Union, which created a difficult situation for these regimes from the start.

On the one hand, these regimes had to follow specific policies required by the Soviet Union and, on the other hand, they tried to conceptualize and implement economic, social and cultural policies that would offer a certain level of popular support and a 'quasi-independence' from Moscow. After a so-called period of normalization during the 1960s, the communist parties started to use alternative strategies and practices to enforce legitimacy. One of them included paternalism practiced as complete obedience of the citizens in relation to the socialist state, which, in return had to secure the fundamental needs/goods (homes, education, employment). The ultimate and undeclared purpose of paternalism was to guarantee a passive obedience and a complicity of the masses in the exercise of authority.

Even though different methods were used by communist parties in different countries, they all illustrate the impossibility of reforming the system from within. By appealing to paternalism and/or despotism the political systems distanced themselves from modernization and rule of law (Solnick, 2002). The combination of paternalism and subjugation created a culture of passive acceptance of the regime and the state became an authoritarian association with the role of deciding over individual choices and destinies and of securing the essential needs of human and social existence. In the end, paternalism did not manage to secure permanent domination of the socialist regimes: 'the demise of Communism elevated nationhood into the logical depository of individuals' hopes, fears, and activity- political, social, and economic' (Kostovicova, 2005: 6).

Another key legacy of the communist regime is related to the state policies of institutionalizing ethnicity and nationalism out of practical socio-economic interests. These measures, which characterized the socialist regimes, did not have the purpose of creating nation-states as they differed from the 'rational, based on statehood and citizenship' nationalism more present in the West (Khazanov, 2003: 79), but they have instead determined the development of necessary political conditions that favour nation building in multi-ethnic societies.

Postcommunist nationalism was thus influenced by the measures taken by the communist state to reinforce national identities and to institutionalize nationhood. Ethnic division has determined a 'self-centred notion of national identity constructed around the quest for national control of the contested homeland' (Kostovicova, 2005: 7). In Yugoslavia these state policies have gradually created 'proto-states' by favouring federal units defined by a majority national group.

In Serbia and the Western Balkans, as a result of ethnic nationalism, making an economic privilege out of political loyalty, the decimation of the middle class, and the states' reluctance to confront the past, societies have emerged as deeply fragmented along the lines of ethnicity, welfare and ideology. In the context of post-1990 Kosovo, the Serbs and the Albanians have paradoxically held similar interpretations of the status of the region and of legal developments given that they have contested each other's authority over the territory: 'although both sides' legal arguments are dubious, nevertheless they exist as "real" in nationalist rhetoric' (Daskalovski, 2003: 21).

Moreover, during communism a centralized political power was crucial for the survival of the state. As a result, the domination of the one-party system was the continuing element that made the socialist society 'incapable of allowing an autonomous "civil society" to develop' (Schwarzmantel, 1998: 104). At the same time, the absence of civil society within ex-communist societies has been influenced by the insufficiency of benefits and links based on wealth, ideology or property relations. The leaders of communist regimes had an extremely ambitious purpose to make the state the only source of authority. In the context of the Central and Eastern European communist regimes it can be observed that they developed a capacity to survive despite the absence of popular support. This situation does not exclude the concern of the political authorities to construct, fake or not, a type of popular support. A fundamental aspect is that those that govern look confident about their right to govern in front of the citizens. Nevertheless, after the fall of communism, 'the sudden change in the nature of the state and state-power has created space for the pursuit of nationalist politics aimed at the capture of a state that was no longer in control of society' (Kostovicova, 2005: 5).

Another potential problem in postconflict multiethnic societies is that of developing *ethnic sovereignty*. It is essential to remember here that peace-building includes not only stopping a conflict but the following phase of postconflict efforts to maintain peace. However, in the aftermath of an ethnic conflict, there is a possibility of establishing a political context favourable for the 'victim' side. In other words, one ethnicity can be overprotected and given the attribute of who is 'local' in the eyes of international administrators. Furthermore, ethnic nationalism gained legitimacy in southeastern Europe and the ex-Soviet Union not only as a form of opposition to communism but also as a credible threat to the national state *per se*. Political division determined by unsettled historical problems, political and economic conflicts generated by reforms and international legitimization of the process of self-determination are all factors that have contributed to the escalation of ethnic conflicts in Yugoslavia.

Ethnicity in Prewar and Postwar Kosovo

One of the biggest political and administrative risks in postwar Kosovo has been to emphasize socio-ethnic segregation and even institutionalize ethnic sovereignty. In postwar Kosovo, the contest for political authority was adjudicated by Kosovo Albanians and the leaders of the Kosovo Liberation Army (KLA) in a liberal peace-building framework that, starting with UNMIK, needed to consider carefully the historical, socio-political and cultural factors. It has been generally ignored that in the post-1990 political context of the region, in response to the drastic measures of the Milošević regime, the Kosovo Albanian leadership declared the independence of the 'Republic of Kosova' in 1991 'and started to organize a parallel state, financed by taxes on Albanians in Kosovo and in the diaspora' (Zaum, 2007: 129). This represented a peaceful resistance that even organized unofficial elections and designated Ibrahim Rugova as President, but this only delayed the radical aggressiveness of the Serbian state in parallel with the 'increasing attacks by the Kosovo Liberation Army' (Zaum, 2007: 130).

The violent contest over the autonomy of Kosovo after 1990 reached its climax with the March 1999 NATO bombing campaign against Yugoslavia, which consequently established international authority in Kosovo (UNMIK) through Resolution 1244 of the UN Security Council. The immediate problem with this resolution was the ambiguity of its aim to facilitate transitional administration while developing self-governing institutions, but with no reference to a potential final status of Kosovo: 'UNMIK was effectively tasked to engage in state-building without statehood' (Zaum, 2007: 131). The permanent state-building dilemma installed then was embodied by the policy of *standards before status* as despite the fact that the resolution gave a clear mandate for institution building, it did not decide on the purpose for the authority that the future institutions could eventually have.

Furthermore, the establishment of the Kosovo Transitional Council (KTC) with a purely consultative role was insufficient to prevent alternative sources of authority from taking over at the local level. The unrecognized 'Provisional Government of Kosova' that was led by KLA had the opportunity to appoint mayors and establish 'a parallel governmental structure reporting to its Minister of Local Government, not to UNMIK' (Zaum, 2007: 135). The necessary democratic link between state and society and the creation of civil society were therefore instantly undermined by the external top-down control of the international administration, but at the same time a perennial state weakness was installed under the influence of unofficial substate authority formations.

The concern about substate forms of authority reaches beyond the peril of legitimating warring groups that can provide security for the local population more efficiently than the state authorities. More precisely, in a context where statebuilders have actually started to develop effective forms of central authority capable of ensuring law and order, a more complex problem arises: these new forms of central authority represent the state only in theory while in practice they embody the legacy of nonstate forms of authority. In Kosovo, the liberal peace-building project has 'become implicated in the ethnic, sovereign and territorial dynamics of inclusion and exclusion, cooperation and rejection, and there is little space for democratic politics in between these positions' (Richmond and Franks, 2009: 198).The substate relations of authority are now in peril of being transferred in the public realm of politics and can simulate the centralized character of domestic sovereignty.

Ethnicized Character of Domestic Sovereignty

The liberal-democratic project to implement the 'standards before status' strategy in Kosovo has indirectly favoured an ethnic-based sovereignty by neglecting the particular issues of the postconflict/postcommunist and ethnically divided society. Core liberal values such as pluralism were at stake from the start and continue to be a key challenge for the development of a state with democratic legal authority in Kosovo. Moreover, the resulting local ownership that the international administrators encourage faces the risk of being ethnicized and not in accordance with liberal norms of popular sovereignty: 'citizen participation in decision-making processes has been hindered also by the long-term legacy of viewing the state structures as alien to the domestic context with implications to individual safety and security, identified as a tool in the hands of "the other"' (Keukeleire *et al.*, 2011: 183).

The state is weak and not liberal *per se*. Ethnic sovereignty could win over domestic sovereignty. In contrast to the goal of power sharing to gradually replace international governance with local governance capacity, the peace process and state-building efforts in Kosovo have been undermined by the prominent role of Kosovo Albanians and the result is that 'the central elements of the state are ethnically divided and sustained by foreign assistance and/or donor governments' (Richmond and Franks, 2009: 132). Even though state mechanisms are in place, they may not function because of the pre-established decentralized *illiberal nonstate notions of authority* rooted in ethnic, national, economic or religious ties. Given the detrimental legacy of communism and conflict, state weakness became evident with 'malfunctions in terms of provision of national cohesion and public goods' (Glasius and Kostovicova, 2008: 87). The permanent state weakness is thus both a structural and a political one.

EU State-building: Discourse and Impact on Kosovo

I have examined the principal exogenous and endogenous elements of state weakness from the general theoretical perspective of state-building in relation to a more narrow perspective of the case of Kosovo. Whatever the more important factors are, they all have to be taken into consideration when analysing the role of the EU in Kosovo. Consequently, these factors have constantly been creating implementation challenges for the EU, regardless of its actions as a statebuilder or as an agent of Europeanization in the Western Balkans.

The multifaceted EU presence in Kosovo has been reflected by the intersection of the European Security and Defence Policy (ESDP) and the European Union strategy for Enlargement. As the EU official fact sheet (2008) indicated, the leading role taken by the EU in the international presence in Kosovo had the fundamental overarching objective 'to support the Kosovo authorities at all levels to meet European standards'. It can be affirmed that Europeanization tools have been employed to help Kosovo progress towards European integration in concomitance with state-building objectives: creating democratic and multiethnic institutions, respecting the rule of law, sustainable economic and political development. Hence, through the EU enlargement policy Kosovo's state-building was aided by three components on the ground, namely political, operational and reform driving.

The EU Special Representative in Kosovo is the political representative who supports the local authorities to meet its obligations while promoting overall EU political coordination and who who also had until September 2012 a double-hatted role with extensive executive powers as the International Civilian Representative.

The second component is the European Union Rule of Law Mission in Kosovo (EULEX) with an operational role to monitor, mentor and advise Kosovo's authorities on police, justice, correctional services and customs. The mission thus aims to develop and strengthen a Kosovo independent multiethnic rule of law system while prioritizing immediate problems regarding the protection of minority communities, corruption and the fight against organized crime (EULEX Programme Strategy, 2008).

The third entity is a reform driving European Commission Liaison Office (ECLO) that helps Kosovo in its long-term reforms efforts and that has been deploying enlargement tools under the Stabilization and Association Process (SAP) in support of institution-building, economic development and meeting European standards (democratization, rule of law, legislation).

The Challenge of Limited Statehood

Where states lack the capacity and the willingness to adapt to the EU, the main impediment for the integration of the Western Balkans might be the problem of 'limited statehood' (Börzel, 2010). This has been the key challenge for the EU's presence in Kosovo as it has created problems at all levels. First of all, after 1999 Kosovo has become a subject of international controversy in terms of the implications of the causes of the war, international law, NATO's involvement, relations with Serbia, ethnic tensions, the regional context, the issue of secessionism and all these have been reflected by the continuing contestation of Kosovo's status, territory, identity, legality and sovereignty.

Most importantly, the multilayered contestation of Kosovo has both a domestic and an international character, the multiethnic and multiproblematic north of Kosovo being the centre of attention. As mentioned before, the first period after the 1999 war was defined by the concept of 'status before standards' under the administration of UNMIK, during which standards in terms of governance and human rights were set but with limited implementation in the absence of an agreement on the final status of the province. In other words, the limited statehood of Kosovo under UNMIK raised the questions of who would be the legal and legitimate guarantors and for whom these standards and rights would be applicable.

In 2005 the talks on the status of Kosovo were relaunched and the UN Secretary General named Martti Ahtisaari as the UN Special Envoy at the Kosovo status process negotiations. The two parties involved in the Kosovo issue had completely different positions. While the Serbs were ready to offer Kosovo a large degree of autonomy on condition that it remained part of the Serbian territory, the Pristina officials considered that giving up independent status was unacceptable. In February 2007, at the UN, Martti Ahtisaari presented his plan for the status of Kosovo. According to this plan, the EU and the US would be given the leading role in setting up Kosovo's future. The territory was supposed to become independent under the supervision of an International Civilian Representative with superior powers to the Kosovar government. Members of government could be dismissed by the International Representative if they did not respect the international accord. In addition, the main strategy for implementing the plan was through decentralization in order to find solutions for the *de facto* influence of Serbia over the north of Kosovo. This was perceived as an efficient way of governing multiethnicity in Kosovo but it was not what the Kosovo local leaders had envisaged.

However, prior to starting implementing the Ahtisaari Plan, there was one more obstacle to pass: the approval of a new UN Security Council Resolution and the unanimity of its five permanent members. The right to veto used by Russia on 26 March 2007, obstructed the plans of the Western states as Moscow continued to oppose any potential threat to the territorial integrity of Serbia.

When analysing the relationship between democratization and statehood with reference to political developments in Kosovo, three separate dimensions of statehood can be identified: recognition, capacity and cohesion (Tansey, 2007). The new political entity that emerged as a result of the 1999 NATO intervention had all its three dimensions of statehood either contested or limited by both endogenous and exogenous factors: (i) limited international recognition, denying Kosovo's legal sovereignty, (ii) the challenges of building a new state with new institutional, administrative, legislative and economic capacities and (iii) the divided character of the new territorial entity with a multiethnic society living under the supervision of an international administration and a highly contested state authority.

The analysis of Kosovo's limited statehood suggests two conclusions: first, that international recognition of statehood was not viewed as a prerequisite for democratization and, second, that problems of state capacity or state cohesion present far more fundamental challenges to successful democratic regime change. The post-1999 Kosovo has definitely been following international standards of democratization and despite the administration of UNMIK, local actors have also gradually increased their authority.

Legitimacy Crisis

In the absence of international recognition, the development of domestic political structures in Kosovo has been highly problematic. More precisely, the rather weak character of state institutions has been a major challenge given the impact on governance capacity, the authority of the central institutional and administrative bodies, the limited resources and, as a consequence, the prolonged dependence on alternative administration (external dependency syndrome or substate sources of authority). The widespread weakness of Kosovo's administrative and political governance structure started with the constitutional framework under UNMIK and the establishment of the Provisional Institutions of Self Government (PISG) in 2002 and continued during the gradual development of a statelike apparatus by 2008. Despite the fact that local institutions extended their competences during that period, governance in Kosovo stayed under the ultimate authority of UNMIK. After the 2008 declaration of independence coupled with the adoption of a new constitution in June 2008, the International Civilian Representative (ICR) (also acting as the EU Special Representative (EUSR)) became the final authority in Kosovo (Constitution of the Republic of Kosovo, Art. 147).

However, institutional weakness has not been diminished by these structural reforms and the key challenges continue to be the legitimacy and capacity of the governance structures in Kosovo. Firstly, the Kosovar institutions have been contested by the Serbian minority in the north, which has developed an alternative parallel administrative system and a parallel court that undermines Kosovo's authority. The legitimacy crisis is sustained by severe shortages of civil service expertise and the very limited administrative capacity of local institutions.

In this context, the leading role of the EU has been indicated not only by the €240 million invested in good governance promotion and institution-building projects (EAR, 2006), but also by the deployment of EULEX Rule of Law, the biggest civilian EU mission abroad, thus putting the EU in charge of constructing institutional capacity. It is not a coincidence that the EULEX mission has started in the context of perennial problems in the field of law enforcement and in the local system of justice: limited rule of law and weakness of the judiciary, widespread corruption on all levels of governance and growing organized crime (*EU Enlargement Strategy and Progress Annual Reports,*) (2008–2012).

As in the case of postconflict state-building in Bosnia, implementation has been the main problem for a strategy that hurries to elaborate rules, laws, guiding principles, measures to be taken and so forth but encounters challenges in terms of legitimacy, capacity and the means to implement its decisions. The difficulty of transferring authority to local actors is highlighted by the fact that UNMIK's preliminary role was also to smooth the transition to local ownership. Even supposing structures such as UNMIK manage to put into practice some of its immediate objectives, prolonged external peace-building gradually reduces the chances of efficient and legitimate local ownership.

Kosovo's international legitimacy was contested from the moment it declared independence and it has continued to lack the support of the Security Council. As Surroi (2011) argues, Kosovo's independence has paradoxically confirmed it as an 'unfinished state' given the layers of contestation: territorial/regional (Serbia defending its territorial integrity in the post-Yugoslavian context), global (less than 50% of the UN member states have recognized Kosovo as an independent state and opposition within the Security Council comes from both Russia and China) and the problem of European identity given that five EU member states (Spain, Romania, Slovakia, Cyprus and Greece) have refused to recognize Kosovo.

Apart from the unfinished character of Kosovo as a part of the former Yugoslavia and as part of the international community, there is an unsettled legitimacy problem for Kosovo even within the context of European integration. This is, nevertheless, a challenge for the Europeanization of Kosovo as, on the path to EU membership, the relationship between the two political entities is unclear and the accessing country needs to be recognized as a contractual partner. The problems derived from 'standards before status' continue to exist after the 2008 declaration of independence as, although the EU is helping to build-up Kosovo's domestic sovereignty, its international sovereignty is undermined by the lack of a single policy of Brussels and the negative position of states like Spain and Cyprus.

Postliberal Governance

As regards the responsibility of the EU in southeastern Europe, Chandler (2010) highlights the dual character of the intervention: reinforcing the EU's projection of its power as a civilizing mission while trying to minimize its direct political responsibility derived from this power by developing a *post-liberal discourse*. In other words, instead of using representative legitimacy to legitimize policymaking, 'post-liberal frameworks of governance problematize autonomy and self-government, inverting the liberal paradigm through establishing administrative and regulative frameworks as necessarily prior to democratic choices' (Chandler, 2010: 95). The immediate risk of this model of governance is that of undermining democratic accountability and the legitimacy of governing institutions in states that have legal sovereignty but lack the capacity to sustain political integration. For this reason, Kosovo's contested statehood creates an even more complex challenge for the EU's involvement in the process of state-building.

An inverted logic of liberal state-building that prioritizes institution building rather than democratization faces the downside of lacking popular legitimacy. By trying to diminish the imposing character of external administration, EU state-building has been focusing on developing local ownership and setting up the administrative/ bureaucratic apparatus prior to implementing liberal-democratic principles of governance fully. These arguments regarding the EU's model of governance highlight the negative effect on the relationship between state and society and thus encourage criticisms of the post-liberal state model but, overall, they also discount the endogenous roots of state weakness.

Domestic sovereignty is at stake because of the problems of representative accountability and the state–society fracture that Kosovo is facing. However, the main cause is not the *absence* of mechanisms to integrate society but their *functionality*. The functionality argument, I believe, provides a more consistent response to understanding the relationship between state and society because it focuses on endogenous factors like the inherited distrust for central government and the lack of social cohesion. These elements of distrust, in combination with the influence of post-1990 parallel structures incorporated now as both state and nonstate agents, have jeopardized the independence of the state-building process and the development of a pluralist civil society.

The Future

Kosovo still has many problems to overcome. One of them is state cohesion as, despite the fact that decentralization is on the main agenda of state-building under EULEX, its implementation has been very difficult. Multiethnicity in Kosovo has a special significance not only because of the violent history that on several occasions has transformed the Balkans into the most problematic part of Europe but, especially, because of the context in which Kosovo has departed from the authority of Serbia. In the post-1999 context the argument has been put forward the argument that Kosovo established 'the principle that states can lose their sovereignty over a portion of their territory if they so oppress the majority population there that they rise in revolt and successfully enlist international support for their rebellion' (Ignatieff, 2003: 70). While this argument has been used by the Albanian Kosovars to reject any potential claim from Serbia to reintegrate Kosovo within its territory it has also become a key test for Kosovo to sustain its independence and legitimacy (whether or not it is recognized by the international community).

In the context of the double legacy of communism and conflict, the Europeanization of the Western Balkans has a more complex character than the integration process of the Central-Eastern European countries. Kosovo itself represents a particular example of EU state-building, combining efforts in support of democratization and institutional capacity while highlighting its role in advising and developing sustainable local ownership. In what has been portrayed as a mission with 'enhanced conditionality' (Kostovicova and Bojic-Dzelilovic, 2006), the challenge is not only to fulfil the Copenhagen criteria of political and economic reforms together with the acceptance of the *acquis*, but also to meet conditions related to stability in the area of security as reflected by peace treaties, cooperation with the International Tribunal for the former Yugoslavia and, nonetheless, regional cooperation. The process of the Europeanization of the Western Balkans has been concomitant with a period of 'troubled' and 'permanent' transition of these postcommunist and postconflict societies and a general security threat (Kostovicova,2008: 11). The endogenous element of *sustainable state weakness* is therefore critical for understanding the challenges faced by the EU in the problematic transition of Kosovo.

Conclusion

This chapter affirms my assumptions and my understanding of state weakness in the context of Kosovo by adopting a dual approach that combines exogenous and endogenous problems of postconflict state-building. I claim that the fundamental reason why state-building fails to implement its objectives, including the development of domestic sovereignty, is the perpetual state–society rift. I argue that this fracture is cultivated by both the external influence of international administration (suprastate authority) and a local contest over political authority exercised by nonstate social formations/networks (substate authority).

I also made a clear distinction between 'state failure' and 'state weakness' in support of my evaluation of the challenges for contemporary state-building. I highlighted the role played by both the will of states to provide their population with fundamental political goods and their capacity to do so. Whether we discuss the absence of an appropriate institutional framework and a functional rule of law, the problems of a defective economic system or the lack of social cohesion, I argued that there is an important theoretical gap in the existing literature on state-building: not enough research has been done to integrate the meaning and impact of the local context (contested domestic sovereignty, lack of legitimacy, weak/limited or failing political authority) as a vital cause for states not being able to develop sustainable democratic governance.

The second part of this contribution focused on introducing the understanding of the local context as an alternative approach to the critique of liberal interventionism. At the same time, I emphasized that both the exogenous and endogenous levels of analysis confirm that the legitimacy crisis of governance is derived from the necessity to identify a provider (will) and guarantor (capacity) of state responsibilities. In this context, political authority in Kosovo is exercised externally through accepted and legitimate administration/supervision by the EU and internally through alternative social formations that inherited the legacy of the parallel state or of other unofficial and ethnicized formations. For these reasons, this chapter also drew attention to the phenomenon that permits substate agents to infiltrate inside the official state apparatus and thus control the state mechanism and simulate key political functions.

This chapter linked the impact of endogenous elements with the role of the EU in Kosovo as regards building domestic sovereignty and implementing a model of good governance. Given the particular challenges that the Europeanization via enlargement framework has been facing in the process of state-building in Kosovo, it will be interesting to see whether, in the long term, the conditionality tools, for instance, are appropriate and sufficient for state-building. I also mentioned Chandler's analysis of postliberal governance so as to highlight the innovative institutionalist approach of the EU in the Balkans that uses two levels of implementation: Europeanization and state-building. It has been extremely challenging for the EU to decide upon a clear and compact strategy for the Western Balkans given the different nature of the mission, the different objectives it involves and the specific nature of the region and of each state in particular. In other words, although the EU has the experience of the Eastern European enlargement, when it had to deal with post-communist countries in transition to democracy and capitalism, the Western Balkans has added a number of major issues: a postconflict environment, severe ethnic problems, limited potential for regional cooperation, extreme poverty, contested and/or limited statehood, problematic borders and the buildup of a controversial new-born state – Kosovo.

As this chapter has shown, endogenous factors can explain the faults of postconflict state-building and the perpetuation of state weakness well in the context of changed and limited domestic sovereignty. The case of Kosovo indicates that it is not necessarily sufficient for the EU to combine efforts in support of democratization and institutional capacity while highlighting its role in advising and developing sustainable local ownership. Any further investigation needs to reiterate not only that Kosovo represents a particular example of EU state-building, but also that it remains a postconflict, postcommunist multiethnic political entity with contested statehood and dispersed authority.

References

Ayoob, M. (2007) State making, state breaking, and state failure. In: *Leashing the Dogs of War: Conflict Management in a Divided World* (eds C. Crocker, F. Hampson and P. Aall), United States Institute of Peace Press, Washington D.C., pp. 95–114.

Bickerton, C. (2007) State-building: exporting state failure. In *Politics Without Sovereignty. A Critique of Contemporary International Relations* (eds C. Bickerton, P. Cunliffe and A. Gourevitch), UCL Press, London, pp. 93–111.

Börzel, T. (2010) The transformative power of Europe reloaded. The limits of external Europeanization, *KFG Working Paper Series*, no. 11, http://userpage.fu-berlin.de/kfgeu/kfgwp/wpseries/WorkingPaperKFG_11.pdf
Brown, C. (2002) *Sovereignty, Rights and Justice*, Polity Press, Cambridge.
Chandler, D. (2004) The problems of 'nation-building': imposing bureaucratic 'rule from above'. *Cambridge Review of International Affairs* 17 (3), pp. 577–91.
Chandler, D. (2010) *International Statebuilding. The Rise of Post-Liberal Governance*, Routledge, Oxford.
Clapham, C. (1996) *Africa and the International System: The Politics of State Survival*, Cambridge University Press, New York, NY.
Daskalovski, Z. (2003) Claims to Kosovo: nationalism and self-determination. In *Understanding the War in Kosovo* (ed. F. Bieber and Z. Daskalovski), Frank Cass, London, pp. 13–30.
EAR Annual Report, 2006, http://ec.europa.eu/enlargement/archives/ear/publications/main/documents/AnnualReportJan-Dec2006.pdf
EU Enlargement Strategy and Progress Annual Reports (2008–2012), http://ec.europa.eu/enlargement/countries/strategy-and-progress report/index_en.htm (last accessed 16. 11. 12)
European Union- Fact Sheet- The EU in Kosovo, February 2008, http://www.consilium.europa.eu/ueDocs/cms_Data/docs/pressData/en/gena/98770.pdf (last accessed 16. 11. 12)
EULEX Programme Strategy (2008), http://www.csfederalismo.it/images/stories/PESD/eulex-kosovo/eulex_programme-strategy.pdf (last accessed 16. 11. 12)
European Commission, Kosovo (2011) *Progress Report*, http://eeas.europa.eu/delegations/kosovo/documents/eu_kosovo/20111018_progress_report_en.pdf (accessed 16 October 2012).
Glasius, M. and Kostovicova, D. (2008) The European Union as a state-builder: policies towards Serbia and Sri Lanka. *Südosteuropa* 56 (1), pp. 84–114.
Gong G W. (1984) *The Standard of 'Civilization in International Society*, Clarendon Press, Oxford.
Grovogui, S. (2007) Postcolonialism. In *International Relations Theories: Discipline and Diversity* (eds T. Dunne, M. Kurki and S. Smith), Oxford University Press, Oxford, pp. 229–45.
Herbst, J. (1996) "Responding to State Failure in Africa", *International Security*, 21 (3), pp. 120–144.
Ignatieff, M. (2003) *Empire Lite: Nation Building in Bosnia, Kosovo and Afghanistan*, Vintage, London.
Khazanov, A. (2003) A state without a nation? Russia after empire. In *The Nation State in Question* (eds T. Paul., G. Ikenberry and J. Hall), Princeton University Press, Princeton, NJ, pp. 79–105.
Kostovicova, D. (2005) *Kosovo: The Politics of Identity and Space*, Routledge, London.
Kostovicova, D. and Bojicic-Dzelilovic, V. (2006) Europeanizing the Balkans: rethinking the post-communist and post-conflict transition. *Ethnopolitics* 5 (3), pp. 223–41.
Krishna, S. (1993) The importance of being ironic: a postcolonial view on critical international relations theory. *Alternatives* 18 (3), pp. 385–417.

Kumar, C. (2008) Corruption and transparency in governance and development: reinventing sovereignty for promoting good governance. In *Re-envisioning Sovereignty: the End of Westphalia*, (eds C. Sampford, T. Jacobsen and R. Thakur), Ashgate, Aldershot, pp. 251–66.

Lemay-Hebert, N. (2008) The "frozen conflict" that turned hot: conflicting state building attempts in South Ossetia. *Central Asia and the Caucasus*, 5 (53), pp. 150–159.

Lake, D. and Rothchild D. (1996) Ethnic Fears and Global Engagement: The International Spread and Management of Ethnic Conflict, *Institute on Global Conflict and Cooperation*, Policy Paper.

Levy, J. (2007) International sources of interstate and intrastate war. In *Leashing the Dogs of War: Conflict Management in a Divided World* (eds C. Crocker, F. Hampson, and P. Aall), United States Institute of Peace Press, Washington D.C., pp. 17–38.

Mayall, J. (1996) Introduction. In *The New Interventionism 1991–1994: United Nations Experience in Cambodia, Former Yugoslavia and Somalia*, (ed. J. Mayall), Cambridge University Press, Cambridge, pp. 3–11.

Mazrui, A. (1995) The blood of experience: the failed state and political collapse in Africa. *World Policy Journal* 12 (1), pp. 28–34.

Medvedev, R. (1989) *Let History Judge: the Origins and Consequences of Stalinism*, Columbia University Press, New York, NY.

Migdal, J. (2001) *State in Society: Studying How States and Societies Transform and Constitute One Another*, Cambridge University Press, Cambridge.

Milliken, J. and Krause, K. (2002) State failure, state collapse, and state reconstruction: concepts, lessons and strategies. *Development and Change* 33 (5), pp. 753–74.

Pond, E. (2008) The EU's test in Kosovo. *The Washington Quarterly* 31 (4), pp. 97–112.

Ponzio, R. (2010) *Democratic Peacebuilding: Aiding Afghanistan*, Oxford University Press, Oxford.

Price, R. (2007) Russian nationalism: creating a civic identity. *Groundings 1*, University Dialectic Society, Glasgow.

Richmond, O. and Franks, J. (2009) *Liberal Peace Transitions: Between Peacebuilding and Statebuilding*, Edinburgh University Press, Edinburgh.

Rotberg, R. (2007) The challenge of weak, failing, and collapsed states. In *Leashing* the Dogs of War (eds C. Crocker, F. Hampson and P. Aall), US Institute for Peace, Washington D.C., pp. 83–94.

Schwarzmantel, J. (1998) *The Age of Ideology: Political Ideologies from the American Revolution to Postmodern Times*, Macmillan, Basingstoke.

Solnick, S. L. (2002) Federalism and State-Building: Post-Communist and Post-Colonial Perspectives. In *The architecture of democracy constitutional design, conflict management, and democracy*. (ed. A. Reynolds), Oxford University Press, Oxford, pp. 171–205.

Surroi, V. (2011) *Unfinished States*. Paper presented at EUISS conference on Western Balkans, www.foreignpolicyclub.org/shkrime/vs04.html (last accessed 17 October 2012).

Tansey, O. (2007) Democratization without a state: democratic regime-building in Kosovo. *Democratization* 14 (1), pp. 129–50.

Tilly, C. (1990) *Coercion, Capital, and European States, AD 990–1990*, Blackwell, Oxford.
Tucker, R. (1999) *Stalinism: Essays in Historical Interpretation*, Transaction, New Brunswick.
Von Einsiedel, S. (2005) Policy responses to state failure. In *Making States Work* (eds S. Chesterman, M. Ignatieff and R. Thakur), United Nations University Press, Tokyo, pp. 13–35.
Weber, M. (1948) Politics as a vocation. In *From Max Weber: Essays in Sociology* (eds H. Gerth and C. Wright Mills), Routledge, London, pp. 77–128.
Weller, M. (2008) Kosovo's final status. *International Affairs* 84 (6), pp. 1223–43.
Zaum, D. (2007) *The Sovereignty Paradox: The Norms and Politics of International Statebuilding*, Oxford University Press, Oxford.

Aisling Lyon

Municipal Decentralization: Between the Integration and Accommodation of Ethnic Difference in the Republic of Macedonia[1]

Introduction

The decentralization process in the Republic of Macedonia[2] has been widely regarded as a success story by regional and international actors alike. It is frequently considered a suitable nonterritorial model of ethnic conflict management that can be replicated elsewhere. The reforms, which form part of a more comprehensive peace process defined by the Ohrid Framework Agreement[3] of 2001, offer limited autonomy to Macedonia's ethnic communities, in particular the ethnic Albanians. By increasing the number of competencies administered at the municipal level, in addition to replicating central government's system of consociational power sharing locally, the reform process seeks to give local, culturally diverse communities greater control over the management of their own affairs and resources.

1 This is a modified version of a paper that was previously published in the Journal on Ethnopolitics and Minority Issues in Europe (JEMIE).

2 Hereafter referred to as 'Macedonia'. It should be noted that the 'Republic of Macedonia' is the constitutional name for the state; however, this name is the subject of dispute with neighbouring Greece. Consequently, the Republic of Macedonia is currently recognized under its temporary name the 'Former Yugoslav Republic of Macedonia' ('FYROM') in its dealings with international organizations such as the UN and EU.

3 Hereafter the 'Framework Agreement'. The Framework Agreement brought an end to approximately six months of armed hostilities between the Macedonian security forces and ethnic Albanian insurgents during 2001. It sought to reinstate, and in some cases enhance, the collective rights of the nonmajority communities, in particular ethnic Albanians, and was signed by the government and ethnic Albanian representatives in the lakeside resort of Ohrid on 13 August 2001.

The purpose of this chapter is to position Macedonia's experience with political, administrative and fiscal decentralization within the ongoing theoretical debate concerning how states deal with ethnic difference. It will begin by outlining how the devolution of power to subnational units such as municipalities may offer an institutional solution for managing and preserving cultural diversity within a unitary state. The chapter will then position this discussion within the wider theoretical debate between integrationists and accommodationists regarding how states should manage cultural pluralism. A review of Macedonia's decentralization process, a rather weak form of self-government in comparison to strategies adopted by other former Yugoslav republics, will then follow. Elements of the reforms will be identified as belonging to either the accommodationist or integrationist approaches to managing ethnic difference. Finally, the implementation of the decentralization reforms, defined by the Ohrid Framework Agreement and subsequent legislation, will be examined.

Defining Decentralization

This contribution focuses on only one of a variety of self-governance arrangements available for the management of ethnopolitical conflict: decentralization to local government/municipal units. Other common forms of self-governance arrangements not discussed here are federalism, territorial, and personal autonomy. I define decentralization as a process by which central–local relations are restructured in a unitary state, through the devolution of competencies from the national to local levels of government (Braathen and Hellevik, 2008: 3; Grasa and Camps, 2009: 21). The process is understood to be an effort to share power vertically between central and local government in the following three dimensions: political, administrative, and fiscal. Whilst decentralization can represent extensive devolution to local governments, it is important not to lose sight of the fact that these self-governing entities remain ultimately subordinate to the authority of central government.

The lack of a constitutionally entrenched guarantee is one of the key attributes of decentralization that differentiates it from other forms of territorial self-governance, principally federalism (Rothchild and Hartzell, 2000: 261; Wolff, 2010: 10). Other characteristics of federalism missing in decentralized states are bicameral legislatures, independent mechanisms of judicial review and exclusive legislative and judicial powers. Unlike federal systems of governance, in decentralized unitary states sovereignty is not divided. Decentralization also differs from autonomy, another form of self-governance, which can be granted on either a territorial or nonterritorial basis. The principal characteristic of autonomy that distinguishes it from both decentralization and many types of federalism is its explicitly ethnic nature (Young, 1998: 60). Ruth Lapidoth (2007: 174–5) defines territorial autonomy as 'an arrangement aimed at granting a certain degree of self-identification to a group that differs from the majority of the population in the state, and yet constitutes the majority in a specific region.' It involves the creation of separate governance structures through which members of a specific ethnic community exercise control over their political, economic or cultural affairs (Hadden, 2005: 34).

Decentralization as a Tool for Mitigating Ethnopolitical Conflict

One of the most frequently cited arguments in favour of decentralization as tool for managing ethnopolitical conflict is its ability to satisfy the demands of spatially concentrated nonmajority groups for limited autonomy over their own affairs. The creation or enhancement of subnational units can allow a group that is a minority at the state level, but which constitute a majority locally, to exercise governmental power in ways that would otherwise be foreclosed if the whole country were one undifferentiated territory (Horowitz, 2007: 958). Importantly, however, it does so whilst maintaining the territorial integrity of the unitary state. Decentralization's promise of limited autonomy also provides greater scope for promoting minority rights and the protection of their cultural identity. In this respect, devolved competencies relating to education, culture, and language policy are of particular importance.

Decentralized institutions not only facilitate better access to political structures and state resources for ethnic minority and opposition groups; they can also restrain the monopoly that central government and majority-dominated political parties have on state power. The distribution of power to different levels of government facilitates a system of checks and balances that sets limits on central government. Decentralization increases the number of arenas in which there are political prizes to be won, so the opportunities for previously disenfranchised groups to participate legitimately in government are enhanced. Local institutions may become 'training ground[s] for democracy', suggests James Manor (1999: 49, 85), relieving dangerous frustrations by providing aspiring politicians with additional openings into the political system. Providing alternative sites of power and patronage can also disperse political conflict away from the centre, thereby lowering its stakes (Roeder, 2005: 52; Treisman, 2007: 14). 'Proliferating the points of power', confirms Donald Horowitz (2000: 598), makes politics 'a much more diffused game'; transforming it from a 'zero-sum' contest into one where different groups can each control some part of the governing apparatus.

Experts have argued that the creation of decentralized institutions can also promote social cohesion locally, in addition to facilitating a more balanced relationship between majority and minority communities at the state level. In ethnically heterogeneous regions, self-government can creates nonviolent platforms for interethnic and intergroup discussion relating to local issues and allocation of resources. Such 'learning laboratories', notes Zoë Scott (2009: 16), can help local politicians build trust among groups and acquire political and conflict resolution skills that can be used in different social arenas. Local government may also serve as an incubator for small ethnic parties that choose to form interethnic and transethnic alliances (Treisman, 2007: 245).

Decentralization is an institution that, if properly designed, can potentially benefit political minorities, who can be induced not to secede from the state, and political majorities, who gain countrywide acceptance of state institutions (Lake and Rothchild, 2005: 122). When threatened with secessionist attempts, federalism, or even partition of the state, decentralization can appear an attractive way of preserving state integrity and of integrating separatist movements. Importantly, decentralization to local governments, as opposed to regional or federal institutions, can also be employed to deliberately fragment the local power bases of secessionist groups into smaller, weaker, nonpolitically significant units (Young, 1998: 32; Horowitz, 2000: 646; Crook, 2002: 300).

Decentralization: Peace Preserving or Conflict Enhancing?

Despite the prevalence of decentralization reforms worldwide, the academic community and, more recently, donor agencies have become increasingly sceptical of decentralization's performance as a panacea for culturally diverse unitary states. The promotion of decentralized governance in ethnically divided societies, some argue, is not devoid of risk and its implementation may even have unwanted effects that can inadvertently exacerbate the causes of conflict (Schou and Haug, 2005; Braathen and Hellevik, 2008; Grasa and Camps, 2009; Wolff, 2010). One of the principal arguments that critics have made against territorial forms of ethnic conflict management, albeit more commonly with regard to ethno-federal and regional governance models than local self-government, is their potential for encouraging the secessionist tendencies of minority groups, whilst equipping groups with the necessary resources with which to secede. The key insight here, note Valerie Bunce and Stephen Watts (2005: 136), is that there is a fine line between legitimating difference and undermining commonality. Rather than building a stronger sense of ownership and affinity with the state, decentralization may in fact accentuate differences between regions, promote citizen identification with ethnic or geographic groups rather than the state, and encourage local politicians to stake out hardline positions in defence of regional or ethnic priorities (Siegle and O'Mahoney, 2007: 1).

Contrary to the commonly held constructivist belief that ethnic identities are fluid and capable of changing over time, drawing tight linkages among the nation, territory, and political power can institutionalize ethnicity, increase its salience in local politics and may encourage group isolation and intergroup distrust (Bieber, 2004: 2; Treisman, 2007: 241). The creation of newly defined territorial units, together with the entrenchment of ethnicity locally, may also lead to the creation of 'local tyrannies' and exacerbate discrimination against small ethnic communities (Manor, 1999: 97; Treisman, 2007: 239). In this respect, decentralization may not only freeze, as opposed to reduce, instances of ethnic conflict – it may relocate them from the national to local level and cause them to become more intense. Unless there is complete homogeneity in each local area, notes Crook (2002: 305), the system will create new 'minorities within minorities', who may be subjected to domination by local elites who capture power by 'democratic' means. Ethnic minorities that have just 'won' autonomy from a central government, add Weller and Wolff (2005: 268), may resent the fact that they will have to share power with other ethnic groups. Discriminatory tactics may also adversely affect women and those who do not share such ethnocentric worldviews (Kälin, 2004: 306; Rebouche and Fearton, 2005).

Accommodation or Integration: 'The Enduring Debate in Conflict Regulation'[4]

The ongoing debate about whether states should accommodate or attempt to integrate the ethnic differences of citizens demonstrates a fundamental normative disagreement over the mechanisms of interethnic cooperation. Each approach proceeds from different

4 This replicates the title of a book chapter written by John McGarry, Brendan O'Leary and Richard Simeon (McGarry *et al.*, 2008b, pp. 41–90).

assumptions and epistemological positions regarding the durability and malleability of politically mobilized ethnic identities. Integrationists, notes Richard H. Pildes (2008: 175), focus primarily on the long-term normative vision of the state, whilst accommodationists are (allegedly) more concerned with the immediate, short-term pressures that states face. In the following section I will briefly summarize the principal differences between the accommodationist and integrationist approaches to managing ethnic difference. I will then position the various arguments concerning decentralization's performance as a conflict-mitigating mechanism within this theoretical debate.

In general terms, accommodationists promote dual or multiple public identities and advocate equality with institutional respect for difference (Choudhry, 2008b: 27). They assume that ethnic identities in segmented societies are resilient and not susceptible to short-term transformation; however, they do not necessarily believe identities are primordial and fixed (McGarry *et al.*, 2008: 52). Accommodationists seek to ensure that each ethnic group has the public space necessary to express its identity, make its own decisions in areas of critical importance, and to protect itself against the majority (McGarry *et al.*, 2008: 42). The result is the design of public policy that permits the institutional expression of differences in the public sphere, such as minority language rights, and the use of consociational power-sharing techniques advocated by Arend Lijphart (1975, 2008) and others (for example, Reilly, 2001; McGarry, 2008).

Integrationists, by contrast, believe political instability and even further conflict are a consequence of group-based partisanship in political institutions, since they empower elites that have a vested interest in maintaining these social divisions. They reject the idea that ethnic difference should necessarily translate into political differences and instead argue for the possibility of a common (civic) public identity (Choudhry, 2008b: 27). Accordingly, integrationists support constitutional strategies that promote a common public identity which transcends, crosscuts, and minimizes ethnic cleavages, without (importantly) demanding ethno-cultural uniformity in the private sphere. Examples of such strategies include common state institutions, 'ethnically blind' public policies, the promotion of individual rather than communal rights, the design of mixed or nonethnic territorial entities, and electoral systems that encourage the formation of pre-election coalitions across ethnic divides. Table 8.1 positions the various claims concerning decentralization's performance as a conflict-mitigating mechanism within this ongoing theoretical debate.

Table 8.1: Decentralization and how states deal with ethnic difference

	Accommodation of ethnic difference	Integration of ethnic difference
Decentralization as a tool for mitigating ethnopolitical conflict	Seeks to address (limited) self-determination claims	Maintains the territorial integrity of the state
	Minority control over political, social, economic affairs	Creates proliferating points of power
	Promotes minority rights and multiple identities	Facilitates inter- and trans-ethnic alliances locally
	Balances the power of the majority	Provides a training ground for local politicians to engage in ethnic bargaining
Decentralization as a conflict enhancer	Does not satisfy demands for autonomy or secession	Sets a dangerous precedent: groups want more
	Provides insufficient protection from the majority	Equips minorities with necessary resources to secede
	Relocates conflict to local level, rather than solving it	Maintains and / or reinforces social divisions
		Citizens lack a sense of unity

Decentralization in the Republic of Macedonia: An Integrationist Approach to Diversity Management with Accommodationist Tendencies

In its Basic Principles, the Framework Agreement declared: 'The development of local self-government is essential for encouraging the participation of citizens in democratic life, and for promoting respect for the identity of communities' (*Official Gazette of the Republic of Macedonia*, 2001b, Art. 1.5). Certainly, the Framework Agreement called for the transfer of 11 new municipal competences;[5] 'a cure against federalisation', remarked one ethnic Albanian politician at the time (*Official Gazette of the Republic of Macedonia,* 2001b; Project on Ethnic Relations, 2003: 11). However, despite common perceptions suggesting the contrary, Florian Bieber (2005: 116) noted how decentralization was framed to conform to European standards, especially the principle of subsidiarity, rather than facilitating fully fledged self-government for the ethnic Albanian community. Ermira Mehmeti (2008: 73), then spokeswoman for the ethnic Albanian party Democratic Union for Integration, remarked how Lijphart's models of nonterritorial corporate autonomy and segmental autonomy along ethnic lines were abandoned during the negotiations in Ohrid because of the government's intention to preserve the unitary character of the state. Given the Macedonian government's substantial and persistent fear of decentralizing power to subnational levels, it is worth examining precisely what impact Macedonia's decentralization process has had on the unitary nature of the state.

Macedonia's decentralization process does indeed represent extensive devolution of political, administrative, and fiscal responsibility to the municipalities, but it does not, as in federal states, constitute a division of central government authority. As the Framework Agreement clearly points out in its 'Basic Principles', 'Macedonia's

5 Those specifically referenced in the Framework Agreement were: areas of public services, urban and rural planning, environmental protection, local economic development, culture, local finances, primary and secondary education, social welfare, and healthcare.

sovereignty and territorial integrity, and the unitary character of the State are inviolable and must be preserved. There are no territorial solutions to ethnic issues' (*Official Gazette of the Republic of Macedonia*, 2001b: Art. 1.2). Municipalities in Macedonia remain ultimately subordinate to the authority of central government even though, significantly, their right to the devolved competences is constitutionally entrenched (*Official Gazette of the Republic of Macedonia*, 2001a: Art. 115). Some of these devolved competences, in addition, remain limited and are not held exclusively by the municipalities. The municipalities are also not directly represented at the central level; instead they participate in institutions of the common, unitary state in order to shape decisions that directly affect them. The only mechanism available to municipalities for influencing central government policy (apart from informal political party channels) is the municipal association 'ZELS', which, despite its energy and despite boasting full membership of all 84 municipalities plus the City of Skopje, is frequently marginalized by central government because of its nongovernmental organization status. If disputes do arise between an individual municipality and central government, no independent mechanisms of judicial review exist and the international community possesses no *formal*[6] mediation role (Weller and Wolff, 2005: 73).

The original design of the territorial reorganization itself, irrespective of the manner in which its implementation was carried out, illustrates the government's fear of promoting territorial disintegration and a desire to fragment the political influence of the ethnic Albanian community. Unlike examples of regional autonomy, the ethnic nature of Macedonia's municipalities is not explicitly recognized. Nonmajority communities cannot fully determine themselves as distinct population groups, but only as subgroups within their local municipality (Wolff, 2010: 24). Even forms of personal autonomy for specific territorially dispersed communities are conspicuously absent from the Framework Agreement and subsequent legislation (Daftary and Friedman, 2008: 287). In contrast with neighbouring Kosovo, Macedonian municipalities comprising a significant

6 Italics are my own.

minority ethnic community do not enjoy any special asymmetrical status (United Nations Security Council, 2007: Annex 3, Art. 4). All 84 Macedonian municipalities have been granted identical competences, regardless of local demographics. Whilst nonmajority communities comprising at least 20% in a particular municipality can use their community language in an official capacity locally, as the former Minister of Local Self-Government, Rizvan Sulejmani (2008: 144) points out, these community languages are not in autonomous official use, but must be used in addition to the Macedonian language. It is worth emphasizing that the recognition of community languages comes as a function of demographics, rather than as a symbolic recognition of their equal status with the state (Macedonian) language. Nowhere in the Framework Agreement is use of the Albanian language, for example, specifically mentioned.

The absence of any regional tier of government, in addition to the sizable number of municipalities which survived the territorial reorganization (contrary to expert advice), also illustrates how anxiety over devolving power to territorially concentrated ethnic groups influenced the particular design of Macedonia's decentralization process. Given the territorial concentration of ethnic Albanians in the north and west of the country, it is of no surprise that the government adopted decentralization reforms that would disperse limited and conditional authority to more than 80 nonethnically defined subunits. Ethnic Albanians currently comprise a majority in 16 municipalities and represent at least 20% of the local population in a further 12 (Statistical Office of the Republic of Macedonia, 2005). This would not have been the outcome had the government endorsed the creation of regional units or indeed an autonomous region. The fact that municipalities are allowed to cooperate and form joint institutions such as public enterprises, but are not allowed to merge with adjacent municipalities, further supports this view (*Official Gazette of the Republic of Macedonia,* 2002: Art. 14; Bieber, 2008: 34). Unlike in neighbouring Kosovo, municipalities located on the borders of kin states are also not allowed to receive financial assistance from them (United Nations Security Council, 2007: Annex 3, Art. 11).

With regard to minority protection mechanisms at the local level, the Framework Agreement replicates most of the consociational provisions foreseen at the state level. Of these provisions, greater use of national languages for nonmajority communities comprising at least 20% in a particular municipality has probably had most impact on the daily lives of citizens (*Official Gazette of the Republic of Macedonia,* 2001b: Art. 7). Previously, the threshold for official use of community languages in Macedonian municipalities had been 50%, although this was rarely respected and was indeed annulled by the Constitutional Court in 1994 (*Official Gazette of the Republic of Macedonia,* 1995: Art. 88; Caca 1980: 96; 2001: 152). With regard to languages spoken by less than 20% of the population within a municipality, the Agreement also allows the possibility for their use as an official language, but the decision to do so remains at the discretion of the local authority (*Official Gazette of the Republic of Macedonia,* 2001b: Art. 6.6).

The consociational principle of nondiscrimination and equitable representation within municipal administrations, council, and committees is another crucial element of minority protection contained in the Framework Agreement[7] (*Official Gazette of the Republic of Macedonia,* 2001b: Art. 4). Although the equitable representation of Macedonia's communities had long been declared a state goal, and was indeed enshrined in the 1974 Constitution of the Social Republic of Macedonia,[8] in 2001 the reality was very different. However, the Framework Agreement does not call for strict ethnic quotas in Macedonia's public administration; state institutions are not obliged by law to employ a certain percentage of a particular ethnic group. This is in contrast to other consociation-inspired political settlements, such as Bosnia's Dayton Agreement (Office of the Higher Representative and EU Special Representative, 1995). Special voting procedures, sometimes referred to as 'double-majority' or 'Badinter-majority'[9] voting, are also envisaged to ensure greater consensus in decision making within municipal councils. They operate along similar lines to Arend Lijphart's concept of minority veto; however, they differ in that the right to use them is not given to one particular community. Instead, certain constitutional amendments and legislation

7 See also Article 8.1 of the amended Constitution (Official Gazette, 2001a).

8 Chapter 11 of the 1974 Constitution of the Socialist Republic of Macedonia, titled 'Equality of Nationalities', stated: 'Municipalities and the Republic ensure that nationalities be proportionately represented in the municipal assemblies ... and be adequately represented in their bodies' (Caca, 2001).

9 Named after the French judge Robert Badinter.

'cannot be approved without a qualified majority of two-thirds of votes, within which there must be a majority of the votes from those claiming to belong to non-majority communities' (Official Gazette of the Republic of Macedonia, 2001b: Art. 5).[10] Joseph Marko (2004/5: 709) has commented that this procedure represents a much weaker mechanism than comparable provisions on veto powers in the constitutions of other ex-Yugoslav republics as it does not constitute full veto power. One reason for this criticism is the fact that use of the special voting procedures is restricted to decision making in only specific areas.[11] Finally, the Framework Agreement re-established Committees for Inter-Community Relations in municipalities where at least 20% of the local population belongs to a certain nonmajority community. Municipalities may also establish committees in areas where local communities comprise less than 20%; however, this decision is at the discretion of the municipal council. Comparable with Lijphart's notion of arbitration mechanisms, the role of these committees is to enable institutional dialogue locally between the different ethnic communities on an equal basis and to settle disputes on issues affecting inter-community relations, for example, decisions requiring the use of special voting procedures. Table 8.2 positions specific features of Macedonia's decentralization process within the accommodationist/integrationist framework.

10 This principle is also enshrined in Article 69.2 of the amended Constitution (Official Gazette, 2001a).

11 Special voting procedures can be used when deciding on the follow areas: culture, use of languages, education, personal identification, use of symbols, and issues pertaining to local self-government (Official Gazette, 2001b, Art. 5.2).

Table 8.2: Accommodation and integration of ethnic difference through decentralization

Accommodation of ethnic difference	Integration of ethnic difference
'The multi-ethnic character of Macedonia's society must be preserved and reflected in public life' 'The development of local self-government is essential for … promoting respect for the identity of communities'[a]	'Macedonia's sovereignty and territorial integrity, and the unitary character of the State are inviolable and must be preserved.'[b]
Enhanced municipal competencies	Municipalities remain subordinate to central government authority
Increased language rights for non-majority communities	Relatively large number of municipalities (proliferating points of power) and no regional level of government
Consociational arrangements locally: - proportional elections to municipal councils / committees - equitable representation in municipal administration - Special voting procedures - Committees for Interethnic Relations	Symmetrical decentralization: municipalities comprising a significant community do not enjoy special status
	Competencies remain limited and are not exclusive
	Municipalities participate in institutions of the common state
	No formal recognition of the ethnic character of municipalities
	No explicit recognition of communities benefitting from language rights

a Official Gazette, 2001b: Art. 1.3, 1.5.
b Official Gazette, 2001b: Art. 1.2.

Decentralization in the Republic of Macedonia: Discrepancies in Implementation

Poor and inconsistent implementation of the consociational power-sharing arrangements envisaged locally has, however, affected the accommodation of nonmajority community needs, particularly those of the smaller ethnic communities.[12] Whilst greater municipal use of community languages has meant Albanian has now acquired official status in 29 of the 85 municipalities (including the City of Skopje), the Turkish language has only become a working language in four, Serbian in one, and Romani also in one. Albanian is also in use in a further 17 municipalities where the community constitutes less than 20% locally, Turkish in another four, and the Vlach language in one (Organization for Security and Co-operation in Europe, 2009: 55). The Albanian language has therefore been recognized (formally if not in practice) in over half of Macedonia's municipalities, whilst community languages other than Albanian are in official use in only 10. This reality prompted the European Commission to conclude in its 2009 progress report on Macedonia that 'little progress can be reported regarding use of the languages of the smaller ethnic communities' (European Commission, 2009: 20). The geographic dispersal of the Turkish, Roma, Serbian and Vlach communities throughout Macedonia means that in most municipalities they fall well below the 20% threshold required to benefit from community language rights. Realization of the enhanced use of community emblems also seems beset with problems.

Equitable representation of all communities within public administration and enterprises is another consociational technique foreseen at the municipal level. However, as with the realization of community language and emblem use locally, progress since 2001 on achieving proportionality in municipal administrations has been slow and inconsistent. The European Commission's progress reports

12 For example the Turks, Roma, Serbs, Bosniaks and Vlachs, which, according to the 2002 Census, constitute 3.85%, 2.66%, 1.78%, 0.84% and 0.48% of the national population respectively.

on Macedonia for 2009 and 2010 note how the representation of the smaller communities, particularly the Turkish and Roma, in the civil service remains low (European Commission, 2009: 21; 2010: 22). Limited use of other accommodative mechanisms, such as special voting procedures in municipal councils and the work of municipal Committees for Inter-Ethnic Relations, furthers the impression that not all the needs of Macedonia's ethnic communities are being accommodated equally. With regard to the use of special voting procedures, research compiled during 2006 suggests this practice is 'rarely respected on the local level' (Association for Democratic Initiatives, 2006; Institute for Regional and International Studies, 2006: 14). Fieldwork undertaken by the author in selected multiethnic municipalities in June 2010 found that the situation has not changed significantly since then. An increasing volume of research regarding the effectiveness of the Committees for Inter-Ethnic Relations established in over 30 multiethnic municipalities also raise doubts regarding the equitable accommodation of nonmajority community needs (Community Development Institute, 2007; Forum, 2008; Organization for Security and Co-operation in Europe, 2009; European Commission, 2010; United Nations Programme to Enhance Inter-Ethnic Dialogue and Collaboration, 2010: 5). In particular, the membership of these committees has been the focus of much criticism. Smaller communities, notably the Roma, are often not represented in their local committees and, where smaller communities are represented, they are frequently outnumbered by representatives of larger local communities, notably Macedonians and ethnic Albanians (ZELS, 2010).

Conclusion

This chapter has positioned Macedonia's experience with decentralization within the ongoing debate concerning how states deal with ethnic difference. After discussing the principal arguments concerning decentralization's performance as a conflict-mitigating mechanism, the chapter examined the specific design of Macedonia's decentralization process and located it within the debate between those who advocate integration as a strategy for managing cultural pluralism in multiethnic states and those who support a more accommodationist approach. Discrepancies between the *de jure* provisions and *de facto* implementation of Macedonia's decentralization reforms were also considered, along with their impact on the accommodation and/or integration of Macedonia's nonmajority communities.

Macedonia's experience with decentralization raises questions about whether focusing on the perceived dichotomy between integrationist and accommodationist approaches is the correct way to consider the various options available in the constitutional design of divided societies. Despite representing alternative strategies for managing ethnic diversity, the differing approaches to accommodating and integrating pluralism are not mutually exclusive and can be combined in different ways. This is no more apparent than in post-Ohrid Macedonia within the context of designing decentralization reforms. Whilst municipal decentralization in Macedonia, with its emphasis on preserving the unitary nature of the state, represents an integrationist approach to diversity management first and foremost, its combined use of consociational techniques within municipalities implies elements of accommodation. This is an important observation that should be considered in the design of future state building and power-sharing arrangements in multiethnic states.

However, the strength of the state's accommodationist approach to cultural diversity varies in its treatment of Macedonia's different ethnic communities. The decentralization reforms, in addition to the minority protection mechanisms envisaged locally, favour larger, territorially concentrated communities at the expense of those dispersed throughout the country. The reason for this is partly a result of distorted and inconsistent implementation of the law at the municipal level and partly because the Framework Agreement was never designed to offer equal cultural rights to all Macedonia's ethnic communities. The principal aim of the Framework Agreement in 2001 had been to accommodate the grievances of the ethnic Albanian community and, in doing so, to avert further conflict. It should come as no surprise, therefore, that almost ten years on, the Agreement is failing to offer equal protection for the cultural rights of all Macedonia's ethnic communities. The successful accommodation or integration of nonmajority communities, as McGarry (2008: 29) have observed, is therefore a product of demography. Accommodation may be necessary when groups exist 'powerful enough to resist assimilation but not strong or united enough to achieve secession'; whilst integration is more likely to succeed with respect to dispersed ethnic groups, such as Macedonia's smaller communities.

Implementation of Macedonia's decentralization reforms since 2004 has also diverged from the normative values envisaged in the Framework Agreement and subsequent legislation. This has altered the delicate balance decentralization was intended to represent between accommodationist and integrationist approaches to diversity management, and may have wider consequences for the equilibrium of the wider Framework Agreement.

References

Association for Democratic Initiatives (ADI) (2006) *Power Sharing – New Concept of Decision Making Process in Multicultural Municipalities*, ADI, Gostivar.

Bieber, F. (2004) *Institutionalizing Ethnicity in the Western Balkans Managing Change in Deeply Divided Societies*, European Centre for Minority Issues, Flensburg.

Bieber, F. (2005) Partial implementation, partial success: the case of Macedonia. In *New Challenges for Power-Sharing: Institutional and Social Reform in Divided Societies* (eds D. Russell and I. O'Flynn), Pluto, London, pp. 107–22.

Bieber, F. (2008) Power-sharing and the implementation of the Ohrid Framework Agreement. In *Power Sharing and the Implementation of the Ohrid Framework Agreement*, Friedrich Ebert Stiftung, Skopje, pp. 7–40.

Braathen, E. and Hellevik, S. (2008) Decentralization, peace making and conflict management: from regionalism to municipalism. *Journal of Peace, Conflict and Development* 12, http://www.peacestudiesjournal.org.uk/dl/Decentralisation%20Peace%20Making_%20Einar%20Braathen%20and%20Sirin%20Bjerkreim%20Hellevik.pdf.

Brancati, D. (2008) *Peace by Design: Managing Intrastate Conflict through Decentralization*, Oxford University Press, Oxford.

Bunce, V. and Watts, S. (2005) Managing diversity and sustaining democracy: ethnofederal versus unitary states in the postcommunist world. In *Sustainable Peace – Power and Democracy after Civil Wars* (eds. P. Roeder and D. Rothchild), Cornell University Press, Ithaca, NY, pp. 133–58.

Caca, G. (1980) *The Constitutional Development of the Socialist Republic of Macedonia*, Grafichki zavod Gotse Delchev, Skopje.

Caca, G. (2001) Status and rights of nationalities in the Republic of Macedonia. In *The New Macedonian Question* (ed. J. Pettifer), Palgrave, Basingstoke, pp. 148–66.
Choudhry, S. (ed.) (2008a) *Constitutional Design for Divided Societies: Integration or Accommodation?* Oxford University Press, Oxford.
Choudhry, S. (2008b) Bridging comparative politics and comparative constitutional laws: constitutional design in divided societies. In *Constitutional Design for Divided Societies: Integration or Accommodation?* (ed. S. Choudhry), Oxford University Press, Oxford, pp. 3–40.
Community Development Institute (2007) *Committees for Interethnic Relations: Establishment, Mandate and Existing Experiences,* CDI, Tetovo.
Crook, R.C. (2002) Decentralization and good governance. In *Federalism in a Changing World: Learning from Each Other* (ed. R. Blindenbacher), Mass Market, St. Gallen, pp. 3–40.
Daftary, F. and Friedman, E. (2008) Power-sharing in Macedonia? In *Settling Self-Determination Disputes: Complex Power-Sharing in Theory and Practice* (eds B. Metzger, M. Weller and N. Johnson), Brill, Leiden, pp. 265–306.
European Commission (2009) *The Former Yugoslav Republic of Macedonia 2009 Progress Report,* European Commission, Brussels.
European Commission (2010) *The Former Yugoslav Republic of Macedonia 2010 Progress Report,* European Commission, Brussels.
Forum – Center for Strategic Research and Documentation (2008) *Commissions for Inter-Ethnic Relations in Municipalities of Macedonia,* Forum CSRD, Skopje.
Grasa, R. and Camps, A. (2009) *Conflict Prevention and Decentralized Governance,* International Catalan Institute for Peace, Barcelona.
Hadden, T. (2005) Integration and autonomy: minority rights and political accommodation. In *Power Sharing: New Challenges for Divided Societies* (eds I. O'Flynn and D. Russell), Pluto Press, London, pp. 30–44.
Hannum, H. (2004) Territorial autonomy: permanent solution or step toward secession? In *Facing Ethnic Conflicts: Towards a New Realism* (eds A. Wimmer, R. Goldstone, D. Horowitz, U. Joras, C. Schetter), Rowman & Littlefield Inc., Lanham, pp. 274–82.
Horowitz, D. (2000) *Ethnic Groups in Conflict,* University of California Press, London.
Horowitz, D. (2007) The Many Uses of Federalism. *Drake Law Review.* Vol. 55. pp. 953 - 966.
Institute for Regional and International Studies (2006) *The Process of Decentralization in Macedonia: Prospects for Ethnic Conflict Mitigation, Enhanced Representation, Institutional Efficiency and Accountability,* IRIS, Skopje.
International Crisis Group (2003) *Macedonia: No Room for Complacency,* ICG, Skopje.
Kälin, W. (2004) Decentralized governance in fragmented societies: solution or cause of new evils? In *Facing Ethnic Conflicts: Towards a New Realism* (eds A. Wimmer, R. Goldstone, D. Horowitz, U. Joras, C. Schetter), Rowman & Littlefield Inc., Lanham, MD, pp. 301–11.
Lake, D. and Rothchild, D. (2005) Territorial decentralization and civil war settlements. In *Sustainable Peace – Power and Democracy after Civil Wars* (eds P. Roeder and D. Rothchild), Cornell University Press, Ithaca, NY, pp. 109–32.
Lapidoth, R. (2007) *Autonomy,* United States Institute of Peace, Washington, D.C.

Lijphart, A. (1975) *The Politics of Accommodation: Pluralism and Democracy in The Netherlands,* University of California Press, London.
Lijphart, A. (2008) *Thinking About Democracy: Power Sharing and Majority Rule in Theory and Practice,* Routledge, Abingdon.
Manor, J. (1999) *The Political Economy of Democratic Decentralization,* World Bank, Washington D.C.
Marko, J. (2004/5) *The Referendum on Decentralization in Macedonia in 2004: A Litmus Test for Macedonia's Interethnic Relations. European Yearbook for Minority Issues* 4. Martinus Nijhoff Publishers, Leiden.
McGarry, J. (2008) Power-sharing theory: lessons from the complex power-sharing project'. In *Settling Self-Determination Disputes: Complex Power-Sharing in Theory and Practice* (ed. B. Metzger, M. Weller and N. Johnson), Brill, Leiden, pp. 691–720.
McGarry, J., O'Leary, B., and Simeon, R. (2008) Integration of accommodation? The enduring debate in conflict regulation. In *Constitutional Design for Divided Societies: Integration or Accommodation?* (ed. S. Choudhry), Oxford University Press, Oxford, pp. 41–88.
Mehmeti, E. (2008) Implementation of the Ohrid framework agreement. In *Power Sharing and the Implementation of the Ohrid Framework Agreement,* Friedrich Ebert Stiftung, Skopje, pp. 67–88.
Office of the Higher Representative and EU Special Representative (1995) *The General Framework Agreement for Peace in Bosnia and Herzegovina,* OHR, Sarajevo.
Official Gazette of the Republic of Macedonia (1995) Law on Local Self-Government No. 52/1995, Government of the Republic of Macedonia, Skopje.
Official Gazette of the Republic of Macedonia (2001a) Constitution of the Republic of Macedonia. Government of the Republic of Macedonia, Skopje.
Official Gazette of the Republic of Macedonia (2001b) Framework Agreement, Government of the Republic of Macedonia, Skopje.
Official Gazette of the Republic of Macedonia (2002) Law on Local Self-Government No. 5/2002. Government of the Republic of Macedonia, Skopje.
Organization for Security and Co-operation in Europe Spillover Monitoring Mission to Skopje (OSCE) (2009) *Decentralization Survey,* OSCE, Skopje.
Pildes, R. (2008) Ethnic identity and democratic institutions: a dynamic perspective. In *Constitutional Design for Divided Societies: Integration or Accommodation?* (ed. S. Choudhry), Oxford University Press, Oxford, pp. 173–201.
Project on Ethnic Relations (2003) *Macedonia's Interethnic Coalition: The First Six Months,* PER, Mavrovo.
Rebouche, R. and Fearton, K. (2005) Overlapping Identities: Power Sharing and Women's Rights. In: O'Flynn, I. and Russell, D. eds. *Power Sharing: New Challenges for Divided Societies,* Pluto Press, London. pp. 155–171.
Reilly, B. (2001) *Democracy in Divided Societies: Electoral Engineering for Conflict Management (Theories of Institutional Design),* Cambridge University Press, Cambridge.
Roeder, P. (2005) Power dividing as an alternative to ethnic power sharing. In *Sustainable Peace – Power and Democracy after Civil Wars* (eds P. Roeder and D. Rothchild), Cornell University Press, Ithaca, pp. 51–82.

Roeder, P. and Rothchild, D. (eds) (2005) *Sustainable Peace – Power and Democracy after Civil Wars*, Cornell University Press, Ithaca, NY.

Rothchild, D. and Hartzell, C. (2000) Security in deeply divided societies: the role of territorial autonomy. In *Identity and Territorial Autonomy in Plural Societies* (eds W. Safran and R. Maiz), Frank Cass Publishers, London, pp. 254–71.

Schou, A. and Haug, M. (2005) *Decentralization in Conflict and Post-Conflict Situations*, Norwegian Institute for Urban and Regional Research, Oslo.

Scott, Z. (2009) *Decentralization, Local Development and Social Cohesion: An Analytical Review*, Governance and Social Development Resource Centre, Birmingham.

Siegle, J. and O'Mahoney, P. (2007) *Assessing the Merits of Decentralization as a Conflict Mitigation Strategy*, Development Alternatives, Bethesda, MD.

Statistical Office of the Republic of Macedonia (2005) *Census of Population, Households and Dwellings in the Republic of Macedonia, 2002*, Government of the Republic of Macedonia, Skopje.

Sulejmani, R. (2008) Consensus democracy and power-sharing in Macedonia. In *Power Sharing and the Implementation of the Ohrid Framework Agreement*, Friedrich Ebert Stiftung, Skopje, pp. 131–64.

Treisman, D. (2007) *The Architecture of Government: Rethinking Political Decentralization*, Cambridge University Press, New York, NY.

United Nations Programme to Enhance Inter-Ethnic Dialogue and Collaboration (2010) *Results of a Participatory Assessment National and Local Capacities for Strengthening Inter-Ethnic Dialogue and Collaboration*, United Nations, Skopje.

United Nations Security Council (UNSC) (2007) *Comprehensive Proposal for the Kosovo Status Settlement*, United Nations, New York, NY.

Weller, M. and Wolff, S. (2005) *Autonomy, Self-governance and Conflict Resolution: Innovative Approaches to Institutional Design in Divided Societies*, Routledge, Abingdon.

Wolff, S. (2010) *Approaches to Conflict Resolution in Divided Societies: The Many Uses of Territorial Self-Governance. Ethnopolitics Papers 5*, http://centres.exeter.ac.uk/exceps/downloads/Ethnopolitics_Papers_No5_Wolff.pdf (accessed 19 October 2012).

Young, C. (1998) *Ethnic Diversity and Public Policy*, St. Martin's Press, New York.

ZELS (Association of the Units of Local Self-Governance of the Republic of Macedonia) (2010) Membership Data for Municipal Committees for Inter-Ethnic Relations, Skopje. Unpublished.

Simonida Kacarska

The Framework Convention for Protection of National Minorities in the EU Accession Process – the Case of the Republic of Macedonia[1]

Introduction

As a candidate country for EU membership, the Republic of Macedonia is subject to conditionality related to minority policies, primarily through the Copenhagen criteria for accession.[2] According to the first Copenhagen criterion, in order to join the EU a new member state must ensure the stability of institutions guaranteeing democracy, the rule of law, human rights and respect for and protection of minorities.[3] Conditionality in relation to the protection of minorities was an important element of the enlargement round that was completed in 2007 with the accession of Bulgaria and Romania to the EU. In the absence of *acquis* related to minority policies, research has shown that, in the case of the Eastern enlargement, conditionality in this policy area was focused on the adoption of nondiscrimination directives, governmental strategies and programmes for the inclusion of the Roma minority and the ratification of the Council

1 This chapter is a part of a PhD project I am undertaking in the School of Politics and International Studies at the University of Leeds. An earlier version of the chapter was presented at the RRPP Conference in May 2011.

2 The author recognizes the influence of other international organisations, such as the United Nations, Council of Europe and the Organization for Security and Co-operation in Europe, on minority policies in the region. However, she is primarily interested in examining the role of the EU in the preaccession period.

3 With the Ohrid Framework and the constitutional changes that followed in Macedonia, the term minority was replaced with 'nonmajority communities'. For uniformity of terminology, and due to the term minority being used in the Copenhagen criteria, the chapter will use the term minority.

of Europe Framework Convention on National Minorities (FCNM) (Rechel, 2008).

This chapter extends the research on minority policies in the EU accession process to the Western Balkans and focuses specifically on the use of the FCNM as a benchmarking tool of EU conditionality in the case of Macedonia. The theoretical and methodological approach of this study largely follows the work of Hughes, Sasse and Gordon on the Eastern enlargement (Hughes *et al.*, 2005; Sasse, 2005). Hughes *et al.* argue for the need to study conditionality as a process taking into consideration its formal and informal features, as well as the significance of domestic actors through the use of process tracing as a method. Focusing on the FCNM is necessary because this Convention 'by virtue of its binding character is considered as a breakthrough in minority protection' (Liebich, 2002). As a result of its importance, studies on EU enlargement have stressed the need for a shift 'towards a somewhat more formal incorporation of the Council of Europe monitoring system within the EU pre-accession' (Kochenov, 2006: 341). On the basis of its findings, the chapter argues that conditionality in relation to minorities still suffers from inconsistencies and that the FCNM is not being systematically used by the European Commission (EC) in the enlargement process for the purpose of benchmarking in the political criteria.

The case of Macedonia is instructive for this analysis due to the widely recognized role of the external actors, especially the EU, in the management of its interethnic relations and the devising of minority policies in this country. Macedonia was the first country in the Western Balkans to sign the Stabilization and Association Agreement (SAA) with the EU and the second country (after Croatia) to obtain a candidate status for EU membership. It has been a signatory of the FCNM since 1996 and has already been through three reporting cycles of the Convention. Moreover, the EU has been an active player in fostering the Ohrid Framework Agreement (OFA) in the country and has had significant influence upon power sharing and minority protection (For more on the 2001 conflict and the Agreement, see Engstrom, 2002; Reka, 2008; Hafner-Ademi and Nesik, 2011). Macedonia has been hailed as a success of EU conditionality and as a case of best practice demonstrating successful cooperation between the EU and different international actors in the Balkans. Assessing the role of the Stabilization and Association Process (SAP), Gordon points out that 'the satisfactory resolution of inter-state relations and intra-state majority-minority must lie at the heart of any long-term political stabilization of the [Balkan] region' (Gordon, 2009: 336). As a result, Macedonia can be seen as a critical case for the study of conditionality as well as the consistency of its application among the current candidate countries for EU accession.

This chapter uses qualitative methods: document analysis and open-ended interviews. It is primarily based on EU and national documents prepared for the process of Macedonia's European integration. From the perspective of the EU, it examines the annual reports on the SAP in the period 2001–2004, the progress reports issued from the EC on Macedonia since 2005 and the Accession/European partnerships. While recognizing the use of EU political conditionality in the Western Balkans since 1997 and the Regional Approach, the chapter considers the SAA as a turning point for the EU-Western Balkans relationship, which triggered the preparation of EU and national documents for the purposes of the EU accession. These documents contain the EC assessment on the political criteria and the recommendations that the EU puts forward to the candidate and potential candidate countries concerning the work of the parliament, government, judiciary, anticorruption policy, protection of human rights and minorities and regional cooperation. On the national side, the chapter looks into the yearly National Plans for the Adoption of the *Acquis* (NPAA) and the Contribution to the Progress Reports from the national authorities. In addition, data from open-ended interviews in Brussels and Skopje with EU and national officials, as well as civil society organizations and think tanks conducted in late 2010 and early 2011 have been used.

The research employs process tracing – it examines the development of conditionality and the national response over time. Since the national strategic documents and reports follow the publication of the EC documents, the accession process is suitable for process-tracing analysis. Hence, the data collected through archive and field work are examined at two levels. First, the chapter examines the use of the FCNM through the formal EC and national documents. Second, the study links these findings with interview data in order to trace the use of the FCNM as a benchmark in relation to minority policies.

The chapter is organized in two major sections. The first section provides a background to minority policies as an element of political conditionality in the context of EU accession. It reflects upon the disputed meaning of both these terms and explains how they are used in this research. In addition to elaborating the terms used, this first section presents the rational choice and process-based approach for the study of EU conditionality and their suitability for the study of minority policies as a non-*acquis* policy area. Arguing in support of the latter approach for the study of minority polices, this section also sets the framework for the analysis. The empirical analysis is presented in the second part of the chapter and studies the use of the FCNM as a benchmarking tool in the minority protection conditionality since the signing of the SAA in 2001.

Minority Policies and EU Political Conditionality

Despite their use in the literature, agreed definitions of minority policies and conditionality are missing, both within literature and in practice. The meaning of the term 'respect for and protection of minorities' as used in the EU accession context is still subject to debates. Research on the Eastern enlargement has demonstrated that there is no common understanding of minority protection in the EU. From a legal perspective, De Witte concludes that the meaning of the term respect for and protection of minorities as included in the Copenhagen criteria has not been developed in EU law (De Witte, 2002). Kochenov emphasizes that 'a definition of "minority" is nowhere to be found in the Copenhagen-related documents, leaving it to the candidate countries to determine whom the Commission was asking them to respect and protect' (Kochenov, 2008: 30). In essence, the literature considers minority protection as a soft norm, which is under development and is mostly relevant in the EU's external relations (Schimmelfennig, 2002). Sasse, in her work on the previous enlargement, argues that minority protection as enshrined in the Copenhagen criterion, lacks foundation in EU law – it is a social and political construct (Sasse, 2008: 30). The lack of a common standard of minority rights on the one hand, and their inclusion in the EU accession policy, on the other, carry important implications for the analysis of minority rights. As demonstrated by research in this area, these factors make the assessment of the impact of policies increasingly context-specific and dependent on the EC's inclusion or noninclusion of certain aspects of minority policies in the EU accession process (Swimelar, 2008; Rechel, 2009a; Schwellnus *et al.*, 2009).

Similarly as is the case with minority policies, 'conditionality' has also been subject to numerous redefinitions. Political conditionality in its widest terms is a policy instrument that involves 'the linking of development aid to demands concerning human rights and (liberal) democracy in recipient countries' (Sørensen, 1993: 2). This wide notion of political conditionality is most commonly used in relation to development studies and, although it shares some similarities with EU political conditionality, there is a substantial difference between the two. The main instrument used in the former is the threat of the reduction or ending of development assistance funds. In turn, the main instrument used in EU political conditionality is the carrot of EU membership, while the main threat is exclusion (Uvin, 1993: 67–8). In light of this difference, Smith defines political conditionality as a mechanism that entails the linking of perceived benefits of membership in the organization to the fulfilment of conditions relating to the protection of human rights and the advancement of democratic principles (Smith, 2001: 37). When dealing with EU conditionality, the chapter will use this latter definition and focus on the literature linked with the EU accession process, rather than general conditionality literature.

The dominant approach for the study of political conditionality in the enlargement literature has been rational institutionalism. Schimmelfennig and Sedelmeier have developed three models for the examination of the effectiveness of conditionality – the external incentives model, the social learning model and the lesson drawing model – which were applied in democratic and *acquis* conditionality. In their research, conditionality is understood as a bargaining strategy of reinforcement by reward, under which the EU provides external incentives for a target government to comply with its conditions (Schimmelfennig and Sedelmeier, 2004). The conclusions of their research indicate that rule transfer from the EU to the Central and Eastern European (CEE) and the variation in its effectiveness are best explained according to the external incentives model and are linked to the high credibility of EU conditionality and the low domestic costs of rule adoption. Furthermore, these authors have shown that the effectiveness of EU conditionality depends on the initial conditions – EU influence was less effective with respect to democratic conditionality but was pervasive in terms of *acquis* conditionality (Schimmelfennig and Sedelmeier, 2005: 210). Bearing in mind that the credibility of political conditionality with respect to minority policies is quite low because of its contested nature and high domestic costs, the chances for success of the external incentives model are low. In light of these bleak predictions for success, Sasse has argued that the link between low domestic adoption costs and effective conditionality undermines the very notion of conditionality (Sasse, 2009).

Although a leading analytical tool for the study of the effectiveness of EU conditionality, the external incentives model faces difficulties in the accommodation of minority policies. First, core preconditions for the success of the external incentives model are the clarity of, and consensus on, the rules, which, as was already explained, is not the case with minority policies. Brusis thus concludes that EU policies are likely to have a more tangible direct impact on issues where the EU has a more prescriptive *acquis* (Brusis, 2005: 316). Moreover, the external incentives model has been under criticism because of the risk to overestimate the effects of the EU conditionality. Bearing in mind that the processes of Europeanization occurred at the same time as the democratic transformation of these societies, the separation of the developments linked to each of them is increasingly difficult. As a result, demonstrating causal links between the impact of the externally induced conditions and domestic policy choice have been increasingly difficult. Analysing the use of EU conditionality in the regionalization in the Czech Republic and Slovakia, Brusis argues that 'domestic factors were of key importance for the trajectories and outcomes of regionalization' (Brusis, 2005: 295). The external incentives model, according to him 'does not allow the interference that the domestic change is driven by EU incentives because the Union applies conditionality or because domestic actors justify their decision as driven by EU conditionality' (Brusis, 2005: 297).

In response, empirical studies of conditionality have pointed to its flexible nature and have proposed process-based definitions attempting to incorporate the variety of actors and influences in its application. Hughes *et al.* have argued that conditionality is better explained as a multiplicity of actors, perceptions, rewards and sanctions, including both its formal and informal features (Hughes *et al.*, 2005). Hence, these authors distinguish between formal conditionality, which embodies the publicly stated preconditions as set out in the broad principles of the Copenhagen criteria, and informal conditionality, which includes the operational pressures and recommendations applied by actors within the Commission to achieve particular outcomes (Hughes *et al.*, 2005: 26). This definition, according to Sasse highlights the pitfalls of linear causality models and the need to take seriously the inherent politicization of conditionality over time (Sasse, 2009: 19). Sasse argues that political criteria are a construct, thereby recognizing that any notion of compliance is a construct and a political judgement (Sasse, 2009: 20). This definition and approach provide for the possibility of examining the process of construction, application of conditionality and its outcome, thereby taking into consideration the changes of conditionality over time.

Generally, research on the previous enlargement is largely inconclusive on the role EU conditionality played in relation to the development of minority policies in candidate countries. On the one hand, studies guided by rational choice institutionalism do not see much space for the impact of the EU in this policy area because of the high domestic costs and the lack of consistency of this norm (Schimmelfennig and Sedelmeier, 2005). These studies have nevertheless been criticized due to the presupposed determinacy of the EU rules by research emphasizing the formal and informal nature of conditionality. Empirical studies belonging to this latter strand of literature have argued that in the thin areas of the *acquis* formal conditionality is reduced, which strengthens informal conditionality, providing the Commission with greater scope for ambiguity in its policy recommendations (Hughes *et al.*, 2004: 527). For example,

Hughes *et al.* disapprove of the tendency of enlargement literature to 'mythologize the positive relationship between conditionality and enlargement' calling for more empirically based studies of the application of conditionality (Hughes *et al.*, 2005). Similarly, in an edited volume on minority policies in the enlargement process, Rechel concludes that 'there might not be a clear cut and consistent trend towards improved systems of minority protection, as much depended on the point of departure at the end of communism, the ethnic make-up of the country, historical legacies, and whether the country experienced territorial changes or not' (Rechel, 2009b: 227). Overall, empirical research emphasizes that it is difficult to make generalizations about the EU's role because of the significance of domestic factors and the need to examine conditionality in light of its interaction at the domestic level.

As a result, it has been argued that a consensus on the norms and rules and their transmission should be at the centre of a meaningful definition of conditionality (Sasse, 2005). In light of these debates, the EU has been using standards on minority protection developed by the OSCE High Commissioner on National Minorities (OSCE HCNM) and the Council of Europe (CoE). Not surprisingly, the FCNM ratification was a point of reference in Eastern enlargement and was used by the EC to assess the progress of the acceding countries. Similarly, it has been argued in the literature that 'the system of standards employed by the CoE during its monitoring is much better articulated than that of the EU' (Kochenov, 2006: 341). Without taking a normative stance on the issue of minority conditionality and using analytical tools developed for the Eastern enlargement, this chapter examines whether, in the case of Macedonia, the EU has been systematically using the FCNM as a benchmark in order to address some of the aforementioned criticisms of conditionality in this area. In light of the elaborated problems in the study of conditionality, the intention of this chapter is to examine the evolution and development of EU conditionality in the specific area of minority policies rather than to focus on its outcome and effectiveness. Thus, the following section will examine empirically whether and how the FCNM has been used by the EU and national authorities in the EU accession process in Macedonia.

FCNM as a Reference Point for Minority Protection – the case of Macedonia

Building upon the discussion of the dilemmas surrounding the study of minority policies and conditionality, this section examines the use of the FCNM as an element of EU political conditionality in Macedonia in two consecutive periods. In the first period between 2001 and 2004 the country was subject to monitoring solely in relation to its SAA obligations. In the post-2005 period, after it was granted the status of a candidate country for membership, it was included in the regular enlargement mechanisms. The need to distinguish between these two periods results primarily from the different mechanisms the EU employs. Whereas in the former period the EC monitored the situation through the SAA yearly reports, in the post-2005 period these were replaced period with more detailed annual progress reports and the European/Accession Partnerships studied below.

SAA period 2001–2004

European Union conditionality between 2001 and 2004 was based solely on the SAA as the main document determining the relations between the EU and Macedonia. Specifically in relation to minority rights, Gordon *et al.* have emphasized that 'although the original Communication from the Commission on the Stabilisation and Association process for the countries of South-Eastern Europe acknowledged the importance of human and minority rights … there was no further mention of this dimension in its early exposition of the six main elements of the SAP let alone in the country specific conclusions' (Gordon *et al.*, 2008: 13). Thus, the SAA only requires respect of minority rights in principle and does not stipulate any specific obligations.

At the national level, the main strategic document that outlines the activities for the government was the Action Plan for implementation of the SAA and the matrix for monitoring its implementation (Government of the Republic of Macedonia, 2001). Structured according to the SAA, this document, while recognizing the need for respect of minority rights in principle, does not contain any specific activities in relation to minority protection, nor does it make a specific reference to the FCNM. In Chapter VII, which refers to Justice and Home Affairs, the following activity is included: '[u]pgrading of domestic legislation in the function of reinforcement of institutions and rule of law ... including continuous active implementation of ratified international documents, as well as acceding and/or ratification of EU, Council of Europe and UN conventions' (Government of the Republic of Macedonia, 2001). Overall, in this main strategic document there are no specific obligations in relation to minorities, or references to the FCNM as a benchmark.

Since 2002, the EC began publishing, on an annual basis, reports on the progress of all the countries included in the SAA process. These reports are not as detailed as the regular progress reports, which the EC started preparing from 2005, but contain references to all the elements of the political criteria, including minority protection. Hence, an examination of the references to the FCNM in the three SAA reports between 2002–2004 illustrates whether the EC has used this Convention as a benchmark in this early period.[4] In the first SAA report of 2002, the EC considers that 'despite formal protection of minority rights under ... the "Framework Convention for the Protection of National Minorities" in 1997, the enforcement of minority rights is a major problem in the country, greatly contributing to the current inter-ethnic crisis' (Commission of the European Communities, 2002). This assessment is to be expected especially having in mind that in the previous year the country was torn by an interethnic conflict. (For an overview of the 2001 conflict and the Ohrid Framework Agreement see Engstrom, 2002; Reka, 2008; Hafner-Ademi and Nesik, 2011.) Nevertheless, the EC does not make any use of the FCNM or its reports. Moreover, in this first report, the EC does not recommend direct measures that need to be undertaken for the advancement of the minority policies.

4 In this same period, the EC dealt with the FCNM ratification as part of the conditionality for the candidate countries at the time.

The reports in the two following years also do not contain any specific references to obligations from the FCNM or its implementation, but only general assessments of the interethnic situation. In the 2003 SAA Progress Report the EC recognizes that 'interethnic relations have undeniably improved since the crisis' and recommends that 'further measures to build confidence and promote dialogue between communities will be vital to support the on-going political process and reinforce the de facto cooperation which often, at local level, allows daily public affairs to be conducted' (Commission of the European Communities, 2003). In the first years after the signing of the OFA it is not surprising that most of the energy at the state level was channelled towards adopting the legislative reforms required for this purpose. My interviewees similarly underlined that, in the case of Macedonia in this period, minority policies were linked to the implementation of the OFA (author's interview with senior civil servant in the Mission of the Republic of Macedonia to the EU, Brussels, November 2010). Besides the focus on the OFA, in this period the EC did not use references to international or European standards, although this was the case later.

The first strategic document that outlines the activities specifically directed towards the fulfilment of EU conditions at the national level was prepared in June 2003 in response to the 2003 SAA Report (Government of the Republic of Macedonia, 2003a). In relation to minority policies, this Action Plan sets out detailed activities for the implementation of the OFA in relation to reconstruction of housing and so forth. From this plan it is evident that the advancement of minority protection was primarily understood in terms of the adoption of the legislative projects related to the OFA without reference to the FCNM. In November 2003, six months after the preparation of the Action Plan mentioned above, a report on its realization was prepared, which puts forward detailed information on the legislative activities undertaken and progress on equitable representation (Government of the Republic of Macedonia 2003b). In this document, the FCNM is mentioned for the first time at the national level in relation to the submission of the first report of the country on the implementation of this convention – however, not in terms of substantive policy advancement. Similarly, in the SAA Progress Report, in the following year, the EC started using the term 'European standards' and made sporadic references to FCNM in relation to minority rights (For more on European standards see Kymlicka, 2006). For example, in 2004 the EC underlines the need for 'efforts to be made to fully apply European standards, such as the implementation of the FCNM of the Council of Europe, [which] would help to build further confidence and sense of loyalty to the State' (Commission of the European Communities, 2004). However, beyond this largely declarative and broad recommendation there was no further use of this instrument by the EC. Similarly, the national strategic documents do not use the FCNM as a reference point with the exception of mentioning the report submitted to the reporting bodies on the implementation of the FCNM, as already explained (See Government of the Republic of Macedonia, 2003b).

In a nutshell, between 2001 and 2004 there are no specific formal conditions and benchmarks attached to the FCNM identifiable in the EU documents. Both the EC and the national staff working on these issues mentioned that especially in this period, the EC was not using the FCNM as benchmarking tool (author's interview with senior European Commission official in Brussels, October 2010; author's interview with senior civil servant in the Ministry of Justice in Skopje, February 2011). National staff drafting the reports for the FCNM, in particular, emphasized that these documents were prepared in a separate procedure and were not deemed as highly important for the EU accession process (author's interview with senior civil servant in the Ministry of Foreign Affairs in Skopje, March 2011). Hence, in the period studied, there was no systematic use of the FCNM as a benchmark in relation to minority conditionality, highlighting the imprecise nature of the conditions in this policy area.

Post-2005 Period – Macedonia as Candidate Country for EU Membership

The previous section examined the use of the FCNM as a benchmark in the EU accession process between 2001 and 2004. The analysis that follows examines the post-2005 period, when the EU introduced more detailed conditionality instruments. In December 2005, the EC granted the Republic of Macedonia the status of a candidate country and since then the country has been included in the regular enlargement mechanisms through the preparation of the annual progress reports and the European/Accession partnerships. These two documents provide important information as they are much more extensive than the SAA reports and they set short-term and medium-term priorities for the acceding countries both in the political and economic criteria, as well as the adoption of the *acquis*. Moreover, the EU documents provide the basis for the preparation of national strategic documents for European integration. Hence, following the publication of the Commission reports on an annual basis, the governments since 2006 have been preparing the NPAA as a strategic document that outlines the activities to be undertaken for the purposes of European integration. Therefore, due to the further 'formalization' of the process, it could be expected that in the post-2005 period the EU conditions would be more structured and consistent and would be met by follow-up at the national level.

Nevertheless, in this latter period too, it is difficult to see a structured application of conditionality and use of FCNM as a benchmarking tool in the EU and national documents or in the interviews conducted. In the post-2005 period, the EU documents on Macedonia do not make more specific use of the Convention for setting any benchmarks or conditions. The ratification of the FCNM by Macedonia is only noted in the 2005 analytical report as factual information without any further follow-up (Commission of the European Communities, 2005). A general reference to the FCNM is also found in the European Partnership of 2006, which puts forward the following short-term priority: 'promote respect for and protection of minorities in accordance with the ECHR and the principles laid out in the Council of Europe's FCNM, in line with best practice in EU member states' (Council of the European Union, 2006). The broad framing of this priority was strongly criticized by my interlocutors at the national level as vague and as very difficult to operationalize through the bureaucratic mechanisms of the enlargement process (author's interview with senior civil servant in the Mission of the Republic of Macedonia to the EU, Brussels, November 2010).

In response to these fleeting references to the FCNM in the EU documents, the first national document that refers to this issue is the 2006 NPAA, which emphasizes that: 'in addition to the obligations arising from this Convention, the basic framework for the minority protection policy in the Republic of Macedonia is the implementation of the Framework Agreement, which largely exceeds the standards laid down by the FCNM' (Government of the Republic of Macedonia, 2006). With this statement, as my interviewees confirmed, the national government questioned the usefulness of the FCNM as a reference point for minority protection due to the advanced national legislation (author's interview with senior civil servant in the Secretariat for European Affairs in Skopje, December 2010). This is also clearly demonstrated in the largely formal approach mentioning the submissions of the regular reports for the implementation of the FCNM in the EU accession documents, without specific use of the Convention or its reports.

The interview data in relation to the FCNM as a reference point or benchmarking for minority rights also provided contradictory opinions. On the one hand, both national and EU officials recognized the potential of the FCNM as a basis for benchmarking in relation to minority policies. In the words of my interlocutors, the FCNM was on the one hand considered as 'useful' and as an instrument used in the preparation of the progress reports (author's interview with senior European Commission official in Brussels, October 2010). Interviewees both from the national level and the EC pointed to the FCNM as a source of reference in this area but at the same time also expressed their doubts about its applicability since the national framework in Macedonia exceeds the requirements of the FCNM. At the EU level, the Commission officials interviewed had differing opinions on the role of the FCNM in the EU system. On the one hand, it was argued that 'while in the past the Council of Europe was clearly chef d'file, today maybe there will be more of complementarity, so there is information exchange' (author's interview with Commission official in Brussels, October 2010). Other EC officials considered the cycle of CoE reporting too long and drawn out, whereas the EC needs more continuous monitoring (author's interview with Commission Official in Brussels, December 2010). Quite contrary to this opinion, another Commission official stressed: 'I am not sure that the EU has much to offer Macedonia in this respect' (author's interview with senior EC official in Brussels, October 2010). It was clear from my contacts with the EC that there is no common stance on this point, which can largely explain the differences in the progress reports examined earlier. External actors engaged in this policy area, such as think tanks at the EU and national level, commented that this discrepancy is likely to go on until the EU develops specific rules in this area (author's interview with senior think-tank analyst in Brussels, October 2010). This specificity connected to the Macedonian context creates problems in the usage and ultimately usefulness of the FCNM as a tool for benchmarking for minority protection in the context of EU conditionality.

Overall, the analysis of the use of FCNM as a benchmarking tool for minority policies points to differing conclusions both in terms of the 'formal' story based on the official documents and the interview data. The EC fleetingly mentions the FCNM its reports and the European/Accession partnerships without any consistency and this is reflected both in the national documents and stakeholders' understandings. National documents have underlined that the domestic framework for minority protection is much more detailed than the FCNM, thereby minimizing its potential to be used as a benchmarking tool. The same inconsistent conclusions are to be drawn from the interviews both at the national level and European level in Brussels since the FCNM is seen as useful in principle, but without any operationalization in the accession process.

Conclusion

This chapter has examined whether and how the FCNM has been used in devising and applying EU conditionality in relation to minority policies in the case of Macedonia. The objective of the analysis was to trace whether, in the case of Macedonia, one can note a systematic use of the FCNM as a benchmarking tool for EU conditionality. The analysis was based on process tracing of official documents prepared by the EC and national authorities for the purposes of Macedonia's accession process. In addition, the author used data from interviews in Brussels and Skopje with EU and national officials, as well as civil society organizations and think tanks working in this area.

In order to set the context in which the study operates, the first section provided clarification on the terminology used and a background on the debates surrounding EU political conditionality and minority protection. Having in mind the difficulties in defining the term 'respect for and protection of minorities' as used in the EU accession process, the chapter applied a context-specific approach to this issue as defined through EU official documents. As for the study of conditionality, the chapter presented the rational choice approach and the alternative process-based approaches to conditionality. Although the rational incentive model is a dominant approach for the study of conditionality, due to its focus on the effectiveness and outcome of conditionality, this chapter looked into alternative understandings of conditionality. The latter process-based approach, due to its emphasis on the fleeting nature of conditionality and the need to study its changes over time, was considered suitable for the study of minority policies as a non-*acquis* policy area. In line with process-based approaches, this chapter traced and examined conditionality in relation to minority policies from its construction at the EU level to its application at the national level.

The empirical analysis dealt with two separate periods – the first between 2001 and 2004, which is referred as the SAA period, and the post-2005 period. The analysis of the former period of enforcing conditionality in the official EU and national documents as well as interviews with officials points to several divergent conclusions. First, the SAA as a document does not stipulate specific criteria or benchmarks on minority protection and this is reflected in the national action plan for the implementation of the SAA. Second, the three SAA progress reports between 2002 and 2004 provide general assessments without specific benchmarks for their implementation. In this period, both the EU and the national documents make only one formal reference to the FCNM without any evident move towards more detailed use of this instrument in the accession process.

The second part of the empirical section examined the post-2005 period when Macedonia became a candidate country for accession. The analysis of the use of the FCNM in the EU and national documents indicates that, as in the case of the Eastern enlargement, there were attempts by the EC to use the FCNM as a reference point for minority protection; however, they were never further developed. Moreover, the interviews at the national level highlighted that the FCNM reference did not make conditionality more specific. At the same time, both national and EU officials recognized the problem of using the FCNM as a reference in relation to Macedonia, as the legislative standards in the country are already quite advanced.

In conclusion, the study of the use of the FCNM in EU conditionality in the case of Macedonia presented in this chapter highlighted that the problem of imprecise EU conditionality in relation to minority policies identified in relation to the Eastern enlargement still persists. The analysis showed the sporadic and largely superficial use of the FCNM in the EU and national documents. The chapter also demonstrated that there is no specific importance attached to the Convention in the context of EU accession by the stakeholders, at the EU or at the national level. Given the lack of systematic use of the FCNM, this research further confirms the findings in the literature emphasizing the context-specific nature of the minority criterion in the EU accession process and the difficulty in devising benchmarks in relation to the political criteria for EU accession.

References

Brusis, M. (2005) The instrumental use of European Union conditionality: regionalization in the Czech Republic and Slovakia. *East European Politics and Societies* 19, pp. 291–316.

Commission of the European Communities. (2002) *Former Yugoslav Republic of Macedonia Stabilisation and Association Report.* Commission Staff Working Paper, Brussels.

Commission of the European Communities. (2003) *Former Yugoslav Republic of Macedonia Stabilisation and Association Report. Commission Staff Working Paper,* Commission Staff Working Paper, Brussels.

Commission of the European Communities. (2004) *Former Yugoslav Republic of Macedonia Stabilisation and Association Report.* Commission Staff Working Paper, Brussels.

Commission of the European Communities. (2005) *Analytical Report for the Opinion on the Application from the former Yugoslav Republic of Macedonia for EU Membership,* Commission Staff Working Paper, Brussels.

Council of the European Union. (2006) Council Decision of 30 January 2006 on the Principles, Priorities and Conditions Contained in the European Partnership with the Former Yugoslav Republic of Macedonia and Repealing Decision 2004/518/EC. Brussels.

De Witte, B. (2002) Politics vs law in the EU's approach to minorities. In: *Europe Unbound: Enlarging and Reshaping the Boundaries of the European Union* (ed. J. Zielonka), Routledge, London.

Engstrom, J. (2002) Multi-ethnicity or bi-nationalism – the framework agreement and the future of the Macedonian State. *Journal on Ethnopolitics and Minority Issues in Europe* 1.

Gordon, C. (2009) The stabilization and association process in the Western Balkans: an effective instrument of post-conflict management? *Ethnopolitics* 8, pp. 325–40.

Gordon, C., Sasse, G. and Sebastian, S. (2008) Specific Report on the EU Policies in the Stabilisation and Association Process. *Mirico Special Report Work Package,* European Academy, Bolzano.

Government of the Republic of Macedonia. (2001) *Action Plan for the Implementation of the Stabilization and Association Agreement between the European Communities and their Member States and the Republic of Macedonia,* Skopje.

Government of the Republic of Macedonia. (2003a) *Action Plan for the Implementation of the Recommendations from the Stabilization and Association Report of the European Commission for the Republic of Macedonia – 2003,* Skopje.

Government of the Republic of Macedonia, (2003b) *Mid-term Report on the Status of Progress of the Stabilisation and Association Process on the Priority Areas Identified in the 2003 EC SAP Report,* Skopje.

Government of the Republic of Macedonia. (2006) *Draft National Plan for the Adoption of Acquis,* Skopje.

Hafner-Ademi, T. and Nesik, I. (2011) Европската Унија и Охридскиот Рамковен Договор *[The European Union and the Ohrid Framework Agreement]*. Ohrid Framework Agreement Case Studies. Macedonian Centre for International Cooperation, Skopje.

Hughes, J., Sasse, G. and Gordon, C. (2004) Conditionality and compliance in the EU's eastward enlargement: regional policy and the reform of sub-national government. *Journal of Common Market Studies* 42, pp. 523–51.

Hughes, J., Sasse, G. and Gordon, C. (2005) *Europeanization and Regionalization in the EU's Enlargement: The Myth of Conditionality (One Europe or Several?)*, Palgrave MacMillan, Basingstoke.

Kochenov, D. (2006) An argument for closer cooperation between the European Union and the Council of Europe in the Field of EU Enlargement Regulation. In *Croatian Yearbook of European Law and Policy*, 2, pp. 311–341.

Kochenov, D. (2008) Summary of contradictions: an outline of the EU's main internal and external approaches to ethnic minority protection, Boston College International and Comparative Law Review 31, pp. 1–51.

Kymlicka, W. (2006) The evolving basis of European norms of minority rights. In: *European Integration and the Nationalities Question*. (eds J. McGarry and M. Keating) Oxford University Press, Oxford.

Liebich, A. (2002) Ethnic minorities and implications of EU enlargement. In: *Europe Unbound: Enlarging and Reshaping the Boundaries of the European Union* (ed. J. Zielonka), Routledge, London.

Rechel, B. (2008) What has Limited the EU's impact on minority rights in accession countries? *East European Politics and Societies* 22, pp. 171–91.

Rechel, B. (2009a) Introduction. In: *Minority Rights in Central and Eastern Europe* (ed. B.Rechel) Taylor & Francis, London.

Rechel, B. (2009b) The way forward. In: Rechel, B. (ed.) *Minority Rights in Central and Eastern Europe*, Taylor & Francis, London.

Reka, A. (2008) The Ohrid Agreement: the travails of inter-ethnic relations in Macedonia. *Human Rights Review* 9, pp. 55–69.

Sasse, G. (2005) EU Conditionality and Minority Rights: Translating the Copenhagen Criterion Into Policy. EUI-RSCAS Working Papers, www.eui.eu/RSCAS/WP-Texts/05_16.pdf (accessed 20 October 2010).

Sasse, G. (2008) The european neighbourhood policy: conditionality revisited for the EU's Eastern neighbours. *Europe-Asia Studies* 60, pp. 295–316.

Sasse, G. (2009) Tracing the construction and effects of EU conditionality. In: *Minority Rights in Central and Eastern Europe* (ed. B. Rechel), Taylor & Francis, London.

Schimmelfennig, F. (2002) Introduction: The impact of international organizations on the Central and Eastern European States–Conceptual and theoretical issues. In: *Norms and Nannies: The Impact of International Organizations on the Central and East European States* (ed. R. Linden), Rowman & Littlefield, Oxford.

Schimmelfennig, F. and Sedelmeier, U. (2004) Governance by conditionality: EU rule transfer to the candidate countries of Central and Eastern Europe. *Journal of European Public Policy*, 11, pp. 661–79.

Schimmelfennig, F. and Sedelmeier, U. (2005) Conclusions: the impact of the EU on the accession countries. In: *The Europeanization of Central and Eastern Europe*. (eds F. Schimmelfennig and U. Sedelmeier), Cornell University Press, Ithaca, NY.

Schwellnus, G., Balazs, L. and Mikalayeva, L. (2009) *It Ain't Over When It's Over–The Adoption and Sustainability of Minority Protection Rules in New EU Member States*, European Integration online papers, http://eiop.or.at/eiop/texte/2009-024a.htm (accessed 20 October 2012).

Smith, K.E. (2001) Western actors and the promotion of democracy. In: *Democratic Consolidation in Eastern Europe* (J. Zielonka and A. Pravda), Oxford University Press, Oxford.

Sørensen, G. (1993) Introduction. *The European Journal of Development Research* 5, pp. 1–5.

Swimelar, S. (2008) The making of minority rights norms in the context of EU enlargement: the Czech Republic and the Roma. *The International Journal of Human Rights* 12, pp. 505–27.

Uvin, P. (1993) 'Do as I say, not as I do': The limits of political conditionality. *The European Journal of Development Research* 5, pp. 63–84.

Part III

Youth in Transition in the Western Balkans

Vladimir Turjačanin and Danijela Majstorović

Construction of Ethnic and State Identity among Youth in Postwar Bosnia-Herzegovina

Bosnian and Herzegovinian 'Identifications' between Scylla and Charybdis

When discussing 'postwar Bosnia-Herzegovina' one can hardly escape descriptions such as 'divided society', 'impossible state' and 'international community's experiment'. In fact, those who tackle the problem of ethnic and the state or national identities in this country will find themselves facing the impossibility of untying the divisive ideological knots and moving towards a 'better future'. Our task within our primary research was to present, position, and describe the ethnic[1] and national identity of youth in Bosnia-Herzegovina (henceforth BiH). In an attempt to to interpret some general trends regarding these rather conflicting identities and to identify their inherent dynamism, we used an interdisciplinary approach and a multimethod analysis. This included a socio-psychological analysis supported by a quantitative, survey research in addition to a qualitative discourse-analytical approach supported by focus groups data.

The main focus of this chapter is to explore both the ethnic and state identities of the youth as the most important forms of social identity in today's BiH and also how they have been instrumentalized, expressed and performed among Bosnian youth. This was

1 The terms 'ethnicity' and 'nationality', especially with regards to research on the former Yugoslavia, are used as synonyms, although the term 'ethnonationality is also in use. To avoid confusion, in this chapter we differentiate between the terms 'ethnic', which refers to 'ethno-national', and 'national' as that refering to the state. The term 'ethnic' will be used with regards to particular identifications of Serbs, Bosniaks and Croats, whereas the term 'national' will be used when referring to state-related (BiH) identity.

done for a number of reasons. First, these youth were socialized in postwar society and they were not directly influenced by the values and dynamics of socialist Yugoslavia. Secondly, we thought that an insight into their current attitudes would be important for predictions about the future of social relations in the country. Thirdly, young people have been more open for communication and more available as a sample, which is relevant given the sensitivity of the social topics in question.

Although there is little systematic empirical data from the prewar period, it is clear that the 1992–1995 war plays a key role in present-day society in BiH. In 1992, BiH became an independent state for the first time in its modern history followed by the 1992–1995 war. The war ended with the Dayton Peace Agreement defining the country as a tri-nation state.[2] Today, BiH is composed of three territorially and politically distinct units: two entities (the Federation of BiH and the Republika Srpska) and the Brčko District. The Federation of BiH is composed of ten regions (cantons), the Republika Srpska is divided into municipalities, whereas the Brčko District consists solely of the city of Brčko. The ruling bodies are established at the cantonal, entity and state level, and each of these regions has its own administrative structures, which contributes to a system of authority that is rather complex, expensive and slow.

Before the war, BiH had a population of about 4.4 million. The largest percentage of the population consisted of the members of the three dominant peoples: Bosniaks (called Muslims at the time) – about 44%, Serbs – about 31% and Croats – about 17%. In addition to the dominant groups, there were Yugoslavs (about 6%) and 'others' (about 2%). A census has not been taken since 1991 for a number of political reasons,[3] so the current population size can only be estimated. According to data from the BiH Statistics Agency, BiH has a population of about 3.8 million.

The 1991 census data show strong feelings of ethnic identity (*nacionalnost*), which were further strengthened by Dayton. It is

2 The contemporary political system in BIH might be a basis for a new term: *tri-nation* state.

3 The 2013 population census in Bosnia-Herzegovina is planned to be organized between 1–15 April 2013.

clear that this is one of the crucial issues in BiH, not only from the standpoint of discourse and social practice, but also in the field of psychological construct analysis. In a situation where ethnic groups in a small territory differ slightly, the religious differences may become basic criteria for difference. According to Altermatt (1996) ethnicizing the society and politics leads to religious conflict and politicization of religion. If we look at historical data, it is clear that religion in BiH has always been a main marker of ethnicity (Bakić, 1994; Velikonja, 2003). The war was a catalyst that resulted in further segregation of ethnic groups in BiH. In our research we found religion along with language and political attitudes toward the state and entity to be the most salient features of ethnic attachment.

Even though religion was less prominent during the period of socialist rule, the overlap between the religious and ethnic identities in BiH has been the greatest of all ex-Yugoslav republics, as religion was a fine line separating the identities conflating the Croat/Catholic and Serb/Orthodox groups in BiH. Today, it is virtually impossible to find an Orthodox or Muslim Croat, or a Catholic or Muslim Serb; they have all homogenized on the basis of the dominant religious affiliation. This similarity did not always exist and, at the time of the 1948 Yugoslav census, citizens of Islamic faith could choose Muslim-Croat, Muslim-Serb, or, the most frequently selected, Muslim-undeclared ethnicity. Beginning in the late 1960s, the Yugoslav government recognized the Muslim Slavs of Bosnia-Herzegovina as a particular 'nation' and not merely as a religious group.

Another important trait when it comes to understanding ethnic identity among the people of BiH is that the dominant Serbo-Croatian – i.e., Croatian-Serbian – language in the Socialist Federal Republic of Yugoslavia (SFRY) has given rise to variations in language and dialect. Today, the language (or languages) of this region have come to represent one of the key features of ethnic identity. Although languages without nations are known to exist (Latin, Ancient Greek, Esperanto …) as well as nations without an official national language (the USA, Australia, Brazil, Argentina …), or nations sharing the same language (the English, Americans …), it seems that language is again being used for the purposes of mobilizing ethnic potential and accentuating differences among peoples.

In terms of structure, that is syntax and lexis, one and the same language is spoken in Croatia, Serbia, Montenegro and BiH. However, in the post-Dayton BiH, there are growing tendencies to separate these languages, at least by their names, followed by arguments about which should be used and why. Today these languages are called Serbian, Montenegrin, Croatian and Bosnian (also Bosniak), not just in BiH but in the whole region, which reflects a one-to-one correspondence between a language and a nation and naming your language a particular way is one of the key factors in performing ethnicity and mobilizing ethnic differences.

Why is it important to study ethnic identity in BiH today? It is not enough to say that these attachments are *made* and as such they can also be *unmade,* as this is easier said than done. The division of real political power in BiH today is based exclusively on ethnicity, which has resulted in ethno-politics as the only visible form of politics in today's BiH. It includes obligatory quotas and the political agency of three major nationalities as 'constitutive peoples', excluding others who are not 'constitutive', such as for example Roma or Jews. However, what on the surface may be read as ethno-politics is a manifestation of the wartime and postwar division of loot in Bosnia, in which ethno-nationalism walked arm-in-arm with neoliberalism securing, with an exception of a handful of ICTY indictees, an almost uninterrupted position of power and discourse proposed by the political and economic, ethnonationalist elites from the early 1990s onwards.

For ordinary people, and, especially, the youth, such a situation, fed by fear and mistrust, precludes the solidarity and common interest that would help them transcend these divisions and rebuild BiH society. Tolerance may not be enough as tolerance discourse alone further ethnicizes and divides people (Majstorović, 2011a) and the legacy of the socialist 'brotherhood and unity' may be beyond restoration for younger generations. One of the aims of this study, therefore, is to generate a better understanding of the society we live in, and to contribute to social science research in general by providing a fuller description of the situation in BiH, 20 years after the 1992–1995 war.

Ethnic Identities and Discourses between Social Constructionism and Performativity

In the literature on nations, nationalism and national – that is, ethnic – identity, terminological confusions often occur. The terms *ethnicity* and *ethnic group* were first used in our[4] literature on sociology and psychology after the 1992–1995 wars. Before that, in SFRY, the terms *nations* and *nationalities* were used when referring to ethnic groups, with the term *nation* referred to larger groups and the term *nationalities* referred to smaller ones. The terms *nation* and *nationality* also denoted ethnicity; rarely were they signifiers of a national identity. Most of the papers on psychology from our region do not make a clear distinction between *ethnicity* and *nation* (e.g. Kuzmanović, 1994; Čorkalo, 1998; Milošević-Đorđević, 2003; Turjačanin, 2005), but there is a consensus in social sciences on using the distinction between *ethnia/ethnic group* and *nation* in relations to the development of a political state – that is, *nation*-state. In this chapter we use the terms *ethnicity/nation/people* as synonyms, but give preference to the term *ethnicity* due to the specific situation in BiH.

Ethnicities, or ethnic identities, are adjusted and construed in political and social space; therefore, once the social context changes it changes the characteristics of the social phenomena (Tajfel and Turner, 1986; Worchel, 1999). People are flexible and adjustable beings, but also beings that resist and that care for freedom of choice, and hence seek to escape from the boundaries of the proposed social categories, according to theory of reactance (Brehm, 1966). The nature of human communities is such that psychological and social phenomena constantly take new shapes and escape permanent definitions. Ethnicity, as a kind of a social categorization, is not permanent, but at this point in BiH it certainly represents the most significant socio-political categorization and mobilization, as it has constitutionally been embedded as such. Ethnicity as a social resource of human identification becomes counterproductive once used against

4 By 'our' we mean the literature in Serbo-Croatian, Serbian, Croatian, Bosnian and other related languages – literature that originates from the Socialist Federative Republic of Yugoslavia (SFRY) or 'former' Yugoslavia.

people – that is, when politicized to the extent that it obstructs the free growth and wellbeing of any person (Allport, 1954; Altermatt, 1996; Worchel, 1999).

What triggers the human mind to construct social reality in ethnically relevant terms and how is it expressed in reality? The multimethod approach that was adopted in this research is a combination of socio-psychological and discourse-analytical approaches that enabled us to see how people tended to perceive and talk about themselves on the continuum of personal and social identifications. We chose this approach in order to be able successfully to theorize social identities, and their perfor mative aspects such as discourse, as a form of social (inter)action (Van Dijk, 1997) in the sense that they are constitutive of social life-building worlds, relationships, objects and, in fact, of doing things. In other words, while discourse constructs social life, in a dialectical way it is also being constructed by social life.

Social identity theory (Tajfel and Turner, 1986; Hogg and Williams, 2000; Haslam *et al.*, 2010) discusses social identities through intergroup relations. The basic motivational force in the construction of social identity involves raising self-esteem through intergroup social comparison whereby the main strategy is to find a comparison that will favour one's own group. Sometimes such comparisons lead one to prioritize one's own social identity over one's personal interests, which has been illustrated by minimum membership experiments (Tajfel, 1970). When we have relatively impenetrable group boundaries, such as ethnic group boundaries for instance, people will socially compare either on the basis of interpersonally accepted standards of comparison (wealth or development) or some idiosyncratic dimension (e.g. morality). The consequences of such social comparisons may result in a positive bias towards one's own group and, often, prejudice and discrimination towards another group.

If there is a real competition for certain resources (e.g. political and economic power), the feeling of threat to one's social identity comes easily and can be a very important factor in the mobilization of ethnic groups (Simpson and Yinger, 1985). The threat can be experienced in other areas of social life, such as norms, values, language and so forth if certain group members perceive that their identity is threatened. This feeling of threat is very often found in the BiH context due to the poor economic situation as different ethnic groups compete for scarce economic resources. Our previous research (Majstorović and Turjačanin, 2011) has also shown that mainstream media play a significant role in the social construction of threat by representing other 'ethnic' social actors as potentially threatening to the ethnic community to which they belong. When threatened, people will express increased attachment to the group and group identification, with the purpose of preserving their self-esteem (Greenberg *et al.*, 1992; Arndt *et al.*, 2002).

The word 'identity', however, tends to ascribe essential importance to the group, instead of analysing it. A number of contemporary scholars have therefore suggested using the term 'identifications', which refers to 'doing', not the 'state' or 'being'. We view identity or identification as social constructs *produced* through a discourse based on the subjective imagining of the nation as a community, with the mother tongue serving as the core of the ethnic identity (Anderson, 1983), and *performed* through stylized repetition of acts (Butler, 1990). Fishman (1980: 63–8) argues that ethnicity entails 'being, doing and knowing'. The *being* of an ethnicity is an inner feeling that goes beyond death and promises eternal life since 'origin and mutual roots can be proven' as is demonstrated by metaphors of 'blood, bones and flesh'. The principle of *doing* means that ethnic identifications entail engagement in certain practices as poems, jokes (which are not told before the members of *Other* ethnicities), cheering, rituals, especially religious rituals, and many other rites and ceremonies where Serbhood, Croathood or Bosniakhood, for example, are performed. In terms of *knowing*, this includes history, myths and legends that transfer intergenerational knowledge, collective memory and history to other group members.

Discourse studies propose several fundamental assumptions related to national identity. A basic premise in understanding identity as a discursive construct is Anderson's (1983) idea of 'imagined communities' in which identity becomes construed and reproduced through discourse as a social praxis. According to seminal study by Stuart Hall (Hall, 1996: 613), national identity can be perceived as a 'narrative' that is reconstrued in different times and contexts. Collective identities do not exist inseparably from individuals, just as individuality cannot exist beyond a society: both collective and individual identities are in a constant process of negotiation, validation and change within individuals who identify themselves with a group or a social category and act in the name of the group, and these two levels are interrelated (Tryanfyllidou and Wodak, 2003).

The discursive-historical method in critical discourse analysis (CDA) perceives identities as contextually dependent, dynamic moments that can be discursively constructed, perpetuated and deconstructed and consequently can assume different forms depending on the context within which they occur (Wodak *et al.*, 1999: 3–4). There is no one, essentially recognized identity; identities are multiple, ambivalent and dynamic. The *strategies* entailed in discursive formation of national identity are based on the triangulation and analysis of large texts (Wodak *et al.*, 2009), which make it possible to identify argument strategies such as topoi and intertextuality (Majstorović, 2007; Majstorović and Mandić, 2011b). According to Heinmann and Viehweger (1991: 215) 'strategies mediate between communicative functions and objectives deducted from the interaction and the social conditions of interacting partners and, on the other hand, the realization of linguistic (or extra-linguistic) means and their structuration.' Simply put, they represent a connection between communicative intentions of the speakers and linguistic means they use in a specific context (Heinmann and Viehweger, 1991: 215). Such discursive strategies and their subjects, although distinctively different, often intertwine and are suitable for social macrostrategies of

- construction;
- perpetuation (justification);
- transformation; and
- disassembling of identitary narratives related to BiH ethnic and national identity.

The aforementioned macrostrategies are *realized* through a series of various rhetoric and linguistic instruments such as argumentative strategies (topoi), rhetoric questions, genre hybrid analysis expressed through recontextualization and intertextualization (Bernstein, 1991; Fairclough, 2003), semantic–paradigmatic constructs such as metaphor, metonymy, synecdoche, presupposition, deixis, speech acts, etc., but also syntactic elements of hypotaxis, parataxis, passive voice and polarity (negation) (Majstorović, 2007).

Researching Ethnicity: A Need for an Integrated Approach

Given our proposed theoretical framework, a combination of quantitative and qualitative research was chosen as the most appropriate approach for this study. Discourse analysis of focus group data gave us a more profound insight in the mechanisms of construction of social phenomena while surveys done on a large sample of respondents provided a basis for testing our hypotheses and generalizing our findings.

By 'youth' we refer to the generation born in the late 1980s and throughout early 1990s, who seldom travel across the entity or state borders, who live in a divided country, go to divided schools where they study about divided histories and languages, thus becoming socialized in the context where togetherness and history are being dismissed 'as if we have never existed' (Turjačanin *et al.*, 2009; Turjačanin, 2011). We wanted to find out how the 'youth' in the contemporary BiH perceive themselves and others, what standpoints they take in relation to ethnic and state characteristics, and how they represent, construe and legitimize their identities and positions in semi(private) domains with regard to the public domain they find themselves in.

We attempted to gain access to half-public discourses through the survey carried out among the student population in the territory of BiH in order to identify how the youth interpret and present not only their own identities but also their everyday lives, how they legitimize their attitudes, and to what extent they include or exclude others. Our aim was to identify the ideological matrices they speak through and pinpoint whose narratives they take over, how fluid and dynamic their discourses are when they talk about themselves and others, and how they articulate their resistance to dominant truths. Furthermore, we were interested in the convictions and doubts they have when they talk about themselves, others and the country they live in.

Data collection for the quantitative part of the study was carried out between December 2010 and March 2011 in several BiH cities. The respondents were fourth-year high-school students and college students in the total of 1899 and the average age of 19.5. There were slightly more female respondents in the sample (57%). In terms of ethnic representation we had 37% of Bosniaks (total 704), 13% of Croats (252), 38% of Serbs (727) and 8% BiH nationals (158).[5] Around 3% said their ethnicity was other (47). In terms of religious affiliation, 40% gave their religion as Islam, 14% said they were Catholics, 38% were Orthodox, 2% gave their affiliation as other, and 7% said they were not religious. We used a convenience sample, which was not absolutely representative, as the last demographic data date from the 1991 census. The questionnaire was four pages long and contained basic demographic data and a few psychological and sociological scales that were used for different analyses. There were mainly multiple choice questions and assessment scales and there were also a certain number of open-ended questions.

The qualitative part of the study included eight focus groups of students from different parts of BiH. We had two groups of Banja Luka students (coded as BL1 and BL2), two groups of Sarajevo students (SA1, SA2), one group of Tuzla students (coded as TZ), one group of students from Pale and East Sarajevo (coded as PAL) and two groups of students from Mostar: one from mostly Bosniak Mostar East (MOE) and one from mostly Croatian Mostar West (MOW). All focus groups were recorded and transcribed while the transcripts were translated into English to ensure maximum clarity of the text. We did not ask respondents about their specific ethnicity: all ethnic and state-related issues were to emerge in the discourse with as much spontaneity as possible but we also knew that respondents wanted to save face and were not as open as they would have been among their close friends and family. We nevertheless extracted

5 As the focus groups preceded the surveys, the issue of Bosnian-Herzegovinian ethnicity/nationality came up so we decided to insert this into the questionnaire. We also left a blank space for respondents to fill in by stating any ethnicity they wanted to.

discourses that were indicative of their attitudes and perceptions towards our research questions.

State, Religion and Ethnic Group Attachment

In view of the importance of ethnic belonging expressed through various attachments, embedded in the everyday life of every BiH citizen by the Dayton constitution, we also wanted to compare the place of ethnic belonging with some other group attachments such as religion, entity, state/national and supernational/EU. The importance of attachment to different communities was also assessed on a scale from 1 (unimportant) to 4 (very important). Table 10.1 shows the mean and variance analysis results for intergroup differences between respondents of different ethnicities.

Table 10.1: To what extent are the following forms of attachments important for you?

	Attachment to …				
	my people	my religion	the entity I live in	the state of Bosnia and Herzegovina	Europe
Bosniaks	3.35	3.36	2.53	3.29	2.65
Croats	3.35	3.53	2.68	2.05	2.41
Serbs	3.45	3.48	2.86	2.07	2.46
BiH	2.73	2.32	1.78	2.97	2.47
F	32.810	81.321	47.613	225.878	5.334
Sig.	0.000	0.000	0.000	0.000	0.000

Generally speaking, of all forms of attachment, the highest scores were attributed to religious affiliation, followed by attachment to a people. Other forms of attachment (to territorial entities, the state of BiH and Europe) proved to be less salient. Within the sample of

Bosniak respondents, the affiliation to religion, attachment to ethnic group and to the state of BiH are regarded as the most important categories, while attachment to the entity and Europe scored relatively low. The Croat and Serb respondents find attachment to their relative peoples and religious affiliation to be of highest importance; these categories are followed by the attachment to the entity and Europe, while these respondents place the importance of attachment to the state of BiH at the bottom of the scale. Respondents of BiH ethnicity believe the sense of attachment to the state of BiH and their people to be the most valuable forms attachments, while they scored relatively low in relation to attachment to the entity and religion affiliation. Even though the differences are statistically significant, the levels of attachment to Europe are similar for all four groups and range around the middle point of 2.5. This, perhaps, may be a starting point for defining mutual goals for different ethnic groups and a fact that must be considered by BiH political opinion makers.

The respondents from these four groups differ most in assessing the importance of attachment to the state of BiH: this form of attachment was most distinctively present with Bosniaks, slightly less with the respondents of BiH ethnicity, and almost equally low with the respondents of Croat and Serb ethnicity. The respondents of the Croat and Serb ethnicity attribute more importance to attachment to the entity and Europe than that to the state of BiH. This is an indication of the apparent problem of fitting their ethnic identity within a broader national identity, demonstrating that Europe is perceived as less threatening to the survival of their respective ethnic identities. Additional evidence of a sense of being threatened occurs particularly in the case of the Croat respondents – 66% of them stated that they were anxious about the future of their people in BiH, compared to 49% of the Serb, 45% of the Bosniak and 32% of the BiH respondents. Furthermore, research confirmed that the respondents of Bosniak ethnicity display deepest emotional ties to the state of Bosnia-Herzegovina, as a territory and as a political community.

How does this phenomenon occur? First, according to the prewar data and postwar statistical estimates, Bosniaks represent the majority in BiH, which means they also represent the most politically influential ethnicity in BiH society. Data obtained in focus groups also illustrate that one aspect of the absence of attachment to the state of

BiH in Croats and Serbs stems from their awareness of the so-called 'backup homelands' (Croatia and Serbia) for whose sports teams they mostly cheer. According to our results, the Bosniak respondents tend to display preference towards Turkey,[6] due to historical and religious ties between the two countries. However, because of the geographical and cultural distance, Bosniaks largely identify with BiH. We should also not underestimate the fact that the conflict in BiH started and developed through two main tendencies: a centripetal tendency, advocated by predominantly Bosniak and Croatian parties, which strove for independence from the Serb-dominated Yugoslavia, and a centrifugal tendency, advocated by Serb parties, which strove to remain in the Serb-dominated Yugoslavia. Today, we have a situation where Bosniak parties advocate a united Bosnia-Herzegovina with a Bosniak majority, as opposed to Serb and Croat parties, which advocate a three-entity solution in order to avoid dominance by one group. These tendencies are visible both in the political discourse as well as in the data that we obtained through our survey.

Defining Ethnic Groups: The Role of Religion and Language

Ethnic and other social groups are implicitly and explicitly defined by means of various characteristics ascribed to them by the group members. These characteristics are sometimes ostensibly different, as is the case with religion in BiH, while sometimes they can be subtle, almost invisible, such as in the case of the language of these

6 One of our Sarajevo focus group provided a series of positive evaluations of the Ottoman rule in BiH and refers to religious tolerance, arguing that Turkey *never forced anyone, but simply set the criteria,* which mitigates the discourse of coercion and euphemistically defines the nature of the Turkish rule, confirming that the Turks *had, of course, occupied these territories.* In this piece of discourse, the respondents tended to normalize the conversation by referring to the historical inevitability of the colonial treatment at the time and emphasizing the fact there was no democracy back then.

groups in BiH. Our respondents assessed important characteristics of their respective peoples using a scale from 1 to 4, where 1 denotes 'completely unimportant', 2 'somewhat important', 3 'rather important' and 4 'very important'. Table 10.2 shows the means and the variance analysis results for intergroup differences between respondents of different ethnicity.

Table 10.2: Characteristics valued as the traits of one's people

	Language	Religion	History	Common background	Territory
Bosniaks	3.37	3.27	3.26	2.95	3.08
Croats	3.59	3.60	3.30	3.00	2.91
Serbs	3.65	3.64	3.46	3.16	3.06
BiH	3.33	2.49	3.31	2.83	2.94
F	22.665	96.619	7.518	10.526	2.801
Sig.	0.000	0.000	0.000	0.000	0.000

	Sense of unity	Customs	Members' appearance	State
Bosniaks	3.26	3.30	1.73	3.24
Croats	3.35	3.45	1.78	2.80
Serbs	3.24	3.57	1.82	2.91
BiH	3.19	3.22	1.49	3.08
F	1.566	18.178	5.288	18.648
Sig.	0.000	0.000	0.000	0.000

In assessing the characteristics mentioned in Table 10.2, we see that the majority of respondents rate all categories highly except the category of physical appearance. If we bear in mind that the mean estimate is 2.5, we see that most estimates exceed this value.

In the assessment of the importance of individual factors, we see that the largest differences occur in the assessment of the importance of religion, which is of most importance for Serb and Croat respondents, slightly less to Bosniak respondents and of least importance to

BiH respondents. The results related to the language and customs are similar: Serb and Croat respondents once again attribute more importance to these categories than the BiH and Bosnia respondents. On the other hand, we find that Bosniak respondents attribute the highest values to the importance of the state to their ethnic group; in this respect Bosniaks are followed by BiH respondents, while Croat and Serb respondents place less value on the same category. It could be said that most Bosniak respondents, significantly more than the Croat and Serb respondents, consider Bosnia-Herzegovina as their own country.

When describing the characteristics of their people, respondents of Bosniak, Serb and Croat ethnicity tend to rely on the traditional cultural-religious model of ethnicity, which defines the ethnic group through language, religion, customs, history and sense of unity. Respondents of Croat and Serb ethnicity attach somewhat greater significance to religion and language, whereas Bosniak respondents focus on the state as a very important signifier. Respondents of BiH ethnicity once again stand out, and exhibit a culture-related view of their own people, giving a relatively low importance to faith and common origin while placing greater importance on language, history, traditions, sense of unity and the state. The main difference between BiH respondents and those who defined themselves as Serbs, Bosniaks and Croats is their understanding of religion as the basis of their ethnic group. For BiH respondents, religion is the least important factor (besides physical appearance). A deeper analysis of socio-demographic data also shows that BiH respondents have more ethnically heterogeneous backgrounds than respondents of the three major ethnic groups: 70% of BiH respondents have relatives of other ethnicities, comparing to 51% of Serbs, 48% of Croats and 44% of Bosniaks. Moreover, 21% of them are descended from ethnically mixed marriages, compared to 10% Croats, 6% Serbs and 5% Bosniaks. We might argue that having heterogeneous experiences 'softens' the impact of religious denomination on ethnicity but since this is only a correlational study, we must treat this issue with caution.

When respondents from the FBiH (mostly Bosniaks), discussed ethnic identities in focus groups, they tended to conflate Serb, Croatian and Bosniak ethnicity with their religion (Orthodox, Catholics,

Muslim). For them Serbs and Croats were people from Serbia and Croatia, while in BiH there were Orthodox and Catholic Bosnians, thus stressing the overarching primacy of the Bosnian identity as a territorial identity.

(MOE, M1): *It would be OK for people who moved from the territory of Serbia but people who were born at the BiH territory and who have lived here all their lives, I think it's funny that they call themselves Serbs … those are unstable people who don't have the courage to face it and say 'ok I am a Bosnian but I am Orthodox.'*

(MOE, F1): *Serbs are the people who should be citizens of Serbia, Croats should be citizens of Croatia, Bosniaks should be citizens of BiH …*

In focus groups of Croats and Serbs, there was no confusion for they used the terms 'national' and 'ethnic' interchangeably and, in discourse, their ethnic identity came first.

(MOW, F1): *Well, if someone asks me, what do we say, we first say 'Croats'.*

(MO): *Croats, OK, mhm.*

(F1): *Croats who live in Bosnia-Herzegovina.*

Whereas the quantitative data show the same for the Bosniaks, despite the fact that BiH was also offered as a category in the questionnaire, our FBiH focus group respondents stressed citizenship or state identity as number one. For them, Croats are only citizens of Croatia and Serbs are from Serbia. Ethnicity, at least discursively, does not exist for most of our respondents from the FBiH, just religion and citizenship. For them, it is impossible for ethnic and state identities to coexist and one should make a choice.

(TZ, F1): *If someone identifies himself or herself as a Croat, then they should go to Croatia, be citizens of Croatia, and that's a Croat … I have a friend, and I ask her 'what are you?' and she says 'I am a Croat', she is not a Croat she is Catholic.*

When asked whether we could all be Bosnians or not, the RS respondents (mostly Serbs) generally answered negatively, using temporal hedges such as phrases 'at this point' or 'not now' or 'perhaps in 50 or 60 years' time', referring to 'healing' processes, which always take time, and alluding to its impossibility by using humour and metaphor. In addition, the respondents referred to the issues from the past that 'cannot be simply erased', claiming we should deal with these issues 'little by little'.

(BL2, F1): *Well, I don't think it's possible right now, since everything is still so fresh,* but, who knows, *sometimes, in 50–60 years from now, when people realize it, of course, if we don't get wiped off at the end of the world they announce for 2012 (laughs), it could unite us (laughs) ...*

F1: *... well, if there was something, some other thing threatening us, all three parties ... we wouldn't argue, but now, without the whole end-of-the-world matter, I doubt it (laughs).*

(PAL, F1): *If say ... all politicians were under thirty, the situation would be much, much better, because, err ... the older hold so much hatred ... I can see it a bit in my parents, they keep trying to explain to me that I should treat everyone the same, but you can't just erase some things that had happened, I mean, I've heard so many war stories errr ... from my mum, my dad ... those are things that stick in your mind, and I think we should deal with them little by little.*

The term 'Bosniak' was very much contested as well: while there were those who refused to refer to themselves as Bosniaks, because of the strong connection with the Muslim religion, there were also those who referred to the historical sources (the topos[7] of history) who took a different view. The former claimed that there were apparently 'atheist Muslims' in Bosnia contending that the Bosniak identity was 'imposed' following the Orthodox-Serb, Catholic-Croatian model. But it is also true that the terms 'Bosnian' and 'Bosniak' were often used interchangeably and they elaborated it by using the topos of history.

(SA2, M1): *The term 'Bosniak' as it is understood today is a result of the Bosniak Congress that happened in 1993. But there weren't only Muslims there. It's a, it's a term that is as old as BiH ...*

(M2): *In this country, it's been forced Bosniak, Serb, Croat ... While the BiH citizenship has been given a minor role ... As long as the role of the BiH citizen isn't given an undisputed priority, we won't have solutions for these things ...*

Respondents from the FBiH mainly insisted on the Bosnian/Bosniak identity for all and there is confusion about which is the correct

7 In critical discourse analysis there has been a lot of polemic about how the noton of topos or topi should be used. Richardson (2004: 230) talks of topoi 'as reservoirs of generalized key ideas from which specific statements or arguments can be generated' while in argumentation theory they have been defined as 'content-related warrants' securing the transition from an argument to a conclusion (Žagar, 2009).

term. Excerpts from the discourse below explain how the problem of establishing a Bosnian nation should be resolved by resorting to a hortatory discourse[8] (Hoey, 2001) or 'descriptions with a cover prescriptive intent aimed at getting people to act in a certain ways on the basis of representations of what it is' (Fairclough, 2003: 96):

> (SA1, M1): *I think we should all refer to ourselves as Bosniaks because we live at the BiH territory, we were born here regardless of our religion, and not Serbs, Croats and Muslims, it makes no sense, it isn't logical …*

> (SA1, M2): *I don't think that anybody should refer to themselves as Bosniaks. Generally, Bosnians and Herzegovinians, there, nobody can deny that. You live here, your parents lived here, your ancestors were buried there …*

Table 10.3 shows that, based on the answers of our respondents, ethnicity in BiH fully coincides with religious affiliation.

Table 10.3: Ethnic and religious self-identification (in percent)

			Denomination		
Ethnicity	Islam	Catholicism	Orthodoxy	Not religious	Other
Bosniaks	95.6	0.1	0.1	3.3	0.9
Croats	0.4	93.6	0.4	4.8	0.8
Serbs	0	0.1	95.8	3.5	0.6
BiH	46.5	8.3	5.1	35.7	4.5

These data show a substantial overlap of ethnicity with religion, but this concurrence of ethnicity and religion is not new. A study conducted in 1988, with a sample of 3120 adults from 37 BiH municipalities, found that 89% of Croat respondents said they were Catholic, 82% of Muslim respondents opted for Islam and 77% of Serb respondents said they were Orthodox (Bakić, 1994). The same survey also showed that 56% Croats, 37% Muslims and 19% of Serbs said they were religious. Furthermore, another study done on a sample

8 Hortatory is a universal discourse genre and a type of argument that aims at influencing conduct based on what has been said.

of the youth in BiH in 1989, showed that only 53% of Croat, 34% of Muslim and 21% of Serb respondents considered themselves religious (Velikonja, 2003). In our sample, only 3–5% of the respondents explicitly stated that they were not religious in the part of the instrument by which we measured the salience of religiosity. Based on the data mentioned above it seems that the signifier of ethnicity in BiH has not changed compared to the period before the war – it is still largely connected to religious affiliation (denomination), but the perception of religion and religious practices has certainly changed. Today's religious practices, including ethnic ones, are much more salient than they were in former Yugoslavia. Construction and perception of identity is mostly achieved through relations with other ethnic groups, especially those who are territorially the closest. In the case of BiH, the most visible distinction is religion, which is different in all three. Three religions are connected with the cultural practice of each BiH people but omnipresent places of worship, such as mosques and churches, also demarcate each people's territory.

The correspondence between religion and ethnicity is not surprising because the connection between religion and ethnicity is often emphasized in everyday discourse. This is particularly evident from the statements made by religious institutions' officials, who often emphasize the existential and cultural link between religion and ethnicity, or the crucial role of religion in the preservation of ethnicity in difficult times. The leader of the Islamic Religious Community in BIH, Dr. Mustafa Cerić, said that 'religious community became the main institutional refuge for Bosniaks',[9] while the former Serb Orthodox Church, patriarch Pavle stated how 'being a Serb necessarily entails being Orthodox'[10] and Pope Benedict XVI claimed that 'Croats are the people of profound Catholic faith.'[11] The

9 See www.medzlis.info/index.php?option=com_content&view=article&id=1101:bonjaci-izmeu-vjerskog-i-nacionalnog-reisu-l-ulema-dr-mustafa-ceri&catid=57:kolumne&Itemid=289 (accessed 22 October 2012).

10 See http://pescanik.net/2007/12/koalicija-za-sekularnu-drzavu (accessed 22 October 2012).

11 See http://www.zg-nadbiskupija.hr/index.php?option=com_content&view=article&id=1375:hrvati-narod-duboke-katolike-vjere&catid=5:aktualnosti&Itemid=82 (accessed 22 October 2012).

correspondence between religion and ethnicity is often approved of in elementary and secondary school textbooks.[12]

Another important signifier of ethnicity in BiH is a language or languages of different names, with subtle differences often used to emphasize the intergroup boundaries. Even though they mostly acknowledge that they speak one and the same language with minor differences, the respondents insisted on calling the language by three different names. Using a language as a means of identification is particularly interesting in groups that use the same or similar language and the term *shibboleth* refers to using a language as a means of detection of members of other social groups, based on dialects or expressions. For instance, if in BiH a person uses a term associated with the Croatian language, such as 'vjerojatnost', it is very likely that this person will be categorized as a member of the Croat ethnic group.

Table 10.4: Ethnic and linguistic identification (in percent)

	The language you speak			
Ethnicity	Bosnian	Croat	Serb	Other
Bosniak	97.7	0.6	1.0	0.7
Croat	2.8	95.6	0.4	1.2
Serb	1.1	0.4	97.7	0.8
BiH	79.4	5.8	8.4	6.5

It is obvious that there is a significant correspondence between ethnicity and language, or rather the name of the language. The Bosnian, Croatian and Serbian (and Montenegrin) languages originate from the former Serbo-Croatian language, which has disappeared with the breakup of Yugoslavia, even though it is practically and morphologically one language with different dialects. Labelling the

12 A second-grade grammar school geography textbook reads: 'The social as well as cultural reality of Bosnia-Herzegovina is characterized by different religions. Serbs are Orthodox, Bosniaks are Muslims, Croats are Catholic and there are some other religions as well.' (Husremović *et al.*, 2007: 131).

language with one's ethnic group name is one way of demonstrating socio-cultural dominance; thus, in BiH, language is used for the purposes of construction of ethnicity (or nation). Interestingly, though, there is no 'Bosniak' or 'BiH' language. Before the war, language was not and could not be used as an element of ethnic identity construction because most of the former Yugoslavia used the standard Serbo-Croat.

Aside from the communicative and linguistic (syntactic), political (constitutional) and emotional criteria also play an important role in defining and legitimizing a language. Among our respondents, two main legitimization strategies of appropriation and colonization predominated: the historical one arguing that 'it's all Croatian' or 'Serbian' because of the historical evidence and the standardized Serbo-Croat language prior to 1992 and the territorial one stating that 'it's all Bosnian' and we should speak Bosnian because you live at the territory of BiH. Another option was to recognize all three languages and call it BHS (Bosnian/Croatian/Serbian).

Both Serb and Croat focus groups' respondents felt confident about their respective ethnic status as constitutive peoples and not ethnic minorities in Bosnia. They said that they speak either Serbian or Croatian. To say that one speaks 'another' language was perceived as betrayal:

> (MOW, F1): *If we said we 'speak Serbian', that would immediately be a betrayal*
> (F2): *of your people*
> (F1): *yeah, that's right*

Proponents of the Bosnian language mainly give political reasons and legitimize their claims in territorial terms, arguing that it is normal for them speak Bosnian because they live in Bosnia. Note the use of the epistemic modal *would* and the deontic modal *should* in these hortatories and the topos of 'normality':

> (TZ, M1): *Regardless if you are from Trebinje or Orašje, you are within the jurisdiction of BiH, so on paper you are, on paper there is BiH, so this should be called Bosnian language.*
> (TZ, F1): *I think we would fully agree that it is one language and that it is the Bosnian language unless we are discussing politics …*
> (TZ, M2): *We lived together for years and we adopted these different words from Bosniaks, Croats, Serbs and it would be the most normal for the language to be called Bosnian for we live in Bosnia and we feel as Bosnians.*

Another argument in favour of the Bosnian language is that it 'existed but was not respected … like a lot other things concerning Bosnians and Herzegovinians weren't respected' for in Tito's times 'everything was a bit hushed up.

> (MOE, M1): The Bosnian language has existed for centuries, it was not invented ten years ago … it existed but it wasn't officially presented as such to the public.

Language names differ based on the school in BiH you go to, but respondents discussed it only in terms of lexical differences and not in terms of structural or syntactic varieties, which are a lot less common. A female student from Tuzla says she 'studied Bosnian in the primary school and Croatian in the secondary school' and said that she does not speak purely Bosnian, because she does not use all Bosnian words, and she does not speak pure Croatian because she does not use only Croatian words, and she occasionally adopts some Serbian words, so the language she spoke was 'a mixture'. There was some confusion as to whether Serbs in Bosnia speak *ekavica* dialect, which was seen as a difference marker between Serbian and Bosnian. A politically correct argument is that it is smartest to have a Bosnian-Serbian-Croatian language as 'it does not insult anyone'.

It is evident that ethnic identities in BiH have been culturalized, especially with regard to religion and language. Currently, in our society, there is a problem of coexistence of ethnic and national identity, at least in the affective realm. This is primarily expressed by groups of respondents of Croat and Serb ethnicity, which do not perceive the state of BiH as their own, and display no significant identification with it. We can assume that it is a feeling of threat to one's ethnic identity coming from a superordinate state identity. In fact, according to our respondents, we can observe two possible solutions to this problem in BiH. The first is the state-dominance model, which emphasizes the primacy of state/national identity and suggests that all groups should primarily identify with the dominant state identity. The second is an ethnic-separation model, which attributes exclusive legitimacy to the category of ethnicity, either completely rejecting the national, or accepting it only as a formal determinant, with no sense of real identification.

In Lieu of Conclusions

During the time of socialist Yugoslavia, the dominant discourse was antinationalist. The predominant ideas were those of Yugoslavhood, brotherhood and unity, which resulted in around 6% of the BiH population identifying themselves as Yugoslavs at the 1991 census. Nationalism was considered retrograde and was even punishable as it did not contribute to social progress. On the other hand there was a certain ambivalence in terms of ethnicity as there was an ethnic quota system as a principle of positive discrimination when it came to political or economic functions. The negative sides of such a system were not visible until the breakup of SFR Yugoslavia and the 1991–1995 wars, which, aside from mass destruction, also brought new forms of social functioning.

Today, after the war in BiH, with the political system based on the 'constituent peoples', or ethnic group of Bosniaks, Croats and Serbs, it is clear that these peoples represent each other's main reference groups. Furthermore, it should be noted that, in such a political context, ethnicity has become a 'realistic' basis for comparison and competition as it relates to the distribution of social and political power in the country. Such a categorization is currently constitutionally embedded. The need for a positive identity is universal, and our research shows that members of each ethnic group manifest this by insisting on their uniqueness, the political rhetoric of exclusivity of their origin, history and culture, and by focusing on differences from the culture of 'others'.

Our respondents differed the most when it came to assessing the importance of attachment to the state of BiH, as most Croats and Serbs seemed to favour their ethnic over their national (state) identity. Yet, the meaning of the Bosnian-Herzegovinian remains both vague and weak and therefore not a substantial basis for potential positive identity for all: while Bosniaks tend to conflate and equate Bosnian with Bosniak and with Serbs and Croats mostly rejecting this identity, we felt that this potential was mostly articulated with respondents from interethnic marriages and a minority with clear, civic and liberal beliefs. Bosnia-Herzegovina, both as a state and as a society, has to deal with the fact that many of its citizens do not perceive the country as *theirs*. One of the questions is how to incorporate these ethnic identities into a new society in a way that is not threatening to anyone. As some of our findings suggest, Europe as an overarching identity, seems to be acceptable for most people in both entities, and certainly more so than the BiH state. This 'promise of Europe' may be seen as a telos of reconciliation and unity for the people of BiH. Although today's situation may give rise to pessimism, we may ask whether a strong and ethnic identity necessarily leads towards conflict. It probably does not as prewar research (Baćević, 1990; Kunovich and Hodson, 1999) shows that the expression of prejudice was least in ethnically mixed areas, such as the prewar BiH. It is more likely that prejudice and discriminatory behaviour originate from the dominant discourses and ideologies and political relations present in the BiH society of today. In answer to the question of whether nonconflicting multiple identities are possible, the answer is not only is it possible but it already exists. In particular, all inhabitants of BiH already exhibit loyalty to the state, since they pay taxes and other duties and participate in its political and social life. Adjustment of multiple identities is possible if we mitigate the politicization of ethnic identities, which, at this point, seems almost impossible. What this study certainly cannot provide is a prescription, the solution to avoid politicization of any of the identities, including ethnic ones; however, it can demonstrate that the potential for change is present in all the communities.

Bosnia-Herzegovina is at a crossroads. It remains a divided society and a dysfunctional state where ethnic tensions are based on rather different commonsensical assumptions of what the situation should be. Yet, similarity and unity do exist despite apparently irreconcilable attitudes. This knowledge may serve as a starting point from which society-building efforts will include, respect and embrace these differences.

References

Anderson, B. (1983) *Imagined Communities: Reflections on the Origin and Spread of Nationalism*, Verso, New York, NY.

Allport, G. (1954) *The Nature of Prejudice*, Addison-Wesley, Cambridge, MA.

Altermatt, U. (1996) *Etnonacionalizam u Evropi (Ethnonationalism in Europe)*, Jež, Sarajevo.

Arndt, J., Greenberg, J., Schimel, J., Pyszczynski, T. and Solomon, S. (2002) To belong or not to belong, that is the question: Terror management and identification with gender and ethnicity. *Journal of Personality and Social Psychology* 83, pp. 26–43.

Baćević, Lj. (1990). *Nacionalna svest omladine*, In: S. Mihailović, R. Nešković, V. Goati, J. Vujović, S. Bjelajac, M. Vasović, B. Kuzmanović, S. Pegan, V. Marković, L. Baćević, D. Pantić, M. Bobić, M. Gaćanović, M. Jilek.; Deca krize. Beograd: IDN – Centar za politikološka istraživanja i javno mnenje.

Bakić, I. (1994) *Nacija i religija*, Bosna Public, Sarajevo.

Bernstein, B. (1991) *The Structuring of Pedagogic Discourse*, Routledge, London.

Brehm, J. (1966) *A Theory of Psychological reactance*, Academic Press, New York, NY.

Butler, J. (1990) *Gender Trouble: Feminism and the Subversion of Identity*, Routledge, London.

Čorkalo, D. (1998) *Nacionalni identitet i međunacionalna tolerancija (National Identity and International Tolerance)*, IUC, Dubrovnik.

Fairclough, N. (2003) *Analysing Discourse: Textual Analysis for Social Research*, Routledge, London.

Fishman, J. (1980) Social theory and ethnography. In *Ethnic Diversity and Conflict in Eastern Europe* (ed. P. Sugar), ABC Clio, Santa Barbara, CA, pp. 84–97.

Greenberg, J., Solomon, S., Pyszczynski, T., Rosenblatt, A., Burling, J., Lyon, D., Simon, L. and Pinel, E. (1992) Why do people need self-esteem? Converging evidence that self-esteem serves an anxiety-buffering function. *Journal of Personality and Social Psychology* 63, pp. 913–22.

Hall, S. (1996) The question of cultural identity. In S. Hall, D. Held, D. Hubert and K. Thompson (Eds.) *Modernity: An Introduction to Modern Societies*, Blackwell Publishers, Cambridge, MA, pp. 595–634

Haslam, S. A., Ellemers, N., Reicher, S. D., Reynolds, K. J., & Schmitt, M. T. (2010). The social identity perspective today: The impact of its defining ideas. In T. Postmes & N. R. Branscombe (Eds.), Rediscovering Social Identity: Core Sources (pp. 340–356). New York: Psychology Press.

Heinmann, W. and Viehweger, D. (1991) *Textlinguistik: Eine Einführung*. Tübingen, Niemeyer.

Hoey, M. (2001) *Textual Interaction*, Routledge, London.

Hogg, M. and Williams, K. (2000) From I to we: social identity and the collective self. *Group Dynamics: Theory, Research, and Practice*, 4, pp. 81–97.

Husremović, D., Powell, S., Šišić, A. and Dolić, A. (2007) *Obrazovanje u Bosni i Hercegovini:* Čemu *učimo djecu? Analiza sadržaja udžbenika nacionalne grupe predmeta*

[Education in Bosnia-Herzegovina: What Do We Teach our Children? Content Analysis of School Textbooks of National Group of Subjects], Open Society Fund, Sarajevo.
Kunovich, R. and Hodson, R. (1999) Conflict, religious identity and intolerance in Croatia. *Social Forces* 78, pp. 643–74.
Kuzmanović, B. (1994) Socijalna distanca prema pojedinim nacijama' [Social distance towards certain nations]. In *Razaranje društva [Destruction of Society]* (ed. M. Lazić.), Filip Višnjić, Beograd.
Majstorović, D. (2007) *Diskurs, moć i međunarodna zajednica [Discourse, Power and the International Community*, Filozofski fakultet u Banjaluci, Banja Luka.
Majstorović, D. (2011a) 'Više od tolerancije: marksističko-feministička kritika (ne) mogućnosti tolerancije u tranzicijskoj BiH' [Beyond Tolerance: a Marxist-feminist critique of (im)possible tolerance in the transitional Bosnia-Herzegovina]. In *Tolerancija u društvu [Tolerance in Society]* (eds V. Turjačanin, D. Majstorović, M. Turjačanin, B. Milosavljević, S. Lovrić, Centar za kulturni i socijalni popravak, Banja Luka.
Majstorović, D. (2011b) What it means to be a Bosnian woman- analyzing women's talk between patriarchy and emancipation. In *Living with Patriarchy- Discursive Costructions of Gendered Subjects Across Cultures* (eds D. Majstorović and I. Lassen), DAPSAC series, John Benjamnis, Amsterdam.
Majstorović, D. and Turjačanin, V. (2011) *U okrilju nacije* [*In the Embrace of a Nation*], CKSP, Banja Luka.
Milošević-Đorđević, J. (2003) Jedan pokušaj klasifikacije teorijskih razmatranja nacionalnog identiteta. [An attempt of classifying theoretical considerations of national identity]. *Psihologija* 36 (2), pp. 125–40.
Mujkić, A. (2011) Bosna i Hercegovina između individualne i kolektivne indiferencije. [Bosnia-Herzegovina between individual and collective indifference]. In *In The Embrace of a Nation- Ethnic and National Identity Among Youth in Bosnia-Herzegovina* (eds D. Majstorović and V. Turjačanin), Center for Social and Cultural Repair, Banja Luka.
Richardson, J. (2004) *(Mis)Representing Islam: The Racism and Rhetoric of British Broadsheet Newspapers,* John Benjamins, Amsterdam.
Simpson, G. and Yinger, M. (1985) *Racial and Cultural Minorities: An Analysis of Prejudice and Discrimination*, Plenum, New York, NY.
Smit, A. (1998) *Nacionalni identitet* [*National Identity*], Biblioteka XX vek, Beograd.
Tajfel, H. (1970) Experiments in intergroup discrimination. *Scientific American* 223, pp. 96–102.
Tajfel, H. and Turner, J. (1986) The social identity theory of intergroup behaviour. In *Psychology of Intergroup Relations* (eds S. Worchel and W. Austin), Nelson, Chicago, IL.
Tryandafyllidou, A. and Wodak, R. (2003) Conceptual and methodological questions in the study of collective identities. *Journal of Language and Politics* 2 (2), pp. 201–23.
Turjačanin, V. (2005) *Nacionalni stavovi mladih bošnjačke i srpske nacionalnosti u BiH*, Filozofski fakultet, Banja Luka.
Turjačanin, V., Kolenović-Đapo, J., Čehajić-Clancy, S., Poljac, E., Kordić, M. and Alić, M. (2009) *Divided Schools in Bosnia-Herzegovina*, UNICEF, Sarajevo.

Turjačanin, V. (2011) Sociopsihološke odrednice etničkih distanci kod mladih u BiH [Sociopsychological determinants of ethnic distance among BiH youth]. In *In The Embrace of a Nation – Ethnic and National Identity Among Youth in Bosnia-Herzegovina* (eds D. Majstorović and V. Turjačanin), Center for Social and Cultural Repair, Banja Luka.

Van Dijk, T. (1997) *Discourse as Social Action: Discourse Studies, Vol. 2: A Multidisciplinary Introduction*, Sage, Newbury, CA.

Velikonja, M. (2003) *Religious Separation and Political Intolerance in Bosnia-Herzegovina*, Texas A&M University Press, College Station, TX.

Wodak, R., De Cillia, R., Reisigl, M., and Liebhart, K. (1999) *The Discursive Construction of National Identity*, Edinburgh University Press, Edinburgh.

Wodak, R., De Cillia, R., Reisigl, M., and Liebhart, M. (2009) *The Discursive Construction of National Identity*, Edinburgh University Press, Edinburgh.

Worchel, S. (1999) *Written in Blood: Ethnic Identity and the Struggle For Human Harmony*, Worth Publishers, New York, NY.

Žagar, I. (2009) Topoi in critical discourse analysis. Šolsko *polje* 20 (5/6), pp. 47–75.

Dragan Stanojević and Smiljka Tomanović

Getting on their Feet? Changes in Economic Status of Young People in Serbia between 2003 and 2011[1]

Cultural and structural constraints on the individualization of young people in Serbia have become a part of current academic discourse. Our intention is to present the extent to which the financial and housing situation of young people and their independence from their parents determine this trend. This chapter is based on the comparison of data from surveys carried out on representative national samples of young people in Serbia in 2003 and 2011. The analysis aims at capturing trends over time, as well as the effects of institutional mechanisms that provide structural constraints or opportunities for young people's agency. Education and employment are considered to be the main resources for economic status, independence and agency, which are also dependent on structural factors. Since we aimed at exploring inter-relation of structures and agency, we analyzed education and employment statuses of young people, but also in relation to their perceptions, strategies, and plans. The key findings are that, in 2011, young people in Serbia were financially and economically dependent on their families to a high degree, and that there was almost no change in comparison to their economic status in 2003. Education, employment, and profession were relevant factors in defining the economic status and agency of a young person.

1 Prepared within the framework of the Regional Research Promotion Programme in the Western Balkans (RRPP), which is run by the University of Fribourg upon a mandate of the Swiss Agency for Development and Cooperation, SDC, Federal Department of Foreign Affairs. The views expressed in the chapter are those of the authors and do not necessarily represent the opinions of the SDC and the University of Fribourg.

Framework

Many contemporary studies have suggested that economic status, comprising income and housing, remains one of the key issues for young people across Europe (e.g. Kovacheva, 2001; Brannen *et al.*, 2002; Walther, 2006; Walther *et al.*, 2009). The economic situation that creates the structural framework for the everyday life of young people has undergone profound changes in both Western and Eastern European countries, with the dissolution both of welfare states and socialist states. The risks for young people in their transition to adulthood are similar both for neoliberal and postsocialist societies: rising unemployment, a precarious labour market and a decline in housing policies and social security systems (Kovacheva, 2001; Walther *et al.*, 2009). This has profound effects on the transitions of young people to adulthood, which become less similar, less linear and less certain. Three aspects of transition to adulthood – transition to work, transition to parenthood, and transition to citizenship – are mechanisms of social integration of young people into society, by their participation in economic reproduction through labour, by their participation in social reproduction through childbearing and by their participation in the political domain through citizenship. Employment, income and housing, which provide young people's economic independence, are crucial prerequisites for the transition to adulthood. Low participation in economic and social reproduction, due to high unemployment and postponement of parenthood, together with low political and civil participation, which are hindering social integration of young people, seem to be common features in all the Balkan countries (Kuhar and Reiter, 2012).

Many studies provided evidence of the increasing importance of family resources in young people's lives and transitions (e.g. Biggart and Kovacheva, 2006; Tomanovic and Ignjatovic, 2010). This makes young people dependent on their families' status and in this way reproduces social inequalities. Reliance on unequally distributed family resources poses restrictions on their opportunities for individualized choices and agency but also reproduces unequal chances for access to education (particularly higher education), which has proved to be one of the key mechanisms of social promotion and integration. In this way, young people coming from families belonging to vulnerable social groups (for example, ethnic groups such as Roma; rural communities; the long-term unemployed) are placed at risk of social exclusion.

The interdependence of institutional structural contexts and individual transitions has been introduced by the concept of *transitional regimes* (Walther, 2006; Walther *et al.*, 2009), based on Esping-Andersen's (1990) typologies of welfare regimes and which distinguishes five types of institutional and policy frameworks that serve as markers of biographical orientation for individuals: social democratic/universalistic, conservative/corporatist/employment-centred, liberal, Mediterranean/sub-protective and postsocialist (Walther *et al.* 2009).

Young people in Serbia, like their counterparts in Central and Eastern Europe, are facing a double transition – transition to adulthood in transitional societies. The status of young people and their transition to adulthood are influenced by the postsocialist transformation in Serbia. Serbian sociologists distinguish two phases: *blocked transformation* in the 1990s and *prolonged transformation* since political changes in 2000. Both phases of the transformation are 'path dependent' and deviate from the model of successful postsocialist transition (Lazić and Cvejić, 2005: 35).

The employment situation for young people is one of the key problems in Serbia[2] and it is now even more acute due to the current global financial crisis. The unemployment rate in Serbia has varied in the last decade, although *youth unemployment* remains consistently high as a proportion of total unemployment. According to the official statistics from the Statistical Office of the Republic of Serbia (Statistics Office of the Republic of Serbia, 2010) the overall unemployment rate in Serbia is 19.2%. The bulk of the registered unemployed in 2010 consisted of young people aged up to 35 (34.7% of the total number), and the unemployment rate decreased with age

2 Over 200'000 young people from 15 to 29 were unemployed in June 2010: 20'750 age 15–19; 82'456 age 20–24 and 99'795 age 25–29, which makes 27% of the age group under 30. In each age group, young women make over 50% of unemployed young people (Unemployment and Employment in Serbia, 2010).

(51.9% at 15–19, 45.1% at 20–24, 32.6% at 25–29 and 22.4% at 30–34). The economic crisis increased the unemployment rate from 13.6% in 2008 to almost one-fifth of the population in 2011 and this mostly affected young people entering the labour market. Young people are most sensitive to any changes in the economy. Young people in Serbia are particularly vulnerable compared to other postsocialist countries.[3] The high inactivity rate of people aged from 15 to 30 (51.5%) is due to them postponing the completion of their education, which 87% of young people give as the main reason for not looking for a job (SLMAR). The economic status of young people in Serbia is marked by prolonged high dependence on family resources due to unemployment and housing problems. Our research findings from 2003 revealed great financial dependence of young people on their parents (Tomanovic and Ignjatovic, 2006).

After the breakdown of Yugoslavia, the socialist housing policy system, which was family oriented, collapsed: there was almost no construction and distribution, while public-sector housing was privatized by the previous tenants. Moreover, since there was no developed housing policy (for example, only very unfavourable commercial mortgages were available from 2005), this has resulted in an extreme housing shortage, causing people to rely mostly on family resources (Petrovic, 2004). The data point to the extremely bad housing situation as a constraint on young people's independence: our study from 2003 has revealed that 77% of younger (17–24), 64% of middle (25–30) and 41% of older (31–35) respondents live in their parents' home (Tomanovic and Ignjatovic, 2006: 278). Young people in Serbia show similar patterns in establishing independent households as their counterparts in the former socialist countries, especially from the former Yugoslav region. On the basis of the European

3 In this regard, Serbia differs from Croatia, where the number of young people among the unemployed is relatively large (22% in the age group 15–24 in 2008) but is equal to the number of older people among the unemployed (Ilišin and Radin, 2007), and from Slovenia, where the rate of unemployment of young people is below 15% in 2010 (Lavrič, 2011: 142). As compared with some postsocialist countries in the region that have recently joined the EU, such as Bulgaria, with youth unemployment rate of 25.8%, or Romania, with youth unemployment rate of 23.2%, the unfavourable status of young people in Serbia is evident.

Values Survey – EVS 2008 (cf. Kuhar, Reiter, 2012) in all the former Yugoslav countries, more than half of the young people aged 18–34 years were living with their parents, in contrast to the EU15 countries where the percentage is 34% (51.5% in EU postsocialist countries). In Serbia, far more than in the EU15 countries and significantly more than in the other countries of the former Yugoslavia, young people live in extended households.[4]

The ongoing reliance by young people in Serbia on family material, cultural and social resources, in housing, employment, and the transition to parenthood has been encouraged by state policy, which has produced a combination of subprotective and postsocialist transitional regimes (Walther *et al.*, 2009). A similar situation of high reliance on family financial and housing resources in the transition to employment and parenthood has also been found in other Balkan countries (Tomić-Koludrović and Leburić, 2001; Kovacheva, 2004; Ule and Kuhar, 2008).

Starting from the conceptual and contextual issues outlined above, the first aim of this analysis is to describe the change in economic status – in terms of financial and housing status – by comparing the data from two surveys: from 2003 and from 2011. The second aim is to explore the relevance of education, employment and profession for particular aspects of economic status: financial independence, housing status and independence. The third aim is to explore whether young people rely mostly on family resources in their agency related to economic status or whether they use institutional mechanisms provided by the social system.

The comprehensive survey was based on national representative sample of 3180 young people aged between 17 and 35 and was carried out in June 2003. Quotas were set for age, gender and employment status (students in secondary schools, university students, the unemployed and employed; CPA/CPS, 2004; Tomanovic and Ignjatovic, 2006). Another comprehensive survey was carried out

4 Living with parents, including those with partner/spouse/children: Slovenia 63.8%, Bosnia and Herzegovina 59.9%, Kosovo 80.3%, Serbia 61.3%, Montenegro 57.6%, and with parents only: Slovenia 53.6%, Bosnia and Herzegovina 43.4%, Kosovo 62.4%, Serbia 37.6%, Montenegro 47.5% (EVS, 2008, cf. Kuhar and Reiter, 2012).

on a national representative sample of 1627 young people age 19 to 35 in March and April 2011 (with quotas set for four age cohorts 19/20, 24/25, 29/30 and 34/35). The latter survey provides data for exploring the relevance of education and employment as the main resources determining a young person's economic status.

Because of a difference in sample design in the two surveys,[5] we will present comparisons between the three relevant groups (employed, unemployed and students, Table 11.1) whenever we compare data.

Table 11.1: Activity status: 2003 and 2011

		Year	
		2003	2011
Activity status	Students (%)	33.70	26.30
	Unemployed (%)	31.50	23.80
	Employed (%)	34.80	49.90
Total (%)		100.00	100.00

Financial Status and Independence of Young People

The financial autonomy of young people is considered to be an essential condition for their independence. We have measured it with four indicators: (i) source of income, (ii) amount of personal income, (iii) total household income per capita and (iv) perception of one's own financial status.

5 The first one was (2003) based on quotas formed according to activity status (one-quarter of secondary school students, university students, employed and unemployed) of young people. The second one (2011) was a simple random sample within the chosen age cohorts. In comparing data, secondary schools students were omitted from the analysis.

The respondents were offered several options in order to establish their sources of income and, more generally, the resources they use to support themselves (Table 11.2).

Table 11.2: Sources of income by age group - survey 2011

		Sources of income (%)			
		Maintained by parents	Supported by parents/ relatives	Supported by partner	Scholarship
Age group	19–20	79.4	9.8	2.5	8.6
	24–25	46.0	18.4	6.1	7.3
	29–30	19.1	17.6	10.6	0.5
	34–35	6.8	14.8	11.5	0.0
Total		38.2	15.2	7.6	4.2

		Sources of income (%)			
		Personal income	Family pension	State support	Rent
Age group	19–20	21.6	2.2	2.2	1.0
	24–25	52.8	1.7	1.2	0.5
	29–30	72.3	0.5	2.8	2.0
	34–35	81.2	0.5	2.0	1.8
Total		56.7	1.2	2.0	1.3

The results show that 38.2% of young people were maintained by their parents and an additional 15.2% stated that their parents help them financially, meaning that more than half of the young people in Serbia depend completely or partially on their parents.

We conducted three chi-square tests for independence of each activity group in order to compare financial dependence of young people in 2003 and 2011 with their source of income. Results show that there was no significant change in the employed group but there was a statistically significant reduction in dependence among students and unemployed young people.[6]

Table 11.3: Financial (in)dependence by activity groups in 2003 and 2011

	Year	Maintained by parents	With personal income (salary, honorarium)
Students	2003	84.8	14.4
	2011	76.4	25.1
Unemployed	2003	63.9	13.2
	2011	50.7	24
Employed	2003	0	100
	2011	0	100

In comparison with the 2003 survey, the number of the young people who claimed to be supported by their parents decreased considerably, and the percentage of those with a personal income rose, which indicates an improving trend in the financial situation of Serbian youth (Table 11.3).

In total, 37.5% of youth had no personal income,[7] and an additional 36.5% have an income that is below the average salary; another 16.6% have average income, suggesting that many young people were not financially capable of living an independent life. Their income was also characterized by high level of variability. As expected,

6 A chi-square test for independence (with Yates continuity correction) indicates a significant association between students in 2003 and 2011 and they source of income, $X^2(1, n=1205)=12.36$, $p < 0.001$, phi $=0.1$. Another chi-square test for independence (with Yates continuity correction) indicates significant association between being unemployed in 2003 and 2011 and source of income, $X^2(1, n=854)=22.48$, $p< 0.001$, phi $=0.17$.

7 In the first age group (19–20) it was 66%, in the second (24–25) 38.6%, in the third (29–30) 26.1% and in the fourth (34–35) 17%.

their income increased with age.[8] The quarter of persons with the highest pay grade amd the third in the top two grades are professionals, while other professions are presented as follows: clerks – 7% in the highest, 21% in the top two grades; technicians and qualified workers – 5% in the highest, 10% in the top two grades. Farmers, non qualified and semi qualified workers, are in the worst position since 50% of them are in the lower pay grades.

The total family income per household member related to profession reveals that young professionals were in the best financial position with 52% in higher pay grades. They were followed by clerks (43%), students (32%) and qualified workers (27%); however, low qualified and semiqualified workers (10% in higher and 45% in lower pay grades) and farmers (17.5% in higher and 50% in lower grades) are in the worst position. In addition, the owners of private businesses, government employees and employees in private sector were in the best positions, whereas farmers and temporary and illegal workers were in the worst situation.

Young people's perceptions of their own financial situation in 2011 revealed some changes and some similarities in comparison with the situation in 2003 (Table 11.4).

We found statistically significant differences between employed and unemployed young people in 2003 and 2011.[9] Perceptions of employed and unemployed young people regarding their own financial situations deteriorated to some extent after 2003. They reveal a

8 For the purposes of the study, we made a five-item scale of monthly personal income (in EUR): 1. (low) 1–140, 2. (moderately low) 141–280, 3.(medium) 281–420, 4. (moderately high) 421–560 and 5. (high) 560+. In the text itself, we will sometimes connect two categories, so that we will talk about higher or lower grades/categories. The average salary in Serbia at the time of the survey was around 350 EUR. We have also made a five-item scale of monthly total household income per capita (in EUR): 1. (low) 1–80, 2. (moderately low) 81–160, 3.(medium) 161–240, 4. (moderately high) 241–320 and 5. (high) 321+.

9 A chi-square test for independence indicates that there is a significant association between being unemployed in 2003 and 2011 and perception of one's own financial situation, $X^2(1, n=1582)=34.8$, $p < 0.001$, Cramer's V = 0.13. Another chi-square test for independence indicates significant association between being employed in 2003 and 2011 and perception of one's own financial situation, $X^2(1, n=1102)=24.86$, $p < 0.001$, phi = 0.15.

Table 11.4: Subjective self-perception of the financial situation

	Year	We cannot afford food	We can satisfy needs for food but not for clothes	Enough for food, clothes, even to save small amounts of money but not enough to buy expensive goods	We can afford expensive things but not a car	We can afford whatever we want	Total
Students	2003	0.4	18.6	46.3	31.4	3.4	100.0
	2011	1.3	19.7	41.7	34.6	2.8	100.0
Unemployed	2003	6.1	32.6	46.0	12.8	2.6	100.0
	2011	7.8	44.8	32.9	13.6	0.8	100.0
Employed	2003	2.9	19.1	50.8	24.0	3.1	100.0
	2011	2.4	27.1	39.8	28.0	2.6	100.0

high level of dissatisfaction among young people with their own financial position and although certain changes have occurred, objectively speaking, their situation is still inadequate in comparison with what they desire and need.

If we look at the marital status of the respondents,[10] single young people are in the worst position with regard to personal income: 57%

10 In our survey sample 66% of young people are single, 25% are married, 5.6% live in cohabitation and less than 3% are divorced.

of them belong to lowest pay grades. The percentage of respondents belonging to the high pay grades is 23.3; 11.3% are married and 7.4% not married. In terms of household income per capita, cohabiting households appear to be in the most financially advantageous situation with 53.5% in higher pay grades. As this form of living together is usually chosen by young people belonging to urban, better educated and wealthier population segments, this correlation is to be expected.

Table 11.5 presents data on the expectations of young people as far as their financial prospects in the next year are concerned.

Table 11.5: Financial expectations for next year (in percent)

	Financial expectations for next year						
Age	Financial dependence from parents	Significant financial support from parents	Less financial support	To financially support parents	Financial independence from parents	Without parents	Total
19–20	47.5	6	21.5	5	19	1	100
24–25	14	5	27	8	43	3	100
29–30	2.5	2	23	14	56	2	100
34–35	1.5	3	18	19	51	7	100
Total %	17	4	23	11	42	3	100

In the first age group (19–20) 47.5% expect that their parents will support them completely, 21.5% think their parents will help them less, and 19% expect to become independent. Starting from the next age group (24–25) the percentage of those who expect to stay completely dependent falls sharply and the percentage of those who expect to be independent rises. At this age most young people have finished education or have been on the job market for some time, so that, in this period, clear expectations and a desire to be financially independent appear. This percentage continues to rise in older generations. At the same time, the number of those who expect to help their parents financially in the near future increases with the respondents' age. Results indicate a low level of financial autonomy among young people but also a high level of financial exchange between generations, which is a characteristic of countries in the Mediterranean region.

Housing Status and Independence of Young People

Another important precondition of economic independence is housing independence. Several domestic studies indicate that the lack of clear strategic goals in the field of housing policy has resulted in low housing mobility during the (post)socialistic period, independent construction and illegal construction (Petrović, 2004: 312). In these conditions, some people choose to pool their limited resources and stay in a joint household for longer.

Housing status confirms the high degree of dependence of young people – 56.4% of young people still live with their parents, while 27% live in their own places (11% in an inherited flat/house, 7% in a rented flat that they pay themselves, 5% in a flat that their parents bought for them and 4% in a house/flat that they bought on their own or with their partner) (Table 11.6 shows the age group distribution).[11]

We conducted three independent chi-square tests (for each activity group in 2003 and 2011) in order to compare housing dependency. We have found that there were no significant difference in scores for students and employed young people. We identified some

11 In the youngest group (19–20) 72% of young people live with their parents (compared to 77% in 2003). In the 24–25 age group, the number of those living with parents is decreasing (65% compared to 64% in 2003). Around 51.5% of the 29–30 age group and 37% (compared to 41% in 2003) of the 34–35 age group still live with their parents.

Table 11.6: Housing status of young people in Serbia (in %)

Age	Housing status: Parental home	Inherited apartment	Apartment bought by parents/ relatives	At my cousins'/ friends'	Apartment bought on my own/with partner	Rented apartment – I pay
19–20	72	2	3	2.5	0	1
24–25	64.5	7	4	1.2	2.5	4.3
29–30	51.5	12.7	6.1	2.8	4.6	11.7
34–35	36.7	24	8.5	1	9.3	11.3
Total %	56.4	11.2	5.3	1.9	4	7

Age	Housing status: Rented apartment – others pay	Student dormitory	Property of spouse/ partner	Other	Total
19–20	8.6	10.3	0.2	1	100
24–25	8.1	5.5	1.7	1.5	100
29–30	3.3	0	4	3.3	100
34–35	2.8	0	3.3	2.9	100
Total %	5.5	4	2.8	2.1	100

improvement among unemployed youth,[12] but overall results indicate that there was no significant change in this sphere of young people's life between 2003 and 2011.

The manner in which young people acquired their first real estate indicates their limited financial ability to acquire an apartment using

12 The chi-square test for independence (with Yates continuity correction) indicates that there is a significant association between unemployed young people in 2003 and 2011 and their housing dependency, $X^2(1, n=1111)=6.7$, $p=0.01$, phi = –0.08.

their own money. In most cases apartments are inherited or people receive financial assistance at the moment of purchase. In such circumstances, social class becomes more significant than personal income, because the purchase of the apartment depends on the amount of accumulated family funds. The most common ways in which they provided their own house/flat were: inheritance (25% in the 34–35 age group, 13% in the 29–30 group), house/flat bought on their own (9.5% in the 34–35 age group, 4.5% in the 29–30 group), house/flat bought by parents (8% in the 34–35 age group, 6% in the 29–30 group), renting a place on their own (12% in the 34–35 age group, 11.5% in the 29–30 group).

The percentage of young people who live independently from their parents/relatives is 29.5% of the total number. Of these, 41.2% live in an inherited flat, 25.5% in a rented flat, 19% in a flat bought by relatives and 15% bought their house/flat on their own. Housing independence correlates with financial independence. Level of education, profession and employment status are the most important conditions for having one's own house/flat. Those with a university degree (9.2% of them) bought their first house/flat; those with lower vocational education followed (6.9%), while those with only a primary education were at the bottom (1.2%). Those working in the state sector are, in this respect, in a slightly better position than the others (8.8% of them bought their first house or flat). Different employment status is most obvious when young people rent a house/flat on their own: 14% of the self-employed rent on their own, as do 14% of business owners, 13.8% of those employed in the state sector and 11% of those with temporary jobs. The share in all the other categories is below 5%. Those with a university degree have a better chance of renting a place independently (15.8%), and the others follow: those with a college degree (11.3%), then those with four years of secondary school (8.6%), while the others are below 5%.

If we look at the relations between housing dependence and education level, we get the following results: in the same household with parents live 81% of those with (unfinished and finished) primary education, 72% with lower vocational education for qualified workers, 58.7% with secondary education and 52.5% with college and university education. Students show the highest degree of housing dependence: 55% of them live with their parents, 17% in a rented flat paid by their parents, 16% in dormitories, while only 3.6% pay their rent on their own. As results show, a higher level of education and a higher income increase the chance of a young person establishing an independent household.

The situation outside the capital city appears to be slightly better as more young people have their own place to live (usually inherited). However, young people in Belgrade, regardless of the high prices (to rent or to buy a flat), more often buy their own home, or their parents buy it for them.

These facts about housing status in many aspects correspond with the results of the 2003 survey, so we can conclude that the housing status of young people has not improved significantly in the period of eight years between the two surveys.

Getting married represents another step towards independence, so it is interesting to see the relation between marital status and housing status: 74% of those who are single live with their parents; around 7% live in a rented flat paid for by their parents; 7% live in a student dormitory; only 5% pay the rent themselves; 3% live in a place bought by their parents and almost none of them (0.2%) bought the house/flat themselves. Among those who are married, 21% live with their parents; 29% in an inherited house/flat; 13% bought it themselves; 11% live in a place bought by their parents; 7% rent a flat that they pay for themselves. Those who cohabit are in the best position: 16% of them live with their parents, and more than-three quarters live in a separate housing unit (26% in an inherited house/flat, 21% in a rented flat that they pay for themselves, 14% bought a house/flat by themselves and 4.5% live in a place bought by their parents). Family formation is usually the strongest incentive to founding own household. Provided that the resources (level of incomes, savings) of family of origin are sufficient, they would be used for enabling independent place of residence for a young married couple.

Only 4% of young people in the whole sample provided the house/flat on their own. Half of them used their own savings and a slightly lower percentage combined different sources of income (for example, they might have sold the inherited property and their parents might have helped them financially). Only around 10% of real-estate owners used the subsidized mortgages provided by the state, which indicates that young people usually rely on personal and family resources for obtaining a place to live and that very few of them use institutional mechanisms to provide the necessary funds to buy a house/flat.

Around three-quarters of young people did not plan to change their housing situation in a period of one year. Among those who do, 9% plan to rent a flat, 4% to take out a loan and buy a flat and 5% plan to leave the country. Those planning to take out a loan and buy a flat belong to the older age groups. The absence of a plan to change a place of residence indicates a lack of options as well as traditionally low residence mobility.

Another interesting fact is that about one-third of those who are completely financially independent[13] of their parents still share living space with their parents when they are in the 34–35 age group, 43% at the 29–30 age group, 60% at the 24–25 age group and two-thirds at the 19–20 age group. In fact, the income of young people is insufficient for independent living and the value of such a communal life is more important than the opportunities and risks of independent life.

Education as the Resource for Economic Status and Independence

One of the starting points of our research was the hypothesis that financial independence is mostly influenced by the level of (formal and nonformal) education and the professional background of a young person. The education of young people represents a family strategy and the most important channel of social mobility, namely intergenerational reproduction of social status.

The period of postsocialist transformation in Serbia was characterized by relative stagnation in the spread of educational opportunities

13 In the whole sample, around 44% of those who were financially independent lived with their parents, 20% in an inherited house/flat, 10% rented a place on their own, 7.5% bought the place themselves and 8% lived in a house/flat bought by their parents.

during the 1990s but also by their significant expansion since 2000. The percentage of young people who finish high school and college/university education has increased. At the same time, increasing commercialization of higher education has reduced the chances for young people from lower social strata to study. Education reform itself does not offer the options of working and studying simultaneously, and this is also due to the underdeveloped economy (with a lack of part-time jobs). This is why young people in education are completely financially dependent on their parents. They may have modest state assistance in the form of loans or grants but this is not sufficient to cover all living expenses during their studies. On the other hand, the labour market remains saturated, so a university degree does not guarantee a safe and well-paid job either. But even under such circumstances, the level of education indicates a strong link with the level of income and opportunities that young people have in life.

The survey confirmed a close connection between the income of young people and their education level. The majority of those in low personal income pay grades are those who have only primary school educational level or less (about 81%). Among the lowest educational category only 3% belong to the high pay grades. Those who have finished secondary school are concentrated around average pay grades, while those with a college degree are slightly better represented in the higher income categories (around 13%). Young people with a university degree are the most common group in higher income categories (35%), while around one-quarter of them falls into lower pay grades. Furthermore, income correlates with the perception of financial status. Only a small percentage of the young people who have not finished primary school falls in this group (about 1.5%), but two-thirds of them do not have enough money even to buy food. In the other education groups, those with a university degree are in the best position. In this group 85% can save some money to buy some expensive goods (which is the case with 71% of those with a college degree, 63% of those with secondary education and around 52% of those with lower vocational or primary school education).

The level of independence from parents was also measured by asking young people how important it is to them to become independent. Education was not only an important factor as a condition for independence but it also influences young people's evaluation of independent life. The percentage of those who do not want to become independent is the highest among those with only primary school education (12.5%), while the percentages for other groups are the following: lower vocational – 9.5%; secondary – 4.4%; college/ university education – around 3%.

Giving up further education depends on the amount of income in the household. Those in lower pay grades gave two main reasons for not continuing education: lack of money (63.5%) and lack of interest in further education (60%). The fact that scholarships for secondary school and university students are slightly more common among those with higher household incomes, as well as those whose parents have a college or university degree, shows that educational opportunities and success largely depend on family cultural and economic capital.

Young people from higher income households[14] and with higher personal educational background[15] tended to invest more in education. As expected, students had the most detailed plans for further education: 30.4% intended to continue education in their town/city, 32.7% in another town/city, 16.5% abroad and about 20% did not plan to continue education. Various experts also had plans for further education: 13.3% planned to continue education in their town/city, 15.3% in another town/city and 8.7% abroad.

The survey also confirms the close connection between education and financial situation. Educated young people not only have higher income but formal education and income also enable them to acquire additional knowledge and skills, which position them better on the job market.

14 Among them, two-thirds had good foreign-language skills and one-fifth were attending a foreign language course over the past year. This contrasted with the lower income groups where only one-third of the young people spoke a foreign language, and only 6.3% attended a foreign language course over the past year. Computer literacy was connected with the household income in a similar way.

15 As many as 43.4% of students attended a foreign language course in the past year – 18.6% of those with a university degree and 16% of those with a college degree.

Employment as the Resource for Economic Status and Independence

As expected, higher income correlates with a better status of profession. As far as employment status is concerned, 40% of the young people who own business (2.2% of the total number) have higher grade incomes. In the state sector, 29% of those with permanent jobs (10.7% of the total number) are in the higher income grades (about half of them have medium-grade incomes, and none of them are in lower grades). In the private sector, 18% of those with permanent jobs (18.7% of the total number) have higher incomes but as many as 55% of them are in the lower income grades. In the group of young people with temporary jobs who work illegally (8.8% of the total) 76% have lower incomes whereas young people with temporary jobs who work legally (5.6% of the total number) are concentrated around medium and moderately low incomes. Perception of one's own financial situation follows objective indicators, so 85% of those whose income is derived from the ownership and management of a company or business can save some money and buy some expensive goods, whereas the percentage of those working in the state sector who can do so is 76.3%, and the percentage of those employed legally in the private sector is 72.1%. As far as employment status is concerned, a high percentage of students expects to be supported by their parents. Most of the others (around half of each group) expect to be financially independent.

The potential for entrepreneurship of young people was also explored through their plans to start their own business. In our survey sample, 6.1% of young people already had a private company, 4% were working on starting their own business and as many as 29.4% had thought about that option (60.4% did not want it, or did not think about it). We were also interested in how active young people were while looking for a job. As many as 19.4% of the unemployed were not looking for a job in any way, 28.4% were trying to find a job with the help of the National Employment Service, 25.8% with the help of friends and relatives, and 17.1% on the Internet. Widespread use of informal channels as a mechanism of job finding suggests instability in the job market, with a high level of competition. The percentage of those relying on their friends and relatives is higher among those with lower education profiles (34.3%) than with secondary education (29.8%), lower vocational education (29%) or with (unfinished and finished) primary education, whereas the percentage of those with a university degree is under 18%. Only 6.1% of young unemployed people were involved in one of the national employment service programmes (4.4% participated in 'The First Chance'– a state-launched programme).

Due to a low standard of living, 24.8% of the young people indicated that they would leave the country, 15.2% would do it because of bleak prospects and 8.6% because of unemployment. Bleak prospects are more often mentioned as the reason by those with higher education (18.3%), while unemployment is more often mentioned by those with lower education (11%).

Concluding Remarks

This analysis confirms the conclusion from the 2003 study that young people in Serbia have a high level of financial and economic dependence on their families. We have detected some changes in the situation regarding their financial status and independence: the share of young people who were completely financially dependent on their parents decreased while the share of those with personal income increased between 2003 and 2011. Young people had more diverse perceptions of what they could afford with their income in 2011 as compared to 2003. The data indicate that opportunities that appeared in the labour market improved the financial position of young people, but not sufficiently for any significant independence (especially with regard to housing).

The findings indicate that young people were almost completely dependent on their parents during schooling and while job seeking; after the beginning of employment, their parents usually continue supporting them (even after they create their own households and families). Despite the fact that, during the eight-year period, an increased number of young people became capable of earning money, the amount of income was still below the level that was necessary for independent living. In this regard, Serbia, together with other postsocialist countries in the Balkans (except perhaps Slovenia), belongs to the postsocialist version of Mediterranean/subprotective welfare regimes (Esping-Andersen, 1990), characterized by insufficiently developed programmes of state support, in which many functions are performed by family (self-) assistance networks, and to the postsocialist/subprotective regime of transition to adulthood (Walther *et al.*, 2009).

Financial status and independence are related to education, employment status and profession. Higher formal education provides better professional status and therefore better financial status for young people. At the same time it also orientates them towards additional education and training, thereby increasing their chances in the labour market. Young people with higher economic and cultural capital stemming from their families are also more eligible for institutional mechanisms such as students' grants and loans, which confirms the thesis that inequality has been reproduced by reliance on family resources.

Young people's agency related to economic independence is also correlated to their education, since independence is more valued among those with higher educational levels.

Unemployed young people mainly relied on informal mechanisms for getting a job, while just a small number of young people took advantage of rather underdeveloped institutional programmes for facilitating employment.

The housing situation was very unfavourable for young people in 2011, and no significant changes were detected in the eight-year period between 2003 and 2011. Education level, profession and activity status were correlated with possession of property: employed professionals with a university education were the most likely to purchase real estate for their needs. Only a small number (one-tenth) of young people who acquired their own living place used subsidized mortgages provided by the state from 2005; they mostly relied on their own resources and resources coming from their families. Related to this situation was low agency of young people concerning housing and independence – two-thirds had elaborated no short-term plans in this regard.

The general conclusion is that the economic status of young people is highly dependent on their family resources, which constitute the restricting or enabling structural framework for their financial and housing situation, as well as for their aspirations and agency. Education and employment are the main preconditions for economic status, so more accessible and diversified institutional mechanisms are needed to facilitate young people's transition from education to work and to independent housing, and to facilitate their agency in the process. In this way, at the social level, young people would be integrated through greater participation in economic and social reproduction, through employment and through family formation. On the individual level, they would develop agency in creating their own life trajectories in dealing with uncertainties, rather than postponing their transition to adulthood.

References

Biggart, A. and Kovacheva, S. (2006) Social change, family support and young adults in Europe. In special issue: M. Du Bois-Reymond and L. Chisholm (eds.) 'The Modernisation of Youth Transitions in Europe', *New Directions for Child and Adolescence Development*, Wiley Periodicals, (Number 113, Fall), pp. 49–61.

Brannen, J., Lewis, S., Nilsen, A. and Smithson, J. (eds) (2002) *Young Europeans, Work and Family: Futures in Transition,* Routledge, London.

CPA/CPS (2004) Centar za proučavanje alternativa/Centre for Policy studies, *Mladi zagubljeni u tranziciji [Young People Lost in Transition]*, CPA/CPS, Belgrade.

Esping-Andersen, G. (1990) *The Three Worlds of Welfare Capitalism,* Princeton University Press, Princeton, NJ.

European Values Study, database, http://zacat.gesis.org/webview/index.jsp?object=http://zacat.gesis.org/obj/fCatalog/Catalog5

Ilišin, V. and Radin, F. (eds) (2007) *Mladi: problem ili resurs [Youth: Problem or Resource]*, IDIZ, Zagreb.

Kovacheva, S. (2001) Flexibilisation of youth transitions in Central and Eastern Europe. *Young* 9 (1), pp. 1–32.

Kovacheva, S. (2004) The role of family social capital in young people's transition from school to work in Bulgaria. *Sociologija* 46 (3), pp. 211–26.

Kuhar, M. and Reiter, H. (2012) Frozen transitions? Young people in former Yugoslavia', In: *1989: Young People and Social Change after the Fall of the Berlin Wall* (eds C. Leccardi, C. Feixa, S. Kovacheva, H. Reiter and T. Sekulić), Council of Europe Publishing, Strasbourg.

Lavrič, M. (ed. (2011) *Youth 2010. The Social Profile of Young People in Slovenia,* Ministry of Education and Sports Office of the Republic of Slovenia for Youth, Lubljana.

Lazić, M. and Cvejić, S. (2005) Stratification changes in Serbian society: a case of blocked post-socialist transformation. In: *Transformation and Strategies. Everyday Life in Serbia at the Beginning of the Third Millennium* (eds A. Milić), ISI FF, Belgrade, pp. 35–59.

Petrovic, M. (2004) Housing status and related strategies of households in Serbia. In: *Transformation and Strategies. Everyday Life in Serbia at the Beginning of the Third Millennium* (eds A. Milić), ISI FF, Belgrade, pp. 173–86.

Republic of Serbia National Employment Service (2010) Unemployment and Employment in Serbia, *Monthly Statistics Bulletin* 94 (June), Belgrade.

Statistics Office of the Republic of Serbia (2010) *Labour Force Survey*, RZZS, Belgrade.

Tomanovic, S. and Ignjatovic, S. (2006) Transition of young people in a transitional society: the case of Serbia. *Journal of Youth Studies* 9 (3), pp. 269–85.

Tomanovic, S. and Ignjatovic, S. (2010) The significance and meaning of family transitions for young people. The case of Serbia in comparative perspective. *Annales – Annals for Istrian and Mediterranean Studies. Series historia et sociologia* 20 (1), pp. 27–40.

Tomić-Koludrović, I. and Leburić, A. (2001) *Skeptična generacija.* Životni *stilovi mladih u Hrvatskoj (Sceptical Generation. Life-styles of young people in Croatia,* AGM, Zagreb.

Ule, M. and Kuhar, M. (2008) Orientations of young adults in Slovenia toward the family formation. *Young* 16 (2), pp. 153–83.

Walther, A. (2006) Regimes of youth transitions. Choice, flexibility and security in young people's experiences across different European contexts. *Young* 14 (1), pp. 119–141.

Walther, A., Stauber, B. and Axel, P. (2009) *Youth: Actor of Social Change,* Final Report, IRIS, Tubingen.

Jana Korunovska Srbijanko, Neda Korunovska Avramovska and Tanja Maleska

The 'Getting Nowhere' Generation: The Transitions of Unemployed Youth in Transitional Macedonia

Introduction

The world is facing a growing youth employment crisis. Developing and developed economies alike are confronted with the challenge of creating decent and sustainable jobs for the large cohort of young people entering the labour market every year. This is especially true in transition countries that have very high unemployment rates, such as Macedonia, where, since the 1990s, the rate has stood constantly above 30% Perhaps the high overall unemployment rates are the reason why this is a marginal issue in Macedonia, while youth unemployment is high on the agenda of the international community.[1]

Recognizing that a failure to successfully integrate young people into the labour market has broader consequences for the future prosperity and development of countries, this chapter tries to illuminate the predictors of youth employment in the Republic of Macedonia. This chapter adds to the growing evidence of a global situation in which young people face increasing difficulties when entering the labour force and confirms that young people in Macedonia are

1 Youth employment is a major focus of the Millennium Development Goals (MDGs) and also the Ministers and Heads of Delegations participating in the High-Level Segment of the Substantive 2006 Session of the Economic and Social Council (ECOSOC) committed themselves to 'develop[ing] and implement[ing] strategies that give youth everywhere a real and equal opportunity to find full and productive employment and decent work' (ECOSOC High-level Segment: Ministerial Declaration, 5 July 2006, E/2006/L.8.).

seriously disadvantaged in the labour market. The report therefore adds urgency to the EU call for development of strategies that aim to give young people a chance to make the most of their productive potential through decent employment.

One of the principal findings is that, while education positively correlates with employment among adults, it loses its predictive power among youth. Furthermore, it is worrisome that the social status and the social networks of youth are the only demographics that successfully predict employment. One positive finding was that there was no telling inequality between the different ethnic groups, between male and female respondents, or between respondents from different places of residence (urban and rural).

This chapter provides empirical assessments of the individual predictors for youth (un)employment in transitional labour markets. It is based on a randomly selected simple sample of 1195 respondents. The data were collected in May and June 2010, via a telephone survey.[2] The project was designed to examine how different levels of education influence the future employment of youth. The relationship between employment and eight other demographic variables (age, gender, ethnicity, social status,[3] social network,[4] place of residence, education attained by respondent's parents and number of children), were also analysed to draw as complete a picture as possible.

The aim was to build an analytical starting block from which Macedonia can identify the main challenges facing youth for the process of designing the policies most suited to its particular situation. At the same time, the chapter calls for the development of coherent and coordinated interventions on youth employment that are based on analytical reviews of labour market information.

2 A detailed description of the methodology and the sample is provided in the appendix.

3 Derived as an index calculated as household income divided by the number of persons that live in the household of the respondent.

4 Measured as the reported number of employed friends and relatives close to the respondent and ranging from 1 = almost all are unemployed to 5 = almost everyone is employed.

This report expands knowledge of the nature and dimensions of youth employment, unemployment and underemployment in transitional economies, such as the countries in the Western Balkans. It provides the first analysis of the relationship between demographic characteristics and employment since the independence of Macedonia.

There are two limitations that should be addressed in our study. The first is its cross-sectional design, which does not allow for a causal interpretation of the findings. The model allows only for statements about relationships between the (statistically labelled) dependent and independent variables. A longitudinal design is needed to address this problem.

The second concerns the demographic characteristic of our sample. Even though randomly selected, the sample does not entirely match the demographics of the Macedonian population, first and foremost because more men than women responded, ethnic groups were underrepresented and the sample was relatively young. Similar research on different and possibly stratified samples is needed to allow for further generalization of our findings.[5] However, in our study we decided against stratification for two reasons. Firstly, the official census data are outdated[6] and we did not want to speculate about or estimate the demographics of the country's population. Secondly, there are no data and no previous research on the subject and our aim was to generate knowledge about the entire population. Thus, the underrepresentation of minorities was not a major concern.

5 Reactor has conducted a follow-up more detailed study on the transition from school to work of the Macedonian youth (Korunovska Srbijanko *et all*, 2012),.

6 The last census, at the time of publication, was from 2002.

Why We Cannot Afford the Youth Unemployment Crisis

Youth Unemployment is Now One of the Most Serious Challenges Facing Macedonia

Macedonia is the European leader in youth unemployment, with 57.1%[7] of Macedonian youth unemployed, making up 18% of the overall unemployment rate, which, continues to be one of the nation's largest problems. With youth unemployment rates well above 80% in certain municipalities, these numbers make unemployed youth a socially disadvantaged group whose interests are either not represented at all or, even when they are, the solutions offered are inadequate to provide significant improvements to the overall position of the youth in the labour market. Furthermore, the fact that the key priority in the EU Accession Partnership is the reduction of impediments to employment creation (addressing in particular the youth) means that this is a pressing problem and one that needs to be researched further before any significant progress is achieved and specific measures for improvement are implemented.[8]

> *very high unemployment rates remains an important issue, especially among youth* (EC Progress Report for Macedonia (2011: 25))

The recent global economic crisis has given the subject of youth unemployment renewed prominence following reports that youth unemployment rates skyrocketed to an all time high[9] in 2010. It is somewhat ironic that as the UN launched the International Year of Youth in August 2010,[10] youth unemployment reached its highest

7 State Statistical Office, Labour Force Survey for 2010, published in 2011 (2010).

8 Council Decision (2008/212/EC), published in the *Official Journal of the EU*, L 80/32 from 19 March 2008.

9 *ILO Global Employment Trends for Youth*, August 2010 – special issue on the impact of the global economic crisis.

10 Launched on 12 August 2010; http://social.un.org/youthyear/ (accessed 26 October 2012).

level on record and was expected to increase.[11] An estimated number of 81 million young people cannot find a job. While the average youth unemployment rate of 13% concerns world leaders and policy makers,[12] it seems as if nobody from Macedonia worries about the 57.1%. The problem did not start under the current government but with such large numbers at risk of being permanently scarred by unemployment, it is now at crisis levels.

The Damaging Effects of Youth Unemployment

The numbers are not just numbers; they matter more than we would like. Unemployment has a negative impact on young people's lives and evidence suggests it does *permanent damage to earnings and employment potential* (the so-called 'wage and employment scar'). Many studies have confirmed that initial spells of unemployment have adverse effects on earnings and future employment (Ryan, 2001; Fares and Tiongson, 2007; Doiron and Gorgens, 2008). For example, using longitudinal data of young people in Norway, Hammer (1997) showed that previous spells of unemployment were the strongest predictor of later periods of unemployment. Bynner and Parsons (2002) summarize the importance of skills gained through employment experience in maintaining a position in the adult labour market by pointing out that those who lack these skills are likely to face difficulties both in entering employment and in sustaining any kind of fulfilling career. They argue that 'the skills acquired through kinds of employment experience become increasingly important in maintaining a position in the adult labour market.' Those who do not have the 'human capital' attributes (Becker, 1975) deemed important by employers, face difficulties not only in entering employment but also in sustaining any kind of fulfilling career.

11 *ILO Global Employment Trends for Youth,* August 2010 – special issue on the impact of the global economic crisis.

12 Joint ILO-IMF conference on the challenges of growth, employment and social cohesion in Oslo http://osloconference2010.org/ (accessed 26 October 2012).

In addition to patchy employment prospects, youth unemployment has *negative effects on the mental and physical health of youth*, both now and in the future. A range of academic studies have found that unemployment increases susceptibility to illness (such as heart attacks later in life, mental stress, helplessness, and loss of self-esteem leading to depression). There is also evidence that the psychological imprint of unemployment persists into later life and that consequences may include difficult relationships, lack of social and political participation, lack of motivation to work and poor physical and mental health (Robins and Rutter, 1990; Hammer, 1997).

Youth unemployment also *increases the probability of antisocial behaviour and exaggerates inequalities.* Studies have found that increases in youth unemployment relate to increases in burglaries, thefts, drug offences and criminality (Atkinson and Hills, 1997; Hammer, 1997). However, the effects are not distributed equally across society. Youth unemployment is interlinked with and exacerbates a range of other inequalities that young people face from birth to entering the labour market. For instance, the evidence suggests that young people are more likely to spend time out of employment, education or training (and be scarred for life as a result) if they are from a less well-off background, come from particular ethnic groups, or are disabled. Of the scarce regional research on the subject, Basic *et al.* (2009) managed to prove this notion and identify especially vulnerable subgroups of unemployed young people in Croatia when taking into consideration age, gender, education, duration in the labour market, place of residence or ethnicity.

The 'Getting Nowhere' Generation: The Transition from School to Work

Our research focused on the transition from school to work, which we argue is probably the most significant determinant of the economic (and social) wellbeing of the individual and, if taken collectively, for influencing the level of development of the country.

Comparative analysis suggests that the transition from education to work is crucial and that youth unemployment is often low in those countries that get it right.[13] In order to do so, governments need to understand the factors that 'push' or 'pull' employment.

Our study focused on two things: firstly, we wanted to test how education relates to the future employment of youth – whether the attainment of additional levels of education positively correlates with youth employability. Secondly, are there lessons to be learned in characterizing factors that influence the difficulty of the transition? Reactor's study was developed to test the hypothesis that the level of education attained has a positive relationship with employment status when the covariates age, gender, ethnicity, social status, social network, place of residence, education attained by respondent's parents and number of children are held constant. We investigated the proposed relationships on two samples: youth (under 29 year old) and older respondents (30+), and used hierarchical logistic regression where employment status (dichotomous variable: employed or unemployed) was the dependant variable and the level of educational attainment and the covariates mentioned above were the independent variables.

The resulting models, both for the youth (15–29) and adults (30–65), had suitable goodness of fit and allowed for generalization of the findings. The model for the whole sample (youth and older) correctly predicted whether the respondents would be employed or not in 70.5% of the cases and explained between 24% and 31% of the variance in the employment status of the respondents (Table 12.1). The model for the older sample correctly predicted 72.5% of the cases and explained from 22 to 29% of the variance in employment status (Table 12.2). Although *the model for the youth sample* correctly predicted 77.2% of the cases, it *did not support our hypothesis that the level of education has predictive power for the employment status of the respondents over that of the control variables.* However, the proposed model had a good fit and explained from 34 to 47% of the employment status variance (Table 12.3).

13 OECD, *Off to a Good Start? Jobs for Youth* (2010); ILO and OECD, *Giving Youth a Better Start* (policy note for G20 summit, 2011).

Table 12.1: Hierarchical logistic regression with the control variables entered in the first step and level of acquired education entered in the second step of the analysis: final model total sample N = 1055

	Variable	B	SE[c]	OR	95%CI OR	
	Constant	–3.41	0.43			
	Gender (female)	0.58	0.15	1.78***	1.32	2.41
	Age (cat.) (youth)	0.51	0.19	1.66**	1.14	2.41
	Place of residence (rural)	–0.34	0.22	0.71	0.46	1.09
	Number of children (no children)					
	One or two children	0.36	0.20	1.43	0.98	2.10
	Three or more children	–0.01	0.30	0.99	0.55	1.78
	Social status	0.37	0.12	1.44**	1.14	1.83
	Social network	0.42	0.07	1.53***	1.34	1.74
	Ethnicity (not Macedonian)	0.11	0.20	1.12	0.75	1.65
	Educational level attained by father[a] (primary)					
	High school graduate	0.35	0.20	1.42	0.96	2.12
	Academic degree	0.15	0.27	1.16	0.68	1.96
	Respondent currently in education (yes)	1.45	0.26	4.27***	2.57	7.11
Step 2	Level of education[b] (high school)					
Step 2	Primary or lower	–0.73	0.23	0.48**	0.31	0.76
Step 2	Academic level	0.26	0.18	1.29	0.90	1.85

Notes: SE = standard error; OR = odds ratio; CI = confidence interval: * $p<0.05$, ** $p<0.01$, *** $p< 0.001$; R^2 (Cox and Snell) = 0.24, R^2 (Nagelkerke) = 0.31; Hosmer and Lemeshow Goodness of Fit Test: chi-square = 7.97 (8), p = 0.436.

a Reference group is no education.
b Reference group is high school.
c Estimated coefficient.

Our study aimed to provide a detailed description of the individual predictors of youth (un)employment in the Republic of Macedonia. It also aimed to provide a comparison between the youth and the older generation of respondents and examine whether the predictors

Table 12.2: Hierarchical logistic regression with the control variables entered in the first step and level of acquired education entered in the second step of the analysis: final model older group (over 29s) N = 604

	Variable	B	SE[c]	OR	95%CI OR	
	Constant	1.28	0.61			
	Gender (female)	0.72	0.20	2.06***	1.39	3.06
	Age	-0.06	0.01	0.94***	0.92	0.96
	Place of residence (rural)	-0.62	0.29	0.54*	0.30	0.96
	Number of children (no children)					
	One or two children	0.79	0.28	2.19**	1.26	3.82
	Three or more children	0.52	0.38	1.68	0.80	3.53
	Social status	0.45	0.17	1.57**	1.13	2.19
	Social network	0.27	0.09	1.31**	1.10	1.57
	Ethnicity (not Macedonian)	0.37	0.27	1.45	0.85	2.48
	Educational level attained by father[a] (primary)					
	High school graduate	0.27	0.25	1.31	0.81	2.13
	Academic degree	0.02	0.34	1.02	0.52	2.00
Step 2	Level of education[b] (high school)					
Step 2	Primary or lower	-0.99	0.29	0.37**	0.21	0.66
Step 2	Academic level	0.32	0.25	1.37	0.84	2.26

Notes: SE = standard error; OR = odds ratio; CI = confidence interval: * $p<0.05$, ** $p<0.01$, *** $p<0.001$; R^2 (Cox and Snell) = 0.22, R^2 (Nagelkerke) = 0.29; Hosmer and Lemeshow Goodness of Fit Test: chi-square = 5.90 (8), p = 0.658.

a Reference group is no education.
b Reference group is high school.
c Estimated coefficient.

for employment are consistent over time. This is especially relevant because of the changing political and economic context in the country over the past 20 years (1991–2011).

The study particularly emphasized education and examined the relationship between education, as one of the most important aspects

Table 12.3: Hierarchical logistic regression with the control variables entered in the first step and level of acquired education entered in the second step of the analysis: final model (Youth) N = 464

	Variable	B	SE(B)[c]	OR	95%CI OR	
	Constant	−11.17	1.36			
	Gender (female)	0.36	0.28	1.43	0.83	2.47
	Age	0.32	0.05	1.38***	1.26	1.52
	Place of residence (rural)	0.05	0.39	1.05	0.49	2.27
	Number of children (no children)					
	One or two children	−0.12	0.40	0.88	0.40	1.93
	Three or more children	−0.36	0.86	0.70	0.13	3.73
	Social status	0.76	0.21	2.14***	1.43	3.22
	Social network	0.52	0.12	1.68***	1.33	2.14
	Ethnicity (not Macedonian)	0.34	0.37	1.41	0.68	2.91
	Educational level attained by father[a] (primary)					
	High school graduate	−0.69	0.46	0.50	0.20	1.24
	Academic degree	−0.99	0.54	0.37	0.13	1.08
	Respondent currently in education (yes)	1.12	0.37	3.06**	1.49	6.30
Step 2	Level of education[b] (high school)					
	Primary or lower	0.01	0.53	1.01	0.36	2.82
	Academic level	−0.26	0.31	0.77	0.42	1.42

Notes: SE(B) = standard error; OR = odds ratio; CI = confidence interval: * $p<0.05$, ** $p<0.01$, *** $p<0.001$; R^2 (Cox and Snell) = 0.34, R^2 (Nagelkerke) = 0.47; Hosmer and Lemeshow Goodness of Fit Test: chi-square = 5.35 (8), p = 0.720.

a Reference group is no education.
b Reference group is high school.
c Estimated coefficient.

of human capital, and employment status in an uncertain transition economy with high unemployment rates. It also analysed whether well known determinants of employment status in the developed Western economies described in the mainstream research literature hold their ground in a fragile economy and a changing political system such as that of the Republic of Macedonia. Our findings are intriguing and more often than not discouraging.

Age Vulnerability and the Labour Market

The study confirmed that young respondents had lower chances for employment than the older respondents, when all other variables were held constant (most notably the level of acquired education and current status of education). Macedonian youth is seriously disadvantaged in the labour market. Being in the youth category cut the chances of employment by half – it was 1.8 times more likely for respondents to be employed if they were older than 29 (Table 12.1). This result confirmed the inequality of youth in the Macedonian labour market and proved that youth alone (when all other socio-demographic characteristics are held constant) predicts unemployment. The results are even more striking because age was a significant predictor of employment even in the youth sample alone: the older the respondents, the more likely that they were employed (1.4 times with each additional year) (Table 12.3).[14]

Within samples, the age correlation occurred in the opposite direction. In the older group (over 29 years of age), the younger the respondents the more likely that they were employed (Table 12.2). This only reaffirms the vulnerability of different age groups on the labour market, suggesting that special measures are needed to redress the situation. Bearing in mind that more than 80% of the unemployed youth and older people (50+) are long-term unemployed (more than one year) is additional cause for concern.

14 Note that education status – i.e. whether respondents were currently in the education system – was held constant.

The Lost (Predictive) Power of Education

Our study confirmed that overall (analysed across the whole sample) level of education had a unique predictive power over and above that of all controls, albeit a very small one. The second step of the analysis (where education is added to the model) is statistically a significant improvement to the model (chi-square (2,14) = 13.42; p = 0.001) although it successfully predicts only one additional case. However small, this confirms our hypothesis that the level of education significantly predicts employment status when controlling for the covariates age, gender, ethnicity, social status, social network, place of residence, education attained by respondent's parents and number of children. It means that education plays a significant role in determining employment in the following way: high-school graduates (as the largest group) were the comparison group, and a jump from high school to university degree made it 1.3 times more likely for respondents to be employed (this jump was not statistically significant). Conversely, not finishing high school made it two (1/0.48) times less likely for the respondents to be employed than if they were high school graduates (Table 12.1).

However, while in the older sample model, the level of education predicts employment over and above the controls and thus confirms our main hypothesis for the older respondents as well (Table 12.2),[15] *in the youth sample model (the group of our main interest) the educational level had no significant influence on the employment status* (Table 12.3).[16] This shows that education has lost its predictive power for employment among Macedonian youth and is the most worrying result of our study.

15 The second step of the analysis (where education is added to the model) is statistically a significant improvement of the model (chi-square (2,12) = 15.07; p = 0.001, although it successfully predicts only five additional cases. The model explains 72.5% of the variance in employment status; an improvement from 71.7% from the model without educational attainment as a predictor.

16 The second step of the analysis (where education is added to the model) is *not* a statistically significant improvement of the model (chi-square (2,13) = 0.72; p = 0.697 and it actually predicts less cases (3) than the model without educational attainment!

The *level of education attained by a respondent's father* in the meantime had no predictive power for employment in either sample.

We also controlled for whether respondents were still studying or not (in high school or at university) and this variable, as expected, had a big impact on the employment status of the respondents. Respondents who were still in the educational process were almost three times less likely to be employed than respondents who had completed education, making it obvious that Macedonian students usually do not engage in part-time (or any kind of) employment while they study. Thus, either this 'habit' or tradition of not working while studying and/or circumstances where student jobs in the country are nonexistent, makes it even harder for Macedonian youth to transfer from education to employment, as they enter the labour market with no working experience whatsoever.

The Need to Know More about Social Networks

The predictions about the influence of the social network and social status on future employment proved to be highly relevant. In the whole sample, *social network* had a positive relationship with employment status: with a unit change in the social network variable (e.g. from *almost all unemployed* friends and relatives to *mostly unemployed* friends and relatives) the respondents were 1.5 times more likely to be employed. Social network maintained its positive relationship with employment status in both the older and younger sample. In the youth sample, both the social status and the social network maintained their strong predictive power for employment status: youth with higher social status and stronger connections (a higher number of employed friends and relatives) were more likely to be employed than their peers with lower social status and weaker social networks.

Similarly, the *social status* of the respondent was also positively related. With every unit change in the social status index, the odds (ratio) that the respondent would be employed were 1.4 times higher (OR = 1.44). That is, the higher the social status of the respondent the greater is the chance that she or he is employed.

Likewise, in the older sample, social status had a strong relationship with employment in the expected (positive) direction: one unit change in the social status index increased the odds for employment 1.6 times. For the youth sample this increase was 1.7 times.

The fact that the predictive power of social status and social network are stronger than that of education is worrying. This is especially true for the younger generation where the social status and social networks are the only demographics besides age that successfully predict employment, whereas the predictive power of education is nonexistent. However, the influence of the social status and social network needs to be examined more closely. The social network was measured on one item and did not distinguish between relatives and friends, nor did it tell us how (or if) this network helped the respondent gain employment. A longitudinal study and more detailed analysis of the social networks is needed in order to permit causal interpretation.

Furthermore, the established relationship between social network and employment status is intuitively expected because employed individuals have more employed friends, because it is natural for people to become friends with their colleagues. Nevertheless, the fact that the answer to this item was one of the only meaningful predictors of youth employment calls for further investigation. It is well known that personal connections are one of the most common routes used when searching for employment, which causes difficulties for disadvantaged groups and families. The finding that individual effort (i.e. educational attainment) makes no difference to the transition to the labour market, while social status and network are the strongest predictors, should alarm the authorities and encourage them to look for and promote alternative routes for employment and to take steps to prevent people with disadvantaged backgrounds from becoming even more disadvantaged.

Taking a look at the other factors, the *gender* of the respondents was also a successful predictor, i.e. women were almost two times (OR = 1.8) less likely to be employed than men. The 30+ female respondents were more than two times less likely to be employed, which is an accurate reflection of the current gender makeup of the labour market. However, one positive finding of our study is that gender inequality in the labour market seems to be disappearing for the younger generations and that young women seem to have as much chance on the labour market as the young man, even though opportunities for both are scarce.[17]

Having children was also related to employment status but only in the older group: having one or two increased the chance of employment more than having three or more. Respondents without children, however, were also less likely to be employed. Specifically, having one or two children made respondents more than twice as likely to be employed compared to the respondents with no children. Having three or more children was statistically comparable to having no children, with both groups faring worse on the labour market than respondents with one or two children. This implies that having more than two children is a potential obstacle for chances on the labour market and makes the current government policies aimed at increasing benefits for women that stay at home and care for three or four children inadequate and uninformed. If the government wants to increase the fertility rate, there is research to suggest that increased women's labour market participation, coupled with providing options for work-life balance could lead to increased fertility rates, rather than prolonged maternity leave and state supported inactivity (Luci and Thevenon, 2011).

On the positive side, there was no telling inequality between the different ethnic groups in either of the samples. Macedonians were just as likely to be (un)employed as respondents from other nationalities. However, except for the Albanians, no other ethnic minority had enough respondents in the study to make a significant contribution to the results and thus this finding must be read with caution. There was no difference between the respondents with different places of residence, but here again respondents from rural areas were in the minority. Interestingly and perhaps counterintuitively, when all things are held equal, respondents from the cities were just as less likely to be employed as their fellow citizens from rural areas, but this was true only for the older sample (30–65).

17 Still, the odds ratio for the younger sample was 1.43, meaning that, even though it was statistically insignificant, there was still a telling difference between the female and male respondents.

Conclusion

In Need of Informed Policy Making

In order to apply results, policies must be aimed at 'real' problems. This requires insight into complex phenomena, and evidence-based policy making. This is far from Macedonian realities. For example, the only research and analysis conducted by the Sector for Research and Analysis of the Labour Market at the Employment Service Agency addresses basic demographics (age, ethnicity, qualifications etc.) of the registered unemployed and an analysis of the skills demanded by the labour market – conducted only twice: for 2008 and 2009/2010.[18] Furthermore, the Labour Force Survey, although improved from year to year, still does not include all indicators and is not in line with the International Labour Organization's guidelines.

It seems, then, that the policy-creation process for their operational programs (and those of the Ministry for Labour and Social Policy) are invented for the purposes of satisfying the needs of the EU Accession Partnership and are not based on any concrete research into the actual situation in the Republic of Macedonia. Given that the vast majority of the two of the most underprivileged groups on the labour market, namely women and youth, are known to be willing to work even when given the chance not to (Reactor – Research in Action, 2010; Korunovska Srbijanko *et al*, 2011), these results call for serious revisions in labour market and education policies.

While the institutions struggle to create adequate measures and policy for the youth, a great risk of brain drain threatens Macedonia. The findings of research that Reactor and the Local Youth Initiative conducted on civic engagement and social inclusion showed that more than 50% of Macedonian high-school children see themselves as having left the country in ten years.[19] A recent World Bank study

18 Letter from the agency sent to Reactor in response to the question 'What studies and analysis has your sector conducted from 2005 to 2010?'

19 *Social Capital of Macedonian Youth, 2011* available at: http://reactor.org.mk/CMS/Files/Publications/Documents/1.3.%20Konfuzija_eng.pdf.

also suggests that Macedonia is a regional leader of the brain drain of educated youth, with almost a third of the youth who emigrated having completed higher education (World Bank, 2011a). All this stresses the need to illuminate the reasons behind high unemployment rates and to make room for more inclusive policy making.

Mismatch of Supply and Demand

Realization that investment in higher education does not pay off in the labour market (especially for the young generation of Macedonians) calls for a closer analysis of the utilization of human capital in the country, the quality of higher education, and the structure of the labour market in Macedonia. The State Employment Agency analysis of labour market demands confirmed that there is a low demand for high-skilled workers. With enrolment rates in tertiary education skyrocketing in recent years (from 60% in 2006/7 to above 80% in 2009/10), there is likely to be more supply than demand for youth with higher education degrees. This could lead to a situation in which employers push up the educational requirements for even basic skill positions. The result is high levels of skills-based underemployment (where employees are overqualified for the work they do).

The mismatch could persist due to the structure of the economy. International organizations state that educational qualifications are not so important for the labour market and, oddly enough, unemployment rates do not decrease with attainment of higher education. This is due to the structure of the economy, which employs a low-skill labour force, for example in agriculture or the textile industry. For instance, in its latest 2011 South East Europe Regular Economic Report the World Bank stated that:

> … unemployment among those with low skills (no education beyond primary) is relatively close to the average unemployment rate. In contrast, low skill unemployment in EU-10 countries is more than double the average unemployment rate. The skill structure of employed reflects the structure of economies: agriculture … is a low skill sector, and so is the textile industry which employs about a quarter of Macedonia's manufacturing sector labour force. (World Bank, 2011b)

This is even more worrying if we take into account the research that they *provide evidence that the penalty for jobless spells may also be higher for more educated workers.* Fares and Tiongson (2007) found that young workers from Bosnia and Herzegovina are more likely to go into unemployment and are less likely to transition out of inactivity, and while higher educational attainment is generally associated with more favourable labour market outcomes, i.e. skilled workers are less likely to be jobless and are less likely to transition from employment into joblessness, the penalty for jobless spells is higher.

In sum, our findings open an important debate about the state and status of youth and human capital in the country, and calls for a serious re-evaluation of the policies and measures currently adopted. We argue that our findings imply that, instead of focusing on incentives and advertisements for motivating young people to further their education beyond high school, greater emphasis must be placed on increasing the quality of higher education and creating jobs that can utilize such highly educated workers. More research on the subject of youth unemployment in Macedonia is needed and a fruitful dialogue between the policy makers and the research institutions is necessary.

Appendix: Method

Data Collection and Sample Description

The data-collection process for the study took place between May and June 2010 yielding a total sample size of 1195 respondents. It was conducted via telephone survey on randomly selected telephone numbers; thus it yielded a simple (nonstratified) sample. The response rate was high (68%), although more men (58.9%) than women (41.1%) responded. The age of the sample ranged from 15 to 65. The mean age was 34 years (M=34.4, SD=12.6); 44.2% of the sample was below the age of 29 and considered to be 'youth'.

The majority of the sample (77.5%) were ethnic Macedonians, followed by 191 (16.2%) ethnic Albanians. Other ethnic minorities included 2.4% Turks, 1.2% Roma, 1.0% Serbs and 1.7% respondents of other (undisclosed) ethnicities; 50.3% of the respondents reported having no children, 38.3% had one or two and 10.5% reported having three or more children. The majority of our respondents (46.4%) lived in a four-member household; 29.6% were either alone or in one- or two-member households; an additional 17.6% lived in five-member households and the rest (6.4%) in larger households.

The monthly household ranged from 0 to 15 000 MKD (ca. 250 EUR) for 35.2% of the respondents; the majority (36.1%) received from 15 001 to 30 000 MKD (250 to 500 EUR); 17.5% from 30 001 to 45 000 MKD (500 to 750 EUR) and 11.2% more than that. This hints at economic hardship for a substantial number of the sample, with only 50 respondents out of 1195 (4.4%) receiving more than 60 000 MKD (ca. 1000 EUR) per household.

The majority of the sample (87.1%) lives in cities or towns and only 12.9% of the sample was from the villages – the rural areas of the country.

Most of our respondents had poor social networks (19.4% indicated that almost none of their friends and relatives were employed whereas 29.1% reported that most of them were unemployed). Less than a third (28.2%) reported having both employed and unemployed friends and relatives and the rest indicated a rich social network (16.2% had most of their friends and relatives employed; 6.8% almost all of them). The education attained by our respondents' parents was as follows: 27.1% had fathers with lower education compared to 35.5% for the mothers; 54.2% had fathers with high-school level education compared to 52.6% for the mothers and 18.7% had fathers with higher education compared to 11.9% who had mothers with higher education.

Regarding the variables of interest, namely education and position in the labour market, the sample characteristics were as follows: 18.2% of the respondents were still in education either in high school or at university; 2.0% had no formal education; 19.5% finished only primary school; 38.6% finished vocational high school; a further 14.5% had academic high school as their highest completed education level; 1.5% had a higher education diploma (2–3 years of university); 22.6% had a university degree; 0.9% had a master's diploma and 0.3% (three respondents) were PhDs.

Almost half of the sample (48.3%) was employed; the other half (51.7%) was unemployed. Of the unemployed, 44.6% were looking for a job, 26.9% were not looking to be employed and 28.2% were unemployed because they were currently studying. Of the employed, 14.5% were independent entrepreneurs (self-employed); 61.2% were employed in the private business sector (30.2% in small private businesses, 21.1% in mid-sized companies and 10.8% in big corporations). Little over a fifth of the sample (22.7%) worked in public administration and the rest (an insignificant 0.7%) worked for the nongovernment/nonprofit sector.

Measures

The questionnaire for the study consisted of 23 questions inquiring about all relevant variables. A detailed educational history, including name and type of all schools attended (e.g. vocational or academic high school) and whether the respondents were currently employed, provided the basis for the dependant and independent variables. Nine additional demographic variables were relevant for the study: *gender* (female = 1, male = 0); age (in years); *ethnicity; place of residence* (urban = 1, rural = 0); *educational level attained by respondent's parents* (ranging from 0 = no education to 7 = PhD); *number of children; social status* (calculated as an index derived from the household income divided by the number of persons in the household) and the (power of) *social network* – the number of employed friends and relatives close to the respondent (ranging from 1 = almost all are unemployed to 5 = almost everyone is employed). Because of the high correlation between the level of education attained by the respondents' parents ($r = 0.78$, $p = 0.000$ for the total and the older samples; $r = 0.74$, $p = 0.000$ for the youth sample) and in order to avoid multicollinearity, in the final analysis we only used the level of education attained by the respondent's father.

Analysis

We used hierarchical logistic regression where all the controls were entered in the first step and the level of education was entered in the second step. The predictive power of education was proven if the second model explained significantly more variance in the dependant variable (employment status) – i.e. if the chi-square of the change was significantly different from zero. We conducted three logistic regressions, the first for the whole sample and then one for each group (youth and older respondents). The predictive power of the control variables was measured by the improvement of the model in the first step and the significance of the Wald statistic – i.e. the beta coefficients – in the last (second) step of the regression. The predictive power of the independent variable (the level of attained education of the respondent) was measured by the improvement of the model in the second step of the analysis and by the significance of the Wald statistic and beta coefficient for education. Listwise deletion was used for all the regressions, which resulted in slightly smaller samples.

Details about means, standard deviations and correlations between the variables are presented in Table 12.4.

Table 12.4a: Means, standard deviations and correlations between variables for the older sample

	M	SD	1	2	3	4	5	6	7	8	9	10
1. Employment status	0.61	0.49	1									
2. Gender	0.38	0.49	−0.13**	1								
3. Age	43.01	10.15	−0.18**	0.07	1							
4. Place of residence	1.14	0.35	−0.09*	−0.07	0.19	1						
5. Number of children (3 cat.)	0.96	0.62	16**	0.03	0.35**	0.17**	1					
6. Social status	1.22	0.77	0.34**	0.07	−0.24**	−0.25**	0.38**	1				
7. Social network	2.84	1.17	0.25**	0.07	0.02	−0.14**	−0.10**	0.45**	1			
8. Ethnicity	0.74	0.44	0.20*	0.11**	−0.01	−0.25**	−0.43**	0.37**	0.25**	1		
9. Education attained by father (3 cat.)	0.78	0.7	0.21**	0.11**	−0.21**	−0.19**	−0.27**	0.85**	0.33**	0.32**	1	
10. Education attained by mother (3 cat.)	0.57	0.63	0.25**	0.08*	−0.30**	−0.16**	−0.32**	0.85**	0.30**	0.29**	0.78**	1
11. Education attained by respondent (3 cat.)	1.07	0.69	0.30**	−0.00	−0.11**	−0.26**	−0.34	0.65**	0.30**	0.32**	0.55**	0.53**

Table 12.4b: Means, standard deviations and correlations between variables for the younger sample

	M	SD	1	2	3	4	5	6	7	8	9	10
1. Employment status	0.33	0.47	1									
2. Gender	0.45	0.50	–0.07	1								
3. Age	23.45	4.14	0.52	–0.15**	1							
4. Place of residence	1.12	0.32	0.01	–0.02	–0.00	1						
5. Number of children (3 cat.)	0.14	0.40	0.13**	0.08	0.32**	0.07	1					
6. Social status	1.60	0.78	–0.00	0.20**	–0.09	–0.23**	–0.29**	1				
7. Social network	2.32	1.10	0.37**	–0.02	0.35**	0.01	0.07	0.09	1			
8. Ethnicity	0.79	0.41	0.02	0.23**	–0.05	–0.21**	–0.23**	0.39**	0.04	1		
9. Education attained by father (3 cat.)	1.09	0.59	–0.08	0.16**	–0.10*	–0.22**	–0.25**	0.86**	0.00	0.37**	1	
10. Education attained by mother (3 cat.)	1.00	0.59	–0.07	0.19**	–0.12**	–0.24**	–0.29**	0.83**	0.05	0.44**	0.74**	1
11. Education attained by respondent (3 cat.)	1.00	0.67	0.28**	–0.01	.59**	–0.10*	–0.07	0.28**	0.34**	0.20**	0.25**	0.22**

References

Atkinson, A. B., and Hills, J. (Eds.) (1997) Exclusion, employment and opportunity, Center for the Analysis of Social Exclusion, *London School of Economics and Political Science*, London

Basic, J., Slehan, M. and Kranzelic, V. (2009) Najugrozenije skupine nezaposlenih mladih u RH: Preliminarni podaci projekta 'Socijalna ukljucenost i strategije zivljenja u Hrvatskoj i Sloveniji u europskom kontekstu. [The most vulnerable groups of unemployed young people in Croatia: Preliminary data from the project 'Social inclusion and living strategies of unemployed young people in Croatia and Slovenia in the European context.] *Ljetopis socijalnog rada* 16 (1), pp. 111–31.

Becker, G. S. (1975). Human capital. *National Bureau of Economic Research*, Washing.

Bynner, J. and Chisbolm, L. (1998) Comparative youth transition research: methods, meaning and research relations. *European Sociological Review* 14 (2), pp. 131–50.

Bynner, J. and Parsons, S. (2002) Social exclusion and the transition from school to work: the case of young people not in education, employment, or training. *Journal of Vocational Behavior* 60, pp. 289–309.

Doiron, D. and Gorgens, T. (2008) State dependence in youth labour market experiences and the evaluation of policy interventions. *Journal of Econometric* 145, pp. 81–97.

European Commission (2011) Republic of Macedonia 2011 Progress Report, SEC (2011) 1203 Final, Brussels available at: http://ec.europa.eu/enlargement/pdf/key_documents/2011/package/mk_rapport_2011_en.pdf

Fares, J. and Tiongson, E. (2007) *Youth Unemployment, Labour market transitions, and Scarring: Evidence from Bosnia and Herzegovina,* World Bank Policy Research Working Paper 4183, http://econ.worldbank.orgFurlong, A (1998) Youth and social class: change and continuity. *British Journal of Sociology of Education* 19 (4), pp. 591–7.

Hammer, T. (1997) History dependence in youth unemployment. *European Sociological Review* 13 (1), pp. 17–33.

Jeffrey, C. (2008) 'Generation nowhere': rethinking youth through the lens of unemployed young men. *Progress in Human Geography* 32 (6), pp. 739–58.

Luci, A. and Thevenon, O. (2011) Does economic development explain the fertility rebound in OECD countries?, *Population and Societies 481*, http://www.ined.fr/fichier/t_publication/1551/publi_pdf2_pesa481.pdf (accessed 30 October 2012)

Reactor - Research in Action (2010) *Women in the Macedonian Economy,* Reactor, [], Skopje.

Ryan, P. (2001) The school to work transition: A cross national perspective, *Journal of Economic Literature,* 39 (1): 34 - 92

Robins, L., and Rutter, M. (1990) *Straight and devious pathways from childhood to adulthood,* Cambridge University Press, Cambridge.

Korunovska Srbijanko, J., Korunovska Avramovska, N. and Maleska, T. (2011) *Social Capital among Macedonian High School Students,* Youth Educational Forum, Skopje.

Korunovska Srbijanko, J., Korunovska Avramovska, N. and Maleska, T. (2012) *Youth and the Labour Market,* Reactor-Research in Action, Skopje (available at:http://reactor.org.mk/CMS/Files/Publications/Documents/Youth%20and%20the%20Labor%20Market%2020121.pdf State Statistical Office (2011) *Macedonia in Numbers,* Skopje, www.stat.gov.mk/PrikaziPublikacija_1_en.aspx?rbr=290 (accessed 26 October 2012).

World Bank (2011a) *Migration and Remittances Fact Book 2011,* second edition, The International Bank for Reconstruction and Development/The World Bank, Washington [

World Bank (2011b) *South East Europe Regular Economic Report,* World Bank, http://siteresources.worldbank.org/ECAEXT/Resources/publications/454763-1321298251856/11411_01_fullreport.pdf (accessed 30 October 2012)

Part IV

The Problematic of Social Reform: Balancing Equity, Efficacy and Economic Viability

Neda Milevska-Kostova

Equity in Health in Macedonia: Socio-Economic and Financial Aspects and Effects of Policy Changes on Access to Prescription Medicines in Primary Healthcare[1]

Introduction

This chapter will investigate equity in health by examining economic aspects of access to prescription medicines and other services in primary healthcare (PHC) in Macedonia, and effects of policy changes in the regulation of PHC there. Such policy changes have occurred in the context of ongoing health reforms.

One of the reasons for implementing the concessional privatization model in PHC in the country was to ensure equitable access. Equitable access is a right guaranteed to every citizen in the Constitution of the Republic of Macedonia (1991, art. 39) and in healthcare legislation. The priorities for reforming the healthcare system involved improvement of the quality, efficiency and effectiveness of the health services, with PHC being among the first segments in line for transformation. The Ministry of Health (MoH), with international technical assistance, has successfully transferred the majority of PHC into the private sector, while introducing the capitation payment model as a major incentive for PHC physicians to assist in the

1 This chapter has been prepared as part of the research project funded by the Regional Research Promotion Programme (RRPP). It describes in more detail the research study, which aimed to explore equity in health from a socio-economic aspect, through effects of policy changes relating to the regulation of prescription medicines and overall access to prescription medicines for general population and vulnerable/marginalized groups in particular.

envisaged shift from secondary care domination to a primary care-led service and reinforcement of their gatekeeper role, thus indirectly improving the efficiency and effectiveness of secondary healthcare.

Initial assessments are showing no significant improvements or savings in PHC and, at the same time, no significant improvements in access to prescription medicines. However, rather than employing simple cost-containment strategies, it might be more important to assess the quality of services provided, and, in particular, the effects of reformed PHC on expenditure at the secondary and tertiary levels.

The chapter, although focused on the context of one country, has a wider regional application in the context of transition economies in Central and South-eastern Europe, particularly with regard to the impact of transition on healthcare systems, especially those originating from similar political systems, and on healthcare insurance and benefits systems.

Health Reform and Privatization in Transition Economies

Since the 1980s, many European countries - developed and developing alike - have become increasingly concerned with the costs of healthcare; the aging of the population; higher levels of chronic diseases and disability on the one hand, and the increasing availability of new treatments and technologies together with rising public expectations on the other hand (Saltman and Figueras, 1997). This has led to an emergent yet steady and sustainable process of reform in healthcare systems across Europe.

The incentives for reforming the healthcare services in Central and Eastern Europe (CEE) and South-East Europe (SEE) were also related to the lack of efficiency and cost-effectiveness of the health services, which were delivered through a centralized system based on the principle of free treatment. They were also characterized by the geographical overconcentration of the healthcare facilities' network and overstaffing in hospitals (EurActiv, 2004).

The focus of health reforms in the transition economies of Central and Eastern Europe (CEE) and Southeast Europe (SEE) since the 1990s has been on the promotion of private-sector healthcare delivery (Saltman and Figueras, 1997). The governments of those countries (Czech Republic, Hungary, Slovenia, Slovak Republic, Poland, and Macedonia, for example) have started to incorporate market conditions for health-service provision and new funding allocation instruments (Cernic-Istenic, 1998).

One of the reforms of particular interest was the introduction of a stronger role for PHC in the countries of CEE and SEE. Primary healthcare reform has been particularly challenging to implement as the rapid transition from command economy to market economy brought financial instability, a decline in expenditure on social services, and inadequate organizational structures (Shkolnikov *et al.*, 2001; Atun *et al.*, 2005). These challenges were justified in terms of improving efficiency and the quality of healthcare services (Nordyke and Peabody, 2002), using a model from developed countries for opening the market to private initiative (Cernic-Istenic, 1998; Nordyke and Peabody, 2002). Transition economies are a particularly interesting research subject as they provide the opportunity for comparing the effects on health of the transition from communist to market-oriented democratic systems (McKee and Nolte, 2004).

The coexistence of public and private PHC providers in low- and middle-income countries has been associated with multiple problems, from differences in quality of care to increased patient loads and lack of preventive and public health services (Roemer, 1984; Cichon, 1991). In some cases, the existence of private PHC providers led to improvement in quality of services (Nordyke, 2002) but there are also studies showing that markets have propelled the provision of a service at minimal cost (Titmuss, 1970), which may affect the quality or even effectiveness of services (Mossialos *et al.*, 2004). However, the relationship of quality of services to cost of care is not the main concern of this research and will not be reviewed or analysed.

In the same spirit, the Republic of Macedonia is undertaking sweeping reforms in its healthcare sector, seeking to improve the efficiency and quality of PHC by strengthening the role of the market in healthcare provision (Figure 13.1) (Nordyke and Peabody, 2002). The private provision of healthcare services was legalized earlier (in 1991) and by 2002 private physicians constituted about 10% of all licensed physicians and 22% of all licensed PHC physicians (Nordyke and Peabody, 2002). The process of privatization in PHC started intensively in 2005 with the introduction of a capitation payment system for PHC providers contracted by the Health Insurance Fund (HIF). The capitation payment model that was introduced is a patient-based capitation model, which means that the physician receives a payment that is dependent on the number and type of patients registered with the physician's practice (Chaix-Couturier *et al.*, 2000). The capitation model also includes incentives for physicians for rational prescribing and performing preventive services. By the end of 2008 a total of 2176 PHC providers had been contracted by the HIF (HIF, 2009), which constitutes 95% of the licensed PHC providers and over 35% of all licensed practicing physicians in the country (LKM, 2010).

Figure 13.1: Development of primary healthcare in Macedonia (adapted from: Nordyke and Peabody, 2002)

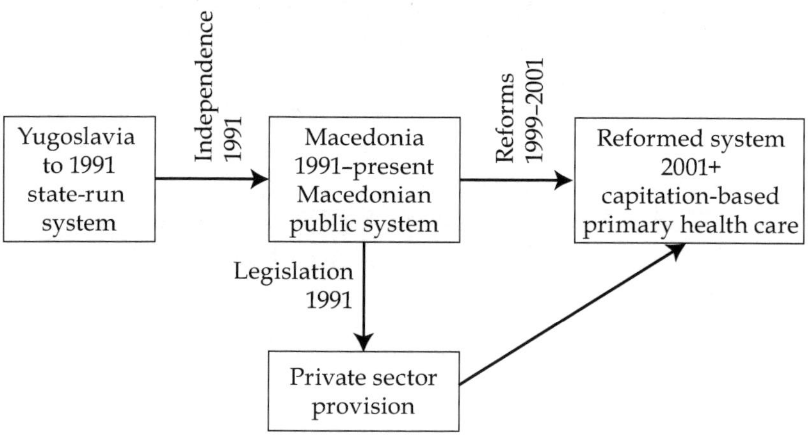

Briefly, the privatization of publicly owned PHC brought market rules into the healthcare sector in Macedonia; the PHC providers that have been working in the public sector as general practitioners (GPs), paediatricians, dentists, gynaecologists, school-medicine doctors and pharmacists have been obliged to open private PHC offices and sign a capitation-based contract with the HIF for payment per registered patient (Gjorgev *et al.*, 2006).

In general, the contract includes two major payment categories: 70% of the capitation fee is transferred each month based on the number of registered patients. The remaining 30% of the capitation fee per registered patient is conditioned with fulfilment of the so-called *preventive goals of the PHC* (Table 13.1): rational prescribing by limiting the number of prescriptions per registered patient (7%), rational referrals and sick leave (4%) and preventive services and early detection of malignancies and deformities in children (combined 19%) (HIF, 2010, 2011). The preventive goals are planned at the beginning of each trimester (as per calendar year), implemented and reported.

Table 13.1: Preventive goals of the primary healthcare, January–March 2010 (adapted from Preventive Goals in PHC, HIF, 2010)

Goal	Description of activities	Indicator	% of capit.	Applicable to
A. General (for all PHC) (total: 11%)				
Prescriptions	Rational use and rational prescribing of medicines on the PLD	Number of prescriptions	7%	All patients
Referrals	Rational referral to higher levels of healthcare	Number of referrals	2%	All patients
Sick-leaves	Rational and justified referral for a sick leave	Number of sick-leave referrals	2%	All patients
B. Other preventive goals (anaemia, asthma, cancer prevention, etc.) (total: 19%)				

Notes: PA = preventive activities, PLD = Positive List of Drugs.

In the early stages of contracting between HIF and PHC providers, a limit was placed on the number of prescriptions, whereby PHC providers could only write two prescriptions per patient per trimester on a cumulative annual basis. Despite this limitation, prescription quantities were still high and not reduced to reasonable levels. The major reason, as identified by the HIF, was that some medicines could be prescribed as multiple packages per prescription (HIF, 2010). In 2009, this was replaced with a more stringent cost-containment policy – a fixed budget for prescribing allowed to the PHC provider in a trimester, adjusted for the number of registered patients. Physician-fixed budgets, especially in PHC, offer an incentive to contain costs (King and Kanavos, 2002) and failure to observe the ceiling reduces the capitation payment.

Figure 13.2: Policy changes affecting primary healthcare with incentives mechanisms

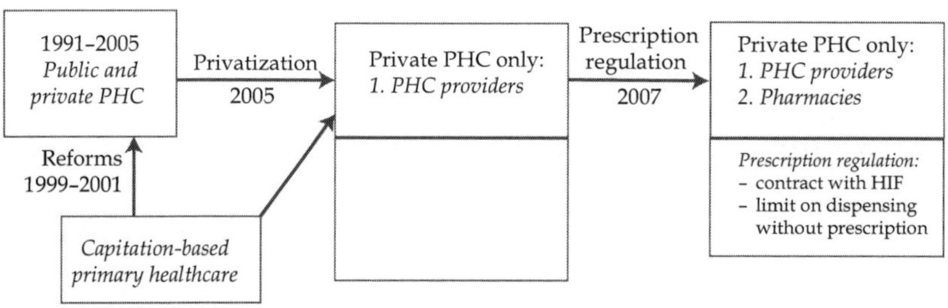

Although commonly called privatization, the process of transformation of the PHC resembles the concession type of transfer of public services (Poole, 2008).

The policy changes described above and in Figure 13.2 have influenced the regulation of the pharmaceutical market and prescribing in particular (Figure 13.3). The supply side, in this case represented by PHC providers and pharmacies, was placed under more stringent regulatory control with regard to the prescription and dispensing of medications.

Having provided a brief background, the next section reviews the literature on the regulation of pharmaceuticals, prescribing and access to prescription medicines in PHC.

Figure 13.3: A simplified flowchart of prescribing in Macedonia

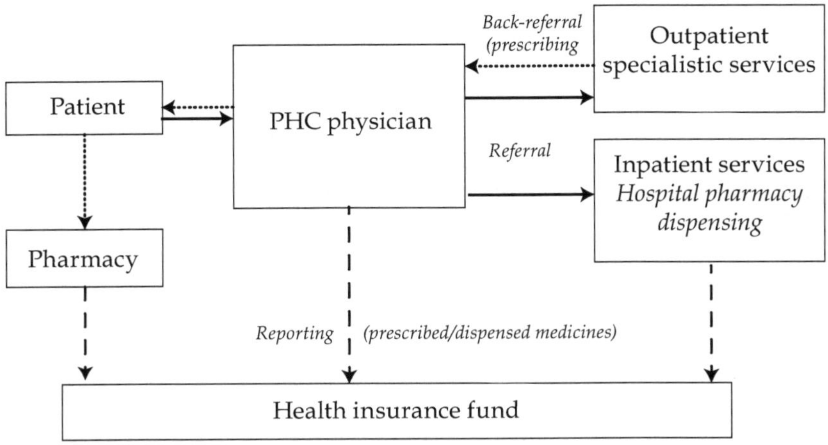

Legend:
Solid line = referral
Dotten line = back-referral: prescribing
Dashed line = reporting

Regulating Prescribing of Medicines in Healthcare Systems

Regulation of the pharmaceutical market is a complex and often very politicized process, as it involves multiple actors, such as government and third-party payers (insurance), prescribing physicians, pharmacists, wholesale suppliers, patients and patient advocacy groups and research-based industries (Mossialos *et al.*, 2004). Trying to balance these interests with effective and efficient pharmaceutical expenditure, countries are applying different controls and incentives in regulating pharmaceuticals, often adjusted to the given context (Permanand and Altenstetter, 2004). In general, these can be divided into regulating the two sides: the supply side and the demand side. Supply-side strategies for optimizing pharmaceutical expenditure are often implemented by regulating pharmaceutical prices and reimbursement levels (Mrazek and Mossialos, 2004). The alternative method of controlling pharmaceutical spending is to influence the behaviour of the groups that generate the demand: doctors, pharmacists and patients (Hutton *et al.*, 1994). These so-called cost-containment policies are usually implemented through measures such as direct fixed price controls, profit controls and reference pricing (Mossialos *et al.*, 2004). Fixed pricing is aimed at securing pharmaceutical prices that are considered reasonable for a given health system (Mrazek and Mossialos, 2004). Profit control (currently unique to UK) is aimed at ensuring that pharmaceutical producers are not making excessive profits on patent-protected products (Department of Health UK, 1999). Reference pricing is a system of setting maximum medicine reimbursement levels per drug that will be paid by the government or the health insurance (Mrazek and Mossialos, 2004; Kanavos and Taylor, 2007).

Prescribing a drug is one of the most frequent therapeutic decisions by general practitioners (Bakker *et al.*, 2007), representing a focal point of contact between doctors and patients and being used as one of the indicators of the quality of medical care (Harding *et al.*, 1985). Despite the traditional teachings that a prescription for a medicine should be necessary, safe, effective and economical at the same time, the prescribing approaches are not always standardized (Bateman *et al.*, 1996). Variations in prescribing have been analysed against both clinical and nonclinical variables (Wilkin *et al.*, 1987; Wilkin and Smith, 1987; Webb and Lloyd, 1994) and results show that nonclinical variables, such as doctors' personal characteristics and experience and patients' expectations also play an important role in the prescription behaviour of the primary physician (Bradley, 1992; Webb and Lloyd, 1994; Wilson *et al.*, 1996), and that much of the prescribing at the GP level cannot be accounted for on purely pharmacological grounds (Bradley, 1992).

Equity in Health: Primary Healthcare and Prescribing

In economic theory, market mechanisms are described in terms of supply and demand. Although the literature provides various and sometimes contradictory definitions of supplier-induced demand (SID) in healthcare (Labelle *et al.*, 1994), there are two most common definitions: 'demand inducement refers to physicians' alleged ability to shift patient's demand for medical care at a given price, that is, to convince patients to increase their use of medical care without lowering the price charged' (Hardley, 1979); 'supplier induced demand is the amount of demand created by physicians, which exists beyond what would have occurred in a market in which consumers are fully informed' (Donaldson and Gerard, 1993).

Both definitions suggest that the physician and the physician's behaviour play a crucial role in deciding the level of demand for healthcare services. However, this chapter is examining SID only as a confounding factor to equity in health in terms of access to prescription medicines, in particular.

In summary, in the transition countries with intensive health reforms, pharmaceutical expenditure control was considered (King and Kanavos, 2002) in an attempt to increase the efficiency and effectiveness of the primary healthcare (Cernic-Istenic, 1998; Nordyke and Peabody, 2002). Some countries have shown a great improvement in the efficiency of their healthcare systems (Franco *et al.*, 2004), whereas, in others, the economic and social benefits of the reforms have not been researched in detail. Research into policy changes in prescription regulation and its effects on prescribing volumes and practices would contribute towards the assessment of how successful the implementation of health reform has been in respect to pharmaceutical expenditure control.

This research looks at equity in healthcare from a socio-economic perspective, and the effects of policy changes of prescription regulation on the access to prescription medicines in the case of Macedonia, where in past years major health system changes have occurred (Nordyke, 2002; Nordyke and Peabody, 2002). As explained above, the policy changes that occurred in the regulation of the pharmaceutical market in Macedonia have affected pharmaceutical companies, healthcare providers and, above all, the patients.

Methodology

In this study a mixed-methods approach will be used to inform different parts of the research question (Campbell and Fiske, 1959; Denzin, 1970; Brannen, 1992; Bryman, 2006). Its recent wide application is justified by the possibilities to address a wider range of questions (O'Cathain *et al.*, 2007), to collect richer and more authentic data (Foss and Ellefsen, 2002) and to enhance the validity of the research (Bradley, 1995). For the quantitative part of the study, secondary data were used to analyse trends over time in demand and supply of medicines before and after the prescription policy changes, using descriptive statistical methods. For the qualitative part of the study, semistructured interviews were used, involving elite interviewing. This method was considered most appropriate because it allowed the research questions to be explored in depth, encouraging detailed responses and also enabling the researcher to probe and challenge responses where appropriate. The qualitative findings were used to complement the quantitative results, for better understanding and explanation. The instruments and sampling are described further in this section. Sample-size calculations are not very commonly used in qualitative research (Sandelowski, 1995); therefore theoretical saturation was used as the criterion to define the sample size when: 'no additional data being found whereby … the researcher becomes empirically confident that a category is saturated' (Glaser and Strauss, 1967). A total of 25 interviews were conducted with representatives from governmental institutions and academia, as well as policy makers and decision makers. The data were analysed using the thematic framework analysis approach.

Findings

Socio-Economic Aspects of Equity in Healthcare

As explained earlier, ensuring equitable access was one of the reasons for implementation of the concessional privatization model in PHC in the country. Equitable access is a right guaranteed to every citizen in the Constitution of the Republic of Macedonia (1991, art. 39), and in healthcare legislation.

Table 13.2 shows that, in most areas, on the level of regional coverage, the population has sufficient access to PHC, as compared to the National Guidelines for Primary Healthcare, defining a population of 2000 per PHC physician (HIF, 2010). The exception is the region of Krushevo, where there is a lack of PHC providers. However, within these regions, the microdistribution of PHC providers (as per the registered address with the HIF) shows a concentration of the PHC in urban areas (over 80%) and a lack of PHC in rural and difficult-to-reach areas. Although the majority of population in the country is urban (54% in the 2002 national census), there is still an evident discrepancy in the coverage of the rural population by PHC physicians.

In order to ensure equitable access to PHC services throughout the whole territory of the country, the model provides incentives for opening a PHC office in rural areas. These incentives are calculated as fixed payments to the PHC physician, regardless of the number of patients registered with the PHC provider. Rural areas for which such conditions are applicable are predefined and revised if necessary.

A problem that has been identified with this approach is that, by using the urban/rural principle, suburban and ghettoized areas are systematically neglected, which leaves marginalized groups in these areas without the desired level of access to PHC services. Most such areas are predominantly settled by Roma and the interest in opening PHC practices is not as high there as in other urban areas. As they are not eligible for incentives, because they would be in rural areas, the provision of PHC services is not satisfactory; and since the PHC practices are the entry point for prescription of medicines, these population groups are excluded from regular supply of prescription

Table 13.2: Ratio of population per PHC provider (GP, paediatrician, school medicine)

HIF Regional office (area covered)	Number of Primary healthcare (PHC) providers	Population in covered area[a]	Population per 1 PHC provider
Berovo	16	13 941	871
Bitola	76	105 644	1390
Brod, Makedonski	9	11 686	1298
Valandovo	8	11 890	1486
Vinica	15	19 938	1329
Gevgelija	29	35 121	1211
Gostivar	74	106 441	1438
Debar	14	26 061	1862
Delchevo	23	25 615	1114
Demir Hisar	7	9497	1357
Kavadarci	40	42 882	1072
Kichevo	32	56 734	1773
Kochani	33	48 846	1480
Kratovo	8	10 441	1305
Kriva Palanka	17	24 964	1468
Krushevo	6	23 252	3875
Kumanovo	96	137 382	1431
Negotino	21	23 757	1131
Ohrid	39	61 256	1571
Prilep	80	82 918	1036
Probishtip	12	16 193	1349
Radovish	22	31 780	1445
Resen	20	16,825	841
Sveti Nikole	15	21 355	1424
Skopje	433	578 144	1335
Struga	34	63 376	1864
Strumica	71	92 625	1305
Tetovo	136	189 066	1390
Veles	48	66 541	1386
Shtip	40	51 808	1295

a The total number of population covered is adjusted to the division of area by the HIF regional office

Sources: HIF Database of contracts in Primary healthcare, HIF official website: www.fzo.org.mk, and State Statistical Office Projections of Population by Municipality in 2010 – SSO, 2011.

medicines. There is no data on the number of PHC providers that have applied for, or have been granted, incentives for opening a PHC practice in rural, remote or hard-to-reach communities, or how many patients have benefited from this equal access measure.

Financial Aspects of Equity in Healthcare

Primary healthcare is fully financed through the Health Insurance Fund (HIF). Established in 2001, based on the Law on Health Insurance, the HIF became a major actor in the collection, pooling, management and allocation of public funds to healthcare in Macedonia. The HIF as an independent public agency also prepares the healthcare services costing and expenditure control policies that are adopted by the government. The sources of revenue of HIF are primarily employment contributions and direct budget transfers for uninsured persons, for services covered through the preventive and curative programmes of the Ministry of Health and for unemployed persons from the Employment Agency. Thus, the social welfare system embraces a total population of almost 2 million (HIF, 2010), and expenditure control for providing a sufficient level of coverage while sustaining satisfactory level of quality of services, is both a necessity and a challenge.

The data on expenditures in PHC (as reported by the HIF) analysed per insured person per year shows a gradual upward trend, with an index of increase in costs of 25.9% for the period 2004–2008. At the same time, the number of insured persons dropped slightly in 2008, despite the previous positive trend; the reason could not be determined, as there were no policy changes at the time (such as opening the market to other insurance companies) that might have caused a shift to other insurance schemes.

Similarly, the indices of drug expenditures in PHC for the period 2004–2008 have shown an upward trend, despite the introduction of cost-containment policies.

However, as disaggregated data are not available for the drug expenditures per health region, it was not possible to measure the equality of the access to prescription drugs reimbursed by the HIF through this study. This, however, remains an issue that deserves further investigation to inform the identified knowledge gap in this area.

Table 13.3: Total expenditures in PHC and expenditures per patient per year (2004–2008)

Year	Number of insured persons	Expenditure in primary healthcare (€)	Expenditure per patient per year (€)	Percentage of total HIF expenditures
2004	1 873 836	71 616 129	38.22	29.92
2005	1 898 334	74 610 627	39.30	29.91
2006	1 938 760	77 753 585	40.10	29.37
2007	1 959 384	82 133 252	41.92	30.75
2008	1 896 012	91 230 387	48.12	28.58
		Index 2008/2004 =	125.90	

Source: HIF Annual Reports for 2004, 2005, 2006, 2007 and 2008.

Table 13.4: Indices of drug expenditures in PHC (2004–2008)

Year index	Index of drug expenditure in PHC
2004/2003	127.86
2005[a]/2004	91.54
2006/2005[a]	91.15
2007/2006	120.91
2008/2007	130.12

a In 2005 there was a price reduction for all medicines of 8.46% on average through bidding for public procurement of prescription medicines.

Conclusions and Discussion

The priorities set in the agenda for reforming the healthcare system involved improvement of the quality, efficiency and effectiveness of the health services, with the PHC being among the first segments in line for transformation. The MoH, with international technical assistance, has successfully transferred the majority of PHC into the private sector, while introducing the capitation payment model as a major incentive for PHC physicians to assist in the envisaged shift from secondary care domination to a primary care-led service and reinforcement of their gatekeeper role, thus indirectly improving the efficiency and effectiveness of secondary healthcare.

Initial assessments are showing no significant improvements or savings in the PHC segment, and at the same time no significant improvements in access to prescription medicines. However, rather than using simple cost-containment strategies, it might be more important to assess the quality of services provided, and even more, the effects of reformed PHC on expenditure at the secondary and tertiary levels.

In conclusion, PHC reform has been examined in terms of its effects on equity of the access to PHC and prescription medicines in the country. The results, showing that the equity has not been completely achieved, should prompt assessment of equity in other segments of PHC (such as referrals and preventive medical check-ups), as they are all constitutionally and legally guaranteed aspects of the current healthcare system. Further to this, and bearing in mind the above results, an analysis of equity of access to healthcare at secondary and tertiary levels would be of great value, as they pose more challenges for achieving equity, not only in the region but on global level.

References

Aberbach, J.D. and Rockman, B.A. (2002) Conducting and coding elite interviews. *Political Science and Politics* 35 (4), pp. 673–6.

Annual Report of the Health Insurance Fund of the Republic of Macedonia (2008) Health Insurance Fund, Skopje, www.fzo.org.mk/WBStorage/Files/gIzvestaj08.pdf (accessed 27 October 2012).

Atun, R.A., Ibragimov, A. and Ross, G. (eds) (2005) *Review of Experience of Family Medicine in Europe and Central Asia. Volume I: Executive summary*. World Bank Report No. 32354-ECA, World Bank, Washington, DC.

Bakker, D.H., Coffie, D.S.V., Heerdink, E.R., van Dijk, L. and Groenewegen, P.P. (2007) Determinants of the range of drugs prescribed in general practice: a cross-sectional analysis. *BMC Health Services Research* 7, 132.

Bateman, D.N., Eccles, M., Campbell, M., Soutter, J., Roberts, S.J. and Smith, J.M. (1996). Setting standards of prescribing performance in primary care: use of a consensus group of general practitioners and application of standards to practices in the north of England. *British Journal of General Practice* 46, pp. 20–5.

Bradley, C.P. (1992) Factors which influence the decision whether or not to prescribe: the dilemma facing general practitioners. *British Journal of General Practice* 42, pp. 454–8.

Bradley, S. (1995) Methodological triangulation in healthcare research. *Nurse Researcher* 3 (2), pp. 81–9.

Brannen J, (ed.) (1992). *Mixing Methods: Qualitative and Quantitative Research*, Ashgate, Aldershot.

Bryman, A. (2006) Integrating quantitative and qualitative research: how is it done? *Qualitative Research* 6 (1), pp. 97–113.

Campbell, D.T. and Fiske, D.W. (1959) Convergent and discriminant validation by the multitrait-multimethod matrix. *Psychological Bulletin* 56, pp. 81–105.

Cernic-Istenic, M. (1998) Privatization of healthcare in Slovenia. *Croatian Medical Journal* 39 (3), pp. 288–97.

Chaix-Couturier, C., Durand-Zaleski, I., Jolly, D. and Durieux, P. (2000) Effects of financial incentives on medical practice: results from a systematic review of the literature and methodological issues. *International Journal for Quality in Healthcare* 12 (2), pp. 133–42.

Cichon M. (1991) Health sector reforms in Central and Eastern Europe: paradigm reversed? *International Labour Review* 130 (3), pp. 311–27.

Denzin, N.K. (1970) *The Research Act*, Aldine Publishing, Chicago, IL.

Department of Health UK (1999) *The Pharmaceutical Price Regulation Scheme*, Department of Health, London.

Donaldson, C. and Gerard, K. (1993) *Economics of Financing Healthcare: The Visible Hand*, Macmillan, London.

EurActiv (2004) Healthcare systems in Central and Eastern Europe. Report on EU Enlargement 2004, European Commission, Brussels.

Foss, C. and Ellefsen, B. (2002). "The value of combining qualitative and quantitative approaches in nursing research by means of method triangulation". *Journal of Advanced Nursing* 40 (2), pp. 242–8.

Franco, A., Alvarez-Dardet, C. and Ruiz, M.T. (2004) Effect of democracy on health: ecological study. *British Medical Journal* 329, pp. 1421–4.

Gjorgjev, D., Bacanovic, A., Cicevalieva, S., Sulevski, Z. and Grosse-Tebbe, S. (2006) The former Yugoslav Republic of Macedonia: health system review. *Health Systems in Transition* 8 (2), pp. 1–98.

Glaser, B. and Strauss, A. (1967) *The Discovery of Grounded Theory: Strategies for Qualitative Research,* Aldine Publishing Company, New York, NY.

Harding, J.M., Modell, M., Freudenberg, S., MacGreggor, R., Nicolas Rea, J., Steen, C.A., Wojciechowski, M. and Yudkin, G.D. (1985) Prescribing: the power to set limits. *British Medical Journal* 290, pp. 450–3.

Hardley, J., Holahan, J. and Scanlon, W. (1979) Can fee-for-service reimbursement coexist with demand creation? *Inquiry* 16, pp. 247–58.

HIF (2009) Book of Rules for the criteria for contracting and the forms of payment for the health services to healthcare settings that are registered for provision to the insured persons of pharmaceuticals that are eligible for dispensing on prescription in primary healthcare. *Official Gazette of the Republic of Macedonia* no. 76/2004, Sluzben vesnik na RM, Skopje, http://slvesnik.com.mk/ (accessed 27 October 2012).

HIF (2010) Planning of the goals for the general practitioners in primary healthcare January-March 2010 [in Macedonian: Планирање на цели за избрани матични лекари од општа медицина за период Јануари-Март 2010], www.fzo.org.mk/WBStorage/Files/Plan%20za%20celi-Opsta%20Medicina.pdf (accessed 27 October 2012).

Hutton, J., Borowitz, M., Oleksy, I. and Luce, B.R. (1994). The pharmaceutical industry and health reform: lessons from Europe. *Health Affairs* 13 (3), pp. 98–111.

Kanavos P. and Taylor D. (2007) Pharmacy discounts on generic medicines in France: is there room for further efficiency savings? *Current Medical Research and Opinion* 23 (10), pp. 2467–76.

King, D.R. and Kanavos, P. (2002) Encouraging the use of generic medicines: implications for transition economies. *Croatian Medical Journal* 43 (4), pp. 462–9.

Labelle, R., Stoddart, G. and Rice T. (1994) A re-examination of the meaning and importance of supplier-induced demand. *Journal of Health Economics* 13, pp. 347–68.

LKM (2010) Macedonian Medical Chamber web site, http://lkm.org.mk/denes.htm (accessed 27 October 2012).

Marrée, J. and Gronewegen, P. (1997) *Back to Bismarck: Eastern European Healthcare Systems in Transition,* Avebury, Hong Kong.

McKee, M. and Nolte, E. (2004). Lessons from health during the transition from communism. *British Medical Journal* 329, pp. 1428–9.

Mossialos, E., Walley, T. and Mrazek, M. (2004) Regulating pharmaceuticals in Europe: an overview. In: *Regulating Pharmaceuticals in Europe: Striving for Efficiency, Equity and Quality* (eds E. Mossialos, M. Mrazek and T. Walley),

European Observatory on Health Systems and Policies Series, Open University Press, London.
Mrazek, M. and Mossialos, E. (2004) Regulating pharmaceutical prices in the European Union. In: *Regulating Pharmaceuticals in Europe: Striving for Efficiency, Equity and Quality* (eds E. Mossialos, M. Mrazek and T. Walley), European Observatory on Health Systems and Policies Series, Open University Press, London.
Nordyke, R.J. (2002) Determinants of PHC productivity and resource utilization: a comparison of public and private physicians in Macedonia. *Health Policy* 60, pp. 67–96.
Nordyke, R.J. and Peabody J.W. (2002) Market reforms and public incentives: finding a balance in the Republic of Macedonia. *Social Science and Medicine* 54, pp. 939–53.
O'Cathain, A., Murphy, E. and Nicholl, J. (2007) Why, and how, mixed methods research is undertaken in health services research in England: a mixed methods study. *BMC Health Services Research* 7, 85.
Permanand, G. and Altenstetter, C. (2004) The politics of pharmaceuticals in the European Union. In: *Regulating Pharmaceuticals in Europe: Striving for Efficiency, Equity and Quality* (eds E. Mossialos, M. Mrazek and T. Walley), European Observatory on Health Systems and Policies Series, Open University Press, London.
Poole Jr. R.W (2008) Privatization. In: *The Concise Encyclopedia of Economics. Library of Economics and Liberty,* www.econlib.org/library/Enc/Privatization.html (accessed 27 October 2012).
Roemer MI. (1984) Private medical practice: obstacle to health for all. *World Health Forum* 5, pp. 195–201.
Saltman, R.B. and Figueras, J. (1997) *European Healthcare Reform: Analysis of Current Strategies.* WHO Regional Publications, European Series No. 72, World Health Organization, Copenhagen.
Sandelowski, M. (1995) Sample size in qualitative research. *Research in Nursing and Health* 18, pp. 179–83.
Shkolnikov, V., McKee, M., Leon, D.A. (2001) Changes in life expectancy in Russia in the mid-1990s. *The Lancet* 357, pp. 917–21.
State Statistical Office 2011. *Population Estimates on June 30, 2010 and December 31, 2010, by gender and age, municipal level and statistical regions* [in Macedonian: Proceni na naselenieto na 30. 06. 2010 i 31. 12. 2010 spored polot i vozrasta, po opstini i po statisticki regioni], State Statistical Offlce, Skopje, http://www.stat.gov.mk/publikacii/2.4.11.14.pdf (accessed November 10, 2012).
Titmuss RM. (1970) *The Gift Relationship: From Human Blood to Social Policy,* Penguin Books, Harmondsworth.
Webb, S. and Lloyd, M. (1994) Prescribing and referral in general practice: a study of patients' expectations and doctors' actions. *British Journal of General Practice* 44, pp. 165–9.
Wilkin, D., Hallam, L., Leavey, R. and Metcalfe, D. (1987) *Anatomy of Urban General Practice,* Tavistock Publications, London.

Wilkin, D. and Smith, A. (1987) Explaining variation in general practitioner referrals to hospital. *Family Practice* 4, pp. 160–9.
Wilson R.P.H., Hatcher J., Barton S. and Walley T. (1996) Influences of practice characteristics on prescribing in fundholding and non-fundholding general practices: an observational study. *British Medical Journal* 313, pp. 595–9.

Notes on Contributors

MARIUS CALU is a PhD student in political science at the School of Politics and International Relations, Queen Mary, University of London. He is working under the supervision of Professor Adam Fagan on the research theme 'Minority Rights in the Process of (Sub) State-Building: The EU's Role in Kosovo and the Question of (Ethnic) Sovereignty'. His research interests include post-conflict peace building and models of democratic governance, EU conflict management and the impact of Europeanization in the Western Balkans. Marius holds a BA in politics and a Masters by Research (MRes) in International Relations at Queen Mary, University of London. His role as a postgraduate researcher has included participation as a speaker and moderator at four international conferences in Serbia, Montenegro, Kosovo and Albania and the publication of one paper in an academic journal specializing in South-East Europe studies and two more forthcoming publications.

PREDRAG CVETIČANIN is the head of the independent Centre for Empirical Cultural Studies of South-East Europe. His current research interests focus on links between social and cultural stratification in South-East European societies. His publications include *Cultural Needs, Habits and Taste of Citizens of Serbia* (CCI, 2007), *Cultural Practices of Citizens of Serbia* (Centre for Study in Cultural Development, 2011, with Marijana Milankov), *The art of making classes in Serbia: another particular case of the possible, Poetics* 39 (6) (2011); *Social and Cultural Capital in Serbia* (editor, CECS, 2012); *Cultural Practices in Boka Kotorska* (Expeditio, 2012). He completed his first degree in sociology at the University of Niš, holds an MA in history and philosophy of arts from the Central European University, Prague, an MA in sociology from the University of Belgrade, an MSc in philosophy of the social sciences from the London School of Economics and Political Science and a PhD in sociology from the University of Belgrade.

CLAIRE GORDON is Teaching Fellow in East European politics at the European Institute, London School of Economics and Political Science, UK. Her current research interests are EU enlargement and conditionality, the EU's relations with the rest of Europe, with a special focus on conflict management and minority protection, and the challenge of Roma inclusion and social cohesion in the Western Balkans. Her publications include *Europeanization and regionalization in the EU's enlargement to Central and Eastern Europe: the Myth of Conditionality* (Palgrave, 2004, with James Hughes and Gwendolyn Sasse), *The stabilization and association process in the Western Balkans: an effective instrument of post-conflict management, Ethnopolitics* 8 (3–4) (2009), and *Measures to Promote the Socio-Economic Situation of EU Roma Citizens* (European Parliament, 2011, with William Bartlett and Roberta Benini). She completed her first degree at the University of Cambridge, holds an MSc in politics and international relations from the University of Birmingham and a DPhil in politics from the University of Oxford.

SIMONIDA KACARSKA is a PhD candidate in the School of Politics and International Studies at the University of Leeds in the UK and a Research Fellow at the University of Edinburgh. She holds research interests in the political transformation of the Balkans and their EU integration. Her publications include *Political parties and the state in the Republic of Macedonia – Implications for Democratic Consolidation, Central European University Political Science Journal* 1 (2008), and *Leaders and laggards in the post-communist road to democracy, Journal of Southeastern Europe* 31/32 (2006). She holds a BA in political science, international relations and European studies from the American University in Bulgaria and an MA in European politics from the University of Sussex. She has also conducted research at the University of Oxford, the University of Kent in Brussels and the University of Siena in Italy.

MARKO KMEZIC, LLM, MES is a senior researcher of the Centre for Southeast European Studies at the University of Graz, Austria since 2007. He studied at Belgrade University and the University of Graz, where he is currently a PhD candidate at the Faculty of Law with a thesis titled *Europeanization by Rule of Law Implementation in the Western Balkans*. Between 2006 and 2008 he worked in Belgrade for the Belgrade Centre for Human Rights. He published extensively on all Western Balkan countries.

Jana Korunovska Srbijanko is a researcher and analyst at Reactor – Research in Action. Currently, she lives in Vienna where she is a research assistant at the Vienna University of Economics and Business. Her research interests include employment policies, with a special focus on youth and women. She is also interested in employability, job insecurity and employees' wellbeing, as well as privacy policy online. Her publications include *Youth Unemployment* (Reactor, 2012, with Neda Korunovska Avramovska and Tanja Maleska), *Predicting Youth Apathy and Exclusion: Macedonian High-school Students and their Relations to their Communities* (Sociologija, 2012, Faculty of Philosophy, University of Belgrade), *Confusion, Capitulation, Resistance: Social Capital among Macedonian High-School Students* (YEF, 2011 with Korunovska Avramovska and Maleska), *Women in the Macedonian Economy* (Reactor, 2010). She studied psychology at the University of Vienna.

Neda Korunovska Avramovska is president of Reactor – Research in Action. Her current research areas include youth participation, inclusion and economic integration, with a special focus on employment policy. She also researches the position of women in the labour market and gender violence, in particular in public spaces. Her publications include *Youth Unemployment* (Reactor, 2012, with Jan Korunovska Srbijanko and Tanja Maleska), *Confusion, Capitulation, Resistance: Social Capital among Macedonian High-School Students* (YEF, 2011, with Jana Korunovska Srbijanko and Tanja Maleska), *Women in the Macedonian Economy* (Reactor, 2010, with Korunovska Srbijanko and Maleska), *Wall of Silence: The implementation of the Right to Free Access to Information* (Open Society Foundation – Macedonia, 2007), *Citizens' Guide to the Courts* (YEF, 2005), and *Street Law textbook and teacher's manual* (YEF, 2000). She studied law at the University St Cyril and Metody in Skopje and is an LLM candidate in Business Law. In 2007, she also specialized in EU institutions, policies and law.

Nemanja Krstić is a teaching assistant in the Department of Sociology, Faculty of Philosophy, University of Niš, Serbia. His research interests include sociological aspects of culture, religion and gender. He is a PhD student in the Faculty of Philosophy, University of Belgrade.

AISLING LYON is a PhD candidate at the Department of Peace Studies, University of Bradford (UK). Her research is on municipal decentralization in the Republic of Macedonia and its capacity to manage ethnic difference. Prior to commencing her PhD studies, she worked in international development, focusing primarily on minority rights protection and conflict prevention in the former Yugoslavia. She was based in Kosovo and the Republic of Macedonia between 2004 and 2006, and again during 2008. During this time she worked at South East European University in Tetovo, Republic of Macedonia as Co-Dean of the Faculty of Public Administration and Manager of the University's Centre for Human Rights. She was also employed in a variety of municipal capacity building projects in Kosovo, in particular supporting the Association of Kosovo Municipalities and the Ministry of Local Government Administration. Aisling was awarded a Masters in East European History (University of Leeds, 2000) and a Masters of Research Methods (University of Bradford, 2009), both with Distinction. She recently completed an International Summer University on federalism, decentralization and conflict resolution at the Institute of Federalism, University of Fribourg/ Freiburg, Switzerland.

DANIJELA MAJSTOROVIĆ is Associate Professor at the English Department in the Faculty of Philology of the University of Banja Luka, teaching courses in discourse/text analysis and cultural studies. Her current research interests include discursive construction of ethnic and gender(ed) identifications in the Balkans, Yugoslav studies, and Balkan postcoloniality with a special focus on foreign interventionism, transition and Europeanization. Her most important publications include *Discourse, Power and the International Community* (Filozofski fakultet u Banjoj Luci, 2007), *Living with Patriarchy* (John Benjamins, 2011, with Inger Lassen, eds), *In the Embrace of a Nation* (Center for Social and Cultural Repair, 2011, with Vladimir Turjačanin, eds), *Construction of Europeanization in the High Representative's discourse in Bosnia and Herzegovina, Discourse and Society 18* (5)

(2007), and *Femininity, patriarchy and resistance in the postwar Bosnia and Herzegovina, International Review of Sociology* 21 (2) (2011). She completed her first degree at the University of Banja Luka, holds an MA in communications from Ohio University and a PhD from the University of Banja Luka.

TANJA MALESKA is a researcher and analyst at Reactor – Research in Action. Her current research interests include youth unemployment, unemployment and inactivity among women, as well as participative planning in urban development. Her publications include *Youth Unemployment* (Reactor, 2012, with Korunovska Avramovska and Korunovska Srbijanko), *Predicting Youth Apathy and Exclusion: Macedonian High-school Students and their Relations to their Communities* (Sociologija, 2012, Faculty of Philosophy, University of Belgrade), *Confusion, Capitulation, Resistance: Social Capital among Macedonian High-School Students* (YEF, 2011, with Korunovska Avramovska and Korunovska Srbijanko), *Women in the Macedonian Economy* (Reactor, 2010). She read English at the University of Vienna, Austria and at the University of Ottawa, Canada.

NEDA MILEVSKA-KOSTOVA, MSc, MCPPM is Executive Director at the Centre for Regional Policy Research and Cooperation 'Studiorum' and executive editor of the *Journal for European Issues "Evrodijalog"*, published by CRPRC Studiorum. She works predominantly in the field of public health policy and healthcare sector reforms in Macedonia and in South-Eastern Europe (SEE). She has a Master of Science from the University of Tokyo and a Master of Public Policy and Management from the Graduate School of Public and International Affairs (GSPIA) at the University of Pittsburgh. Her research and policy interests are in health systems research, health insurance and equitable access to and decentralization of the healthcare services. She was actively involved in preparation of health-related legislation in Macedonia and worked on projects and analyses for various domestic and international institutions and donors, such as the Ministry of Health, UNICEF, GFATM, ECDC, GMS, OSI-Europe, JBIC, JICA, etc. She is currently enrolled in a PhD program at the School of Health and Related Research (ScHARR), University of Sheffield.

SNJEZANA MILIVOJEVIC is Professor of Public Opinion and Media Studies at the Faculty of Political Sciences, University of Belgrade. She is the founding Chair of the Center for Media Research and is an Academic Board member at the Center for Women's Studies. Her main academic interests are in political communication, media policy and regulation, cultural and gender studies and media and public memory. Snjezana Milivojevic co-authored the first media and election study, in *Serbia Televised Elections* (Beograd: Vreme knjige, 1993), contributed to *Serbian Road to War* (Budapest: CEU Pess, 1998), *Media Monitoring Manual* (London: Media Diversity Institute, 2003), and *Television across Europe – Serbia* (Budapest: EUMAP and NMP, 2005) and participated in numerous international research projects in media studies. She was a Chevning Scholar at St Antony's College, Oxford University (2001) and visiting professor for several European and American universities. She was discharged from the University of Belgrade for political reasons pending the repressive University law (1999), and continued her university career in Serbia (2003) only after democratic changes in the country.

JASMINA NEDELJKOVIĆ is a teaching assistant at the Department of Business Psychology, Faculty of Legal and Business Study, Novi Sad, Serbia. Her interests focus on quantitative psychology, research and development in a number of broad areas: measurement, research design, and statistical analysis, as well as mathematical and statistical modelling of psychological and social processes. She completed her first degree at the University of Niš, holds an MSc in Psychology from the University of Niš, and pending is the public defense of her PhD thesis in Psychology at the University of Niš.

JASMINA OPARDIJA is the Programme Manager of the Regional Research Promotion Programme (RRPP) in the Western Balkans at the Interfaculty Institute for Central and Eastern Europe at the University of Fribourg. She holds an MA in East European Studies from the Free University of Berlin and a BA from the Faculty of Political Sciences in Sarajevo (Bosnia and Herzegovina), Department of Journalism. During the period 1999–2007, she was involved in several development and research projects in Bosnia and Herzegovina, focusing on rights-based municipal development and strengthening of civil society and youth activism.

Mina Petrovic is an associate professor in sociology in the Department of Sociology at the Faculty of Philosophy of Belgrade, where she teaches courses on urban sociology, social and spatial exclusion, and environmental sociology. Her latest book, *Transformation of Cities: Towards the De-politicization of the Urban Question* (2009, in Serbian), is devoted to an analysis of the rising socio-spatial inequalities in contemporary European cities. Her latest publications in English include: a chapter on Belgrade's post-socialist urban evolution in the book *The Post-Socialist City, edited by Stanilov* (Springer 2007); and two articles on urban development in Belgrade, published in *Children's Geographies* (8 (2), 141–156 (2010), co-authored with S. Tomanovic); and in *International Journal of Urban and Regional Research* (35 (4), 753–777 (2011), co-authored with S. Hirt).

Dragan Stanojevic is teaching assistant at the Department of Sociology at Faculty of Philosophy, University of Belgrade. He is also junior researcher on the project of the Institute for Sociological Research at the same faculty. He participated in several research and applied projects. His areas of teaching and research policy include sociology of youth, sociology of the family, sociology of religion and quantitative methodology. He is the author of several articles in domestic journals. He has completed BA degrees in ethnology and anthropology, and in sociology in the Faculty of Philosophy, University of Belgrade and he is currently a PhD student in sociology in the same faculty.

Ana Stojanova is a PhD student in political systems and institutional change at the Institute for Advanced Studies in Lucca, Italy. In 2007 she obtained a Master's degree in European studies at the Bulgarian-Romanian Interuniversity Europe Center in Rousse, Bulgaria, spending one semester at Chemnitz University of Technology in Germany. She earned her bachelor degree in economics at the Faculty of Economics in Prilep, Macedonia, where she graduated with honours. Ana's research interests are both theoretical and empirical, and focus on the processes of democratization and democracy consolidation in Eastern Europe, particularly in the Western Balkans. She also has a research interest in voting behaviour, above all elective accountability in the post-communist countries.

SMILJKA TOMANOVIC is Professor of Sociology and the head of the Department of Sociology at the Faculty of Philosophy, University of Belgrade. She is also Senior Researcher and was the Director of the Institute for Sociological Research at the same Faculty (2002–2006). She participated in numerous research projects, applied projects, and also in writing of several policy papers in Serbia. Her areas of teaching, research and policy expertise include sociology of the family, sociology of childhood, sociology of youth, and qualitative methodology. She is the author of three books, several edited volumes, and numerous articles in international and domestic journals.
VLADIMIR TURJAČANIN is Associate professor of Social Psychology in the Department of Psychology, University of Banja Luka, BiH. His current research interests include psychology of ethnic relations, ethnic identity and prejudice in BiH. His publications include *Ethnic Attitudes of Bosniak and Serb Youth in Bosnia and Herzegovina* (Filozofski fakultet u Banjoj Luci, 2005) and *Psychosocial Space and Ethnic Relations of Youth in Bosnia and Herzegovina* (Filozofski fakultet u Banjoj Luci, 2007). He completed his first degree and an MA in social psychology at the University of Belgrade and a PhD in social psychology from the University of Banja Luka.

JELISAVETA VUKELIC is a PhD candidate at the Faculty of Philosophy of the University of Belgrade, Department of Sociology. She is working on the themes such as political participation, environmental activism, environmental citizenship, environmental behaviour and attitudes, social ecology, environmental and spatial sociology. As a researcher, she participates in two projects: Public Participation in Environmental Decision-Making: the case of Bor and Pancevo and The Challenges of the New Integration (Institute for Sociological Research, Faculty of Philosophy). She is a co-author of several papers dealing with environmental issues: *Issues of Environmental Governance in Serbia: Local Authorities' Perspective* (with M. Petrovic, Conference paper, London School of Economic, 2011); *Sustainability of Environmental Activism in Post-socialist Serbia* (with M. Petrovic,

ESA Conference 2011); *Environmental Activism, Awareness and Pro-environmental Behaviour of Serbian Youth* (with D. Stanojevic, conference paper, University of Belgrade, 2011); *Social Capital as a Basis for Collective Action: The Case of Environmental Activism in the two Serbian Towns* (conference paper with I. Petrovic, 2011).

INTERDISCIPLINARY STUDIES ON CENTRAL AND EASTERN EUROPE

Edited by
Christian Giordano, Nicolas Hayoz & Jens Herlth

This new series focuses on the political, economic and cultural changes in Eastern, East-Central and South-Eastern Europe. It publishes scholarly papers presented at the "Eastern European Day" conferences held at the University of Fribourg. These annual conferences examine the various East European countries. Moreover, the series also presents a forum for other conferences held in Switzerland on topics related to Eastern Europe. It aims to reflect on what could be considered the rapprochement of the different branches of Swiss research on Eastern Europe (history, political science, philosophy, Slavic languages). The articles are written in English.

Band 1 Nicolas Hayoz, Andrej N. Lushnycky (eds)
Ukraine at a Crossroads.
269 pp. 2005.
ISBN 3-03910-468-3, US-ISBN 0-8204-7157-7

Band 2 Nicolas Hayoz, Leszek Jesień, Wim van Meurs (eds)
Enlarged EU – Enlarged Neighbourhood.
Perspectives of the European Neighbourhood Policy.
392 pp. 2005.
ISBN 3-03910-624-4, US-ISBN 0-8204-7167-4

Band 3 Nicolas Hayoz, Simon Hug (eds)
Tax Evasion, Trust, and State Capacities.
How good is Tax Moral in Central and Eastern Europe.
379 pp. 2007.
ISBN 978-3-03910-651-6, US-ISBN 978-0-8204-7168-6

Band 4 Andrej N. Lushnycky, Mykola Riabchuk (eds)
Ukraine on its Meandering Path Between East and West.
Interdisciplinary Studies on Central and Eastern Europe.
210 pp. 2009.
ISBN 978-3-03911-607-2

Band 5 Leonidas Donskis (ed.)
A Litmus Test Case of Modernity.
Examining Modern Sensibilities and the Public Domain
in the Baltic States at the Turn of the Century.
314 pp. 2009.
ISBN 978-3-0343-0335-4

Band 6 Marta Dyczok, Oxana Gaman-Golutvina (eds)
Media, Democracy and Freedom.
The Post-Communist Experience.
246 pp. 2009.
ISBN 978-3-0343-0311-8

Band 7 Josette Baer (ed.)
From Post-Communism toward the Third Millenium.
Aspects of Political and Economic Development in Eastern
and South-Eastern Europe from 2000–2005.
272 pp. 2011.
ISBN 978-3-03911-773-4

Band 8 Galina Michaleva, Andrey Ryabov (eds)
Russian Challenges.
Between Freedom and Energy.
240 pp. 2011.
ISBN 978-3-0343-0529-7

Band 9 Nicolas Hayoz, Leszek Jesień, Daniela Koleva (eds)
20 Years after the Collapse of Communism.
Expectations, achievements and disillusions of 1989.
679 pp. 2011.
ISBN 978-3-0343-0538-9

Band 10 Claire Gordon, Marko Kmezic, Jasmina Opardija (eds)
Stagnation and Drift in the Western Balkans.
The Challenges of Political, Economic and Social Change.
325 pp. 2013.
ISBN 978-3-0343-1152-6